Why Are Mexico and the United States So Different?

(México y Estados Unidos: orígenes de una relación, 1819-1861)

Ángela Moyano Pahissa

Originally written and published in Spanish:

first edition:
Editorial Planeta
Mexico City
1987

second edition:
Universidad Autónoma
de Nuevo León
and
Universidad Autónoma
de Querétaro
2002

Translation of the second edition into English by:
Thomas R. Wheaton
Querétaro, México
2019

Reviews

Gordon Mott, former Mexico city bureau chief, Knight-Ridder newspapers:

Angela Moyano Pahissa's remarkable history of United States-Mexican relations in the 19th century provides startling insight into a side of the story Americans have never heard. Her details of the conflict reveal how the United States meddled in, and affected Mexican politics from its independence from Spain right up to the outbreak of the American Civil War. American leaders repeatedly capitalized on Mexico's internal struggles and the weakness of its government to wage campaigns that ultimately led to the seizure in 1848 of what today is most of the Western United States. This is a must read for people who believe in historical accuracy, and who wish to better understand Mexico's attitude toward its northern neighbor today.

Michael Tang, Ph.D., Research Professor, University of Colorado Denver:

Why are Mexicans and Americans so different? is a story that is especially urgent to be read and heard in today's iteration of a conflict that few Americans are aware of, told from a Mexican perspective. From that perspective our awareness is opened to give us a glimpse of the pride, determination, bravery and intelligence of a people who at that time were viewed as racially, culturally, and politically inferior by North Americans. It is a must read to better understand a continent in which most people north of the Mexican border assume that the term "North America" refers to only the United States and Canada.

gain economic access usually at Mexico's expense. Not all treaties were ratified by Mexico.

It is important for the reader to understand that U.S. historical writings and interpretations did not always present the whole picture, where Mexico's actions and motives were simply ignored. Professor Moyano has researched archives and libraries both in the U.S and Mexico to present a more complete and balanced picture of U.S.-Mexico nineteenth-century interaction from Colonial times up to the beginning of the American Civil War..

Table of Contents

Translator's Prologue

When I first visited Venezuela in 1969, two years before moving to Mexico, I had just finished working for three years as a Peace Corps Volunteer in Morocco, had just married a French citizen, and spoke passable French. I thought I was fairly knowledgeable about the world. But even though I should have known better, I was still surprised to see stores in Caracas and Merida referring to themselves as "American". They were Venezuelan, I was American.

Venezuela in those days was developing quickly with fancy hotels on the coast and modern, North American style high rises and stores in the cities, which were connected by limited access highways. Even the food was more North American than tropical Latin American. We could not find a fresh papaya. North American companies' names appeared on buildings and on billboards. It looked like a country closely tied economically to the United States, such as you might expect of a neighboring country like Mexico.

Two years later, we had lived and worked in Puerto Rico for a couple of years and spoke passable Spanish and had a daughter born in Ponce. When we arrived in Mexico City, I thought I was fairly knowledgeable about Latin American culture and Mexico. After all, I grew up in Southern California and had visited Tijuana nearly every weekend that my father was in Korea in the early 1950s. I should have known better, but I expected Mexico City to be like Caracas and was surprised at the great differences in architectural style, the lack of North American companies and businesses, the different lifestyle and food. Everyone ate tacos and enchiladas and mole, and except for Coca Cola, there was not very much North American about it, no MacDonalds, Krystals, or Howard and Johnsons. Even though Mexico is bounded by the United States to the north, it seemed completely different from the United States compared to Venezuela. It was a little disorienting at first.

We spent five years working in Mexico where I earned my MA in anthropology and archaeology, learned Spanish, and developed a pretty good understanding of the vast variety of cultures and geography in Mexico. It is an astoundingly varied country. I even had a recurring dream of being an eighteenth-century Mexican priest walking in sandals in northern Mexico. I harbored thoughts that perhaps I had been a Mexican in a previous life. We returned to the United States with a newly acquired daughter born in Mexico City and an abiding love of the country.

Thirty-five years later, we retired to Mexico where I thought I was fairly knowledgeable about the people, their culture, their history, and current events, and where we still had a few friends left, but where we really had not visited in 25 years. I should have known better. Driving down from the Texas border, there were limited access toll roads, gas stations with nice bathrooms, McDonalds and Carl Jr.'s, shopping centers, Home Depots and Office Depots, Ford and Chevy dealerships, and finally, Querétaro, a beautiful colonial city of about 50,000 people surrounded by a very modern metropolis of 1,000,000, now 2,000,000. So, we settled in, bought a house in the historic district and got involved in the community.

Since I had a masters degree in Mexican culture and thought I knew Mexican history (or at least its prehistory) pretty well, I was feeling confident that I finally knew Mexico. A few years later, when I took a class on the history of Mexican/United States relations at the Universidad Autónoma de Querétaro by the author of this book (see Appendix V), I thought I had a pretty good basic understanding, and that there probably was not much more to learn. I should have known better.

As this class came to a close, we were in the midst of the 2016 United States presidential campaign, where, although some were good people, Mexicans were being called rapists, murders, and thieves with calves as large as cantaloupes stealing our jobs and taking advantage of us in business and international relations. Having read Ángela's book on the history of our mutual relations with a class of Mexican students of about my age (not young!) and hearing them discuss the history and the presidential campaign, I became convinced that North Americans needed to read this book. And since Ángela had never translated it, I volunteered to do it for her.

As you will see in this book, in the United States we learn practically nothing about our nearest neighbor to the south, its people, its views on our respective relationship, and our mutual history. Without examining our own history and biases (which is a difficult thing to do for any people and at which Americans are especially bad), we tend to impose on others our views of the world, our values, and our desires. If nothing else, I hope this book will open the eyes of my fellow North Americans to another point of view on the United States from a well-educated Mexican, and why, not everyone out there loves us, wants to emulate us, or even respects us. Despite what the United States has done to Mexicans in the name of civilization over the past 200 years, they are still warm, forgiving, welcoming, and accepting of us. In the end, that is still something I do not completely understand, and may never understand, but which I appreciate and for which I am thankful.

Tom Wheaton
Centro Histórico
Querétaro, Qro. México
2019

The Author

Dr. Angela Moyano Pahissa was born in Mexico and has lived in Europe and the United States. She received her B.A. in history at the University of Miami in 1968. She obtained her M.A. and then Ph.D in history from the National Autonomous University of Mexico (UNAM), winning a Fullbright scholarship in 1985 to research early North American history at the University of Chicago and traveling throughout the United States. The first chapter in this book is based primarily on that research. She has done research and taught at various institutions in Mexico City and at the University of Monterrey and the Autonomous University of Querétaro in Querétaro, Mexico, where she is currently professor emeritus.

She has received many local, state and national awards for her research, most recently, an honorary award at the XXth International Meeting of the Social Science and Humanities Investigations in 2017; and the *Grand Order of the "Victoria of the Republic"* by the Department of National Defense, the National Academy, and the National Academy of History and Geography for her professional career, support, and appreciation of Mexican History, 2017.

Her specialty has been the history of Mexican relations with the United States and the impacts of those relations in the border areas and the interior. She also has studied and is a recognized scholar on the history of the Second Empire of Emperor Maximilian and Empress Charlotte. She is the author of 17 books on Mexican and Querétano history, and co-author of six more, mostly dealing with Mexican-American border issues.

Translation Notes and Acknowledgements
by Translator

This book has been written from a Mexican perspective, which most Americans are probably unfamiliar with as most of our history books are written by Americans with an American bias. That is one of the main reasons I wanted to translate this work. I wanted to give an American audience a sense of how others see us as a nation, and also because Mexico is our next-door neighbor, has had a long and difficult relationship with us, and is one of our top trading partners. We also rely on Mexican workers to do jobs Anglos do not want to take.

Mexico is in many ways totally unknown to most Americans, who only know Tijuana, Cancun, Acapulco, and the guys down at Home Depot. It is a country with a rich and much longer prehistoric civilization and history than the United States. A university in Mexico and trading ships sailing between Acapulco and the Philippines had existed for eighty years before English settlers landed at Jamestown and the Pilgrims got off the Mayflower at Plymouth Rock.

Mexico has dozens of different indigenous languages and cultures that make it fascinating for anthropologists, and despite being our next door neighbor, Mexico is culturally more different from the United States than is Western Europe.

There is currently talk of building a wall along the border, keeping out alleged rapists and murderers, the "illegal alien" problem, and the World Court case in the Hague against the United States over the exact boundaries between our two countries, a legacy of some of the events in this book. It seems a propitious time for Americans to learn something about the history of our relationship with Mexico and how the border situation got to the point where it is today.

Dr. Ángela Moyano Pahissa's book is one of several on the topic. Because Dr. Moyano is a careful researcher and well-respected by her peers in Mexico and in the United States, where she has lived many years, her book is one of the best on the topic. Plus, it is clearly written. After taking a course by Dr. Moyano in Querétaro, Mexico, where we live and where she has taught at the Universidad Autónoma de Querétaro for over 25 years, and after reading a few of her books, I felt compelled to translate this one as a general overview of the origins of the problem of United States/Mexico relations, our common border, and our cultural differences.

Some readers will no doubt be offended by some of the points she makes, but it is hard to ignore her conclusions and the facts she uses to support them. Others, who have travelled and have learned another culture and language will undoubtedly understand and appreciate what she has to say. I hope that every reader will learn something useful about our two cultures and how and why we are how we are.

Mexicans generally use the term "North American" where people of the United States would use "American". I have decided to keep the Mexican term in this book written from a Mexican point of view to give a Mexican flavor to the text. In the United States we use the term "Ambassador" instead of "Minister". In Mexico, the title "Minister" was used for an ambassador until about 1860. We will use "Minister" when referring to the Mexican ambassador and "Ambassador" when referring to the American ambassador. I will use the term "Anglo-Saxon" as the adjective and "Anglo Saxon" as the noun where Ángela uses the term "anglo-saxon" to refer to the cultural origins and expressions of most of the original English colonists and their descendants. Where she uses "anglo-american", referring to modern day English speakers of European origin, I will use the commonly accepted term in the United States and particularly the Southwest United States, "Anglo".

The Treaty of Guadalupe-Hidalgo is sometimes referred to as the Transcontinental Treaty by North Americans. The term Transcontinentality, an unusual term in English, is used occasionally in this book to refer to the treaty that gave the United States the northern half of Mexico, from Texas to California.

Spanish personal names usually include one or two first names ("nombres") followed by the patronymic and the matronymic called "apellidos" (for example Garcia Rodriquez). People are often referred to by the patronymic or by the patronymic and matronymic, in this case Garcia or Garcia Rodriguez. Using just the "last name" or matronymic, which some North Americans unfamiliar with Spanish naming systems do, is very confusing for Spanish speakers and people familiar with naming practices in the Spanish speaking world. This double last name system is very useful in determining relationships, but can be confusing for North Americans.

River names can be different when referred to by Mexicans or North Americans. The Rio Grande between Mexico and Texas is called the Rio Bravo in Mexico, although most Mexicans recognize Rio Grande as the North American term. I will use the Mexican names, sometimes with the American name in parentheses.

In the following discussion of early nineteenth-century Mexico-United States relations, Santa Anna makes frequent appearances. Santa Anna was not very consistent in his political leanings, and was president on over 12 different occasions often taking different sides politically, sometimes federalist, sometimes centrist, sometimes conservative. This sometimes makes early nineteenth-century Mexican history a little hard to follow.

This is my first attempt at translating an entire book, and it was an enjoyable challenge, in no small part due to the author, Angela Moyano. We met nearly weekly for a period of months after I had made a preliminary translation of a chapter or two and she answered questions I may have had. I then corrected that translation and the following meeting I left it with her to read after discussing new questions on the preliminary translation of the most recent chapters. She was, like me, more interested in getting the feeling and meaning of the book correct rather than in a word by word translation. This meant shortening sentences and occasionally rearranging wording. She made the experience educational as well as very pleasant. I would also like to acknowledge and thank Gordon Mott and Ken Cott for reading over the draft, making corrections, for being encouraging, and for their reviews. Lastly, I want to express my deep thanks and appreciation to my old Morocco Peace Corps friend and colleague (had to get the Peace Corps in there somewhere), Dr. Michael Tang of the University of Denver and VERI Books, LLC, who copy edited the book in preparation for publication. It always pays to have another pair of eyes look over a manuscript, and he has some really great eyes plus editing skills. Thanks Mike.

All maps have been redrawn from the often illegible copies in the original. Any errors are the responsibility of the translator.

Copy edited by VERI Books, LLC

INTRODUCTION

The United States and Mexico have had innumerable problems since the start of their diplomatic relations at the end of the War for Independence from Mexico. Spain and France experienced a similar situation, as did Italy and Austria, to name only a few countries that bordered each other. The history of the relations between neighbors is plagued with problems, especially when their cultural traditions are totally different. If language unites them, then at least their differences are diminished, as in the case of Germany and Austria, the United States and Canada In the present case, the situation is complex. The United States is a product of a combination of European cultures on an English base and never having been culturally mixed with North American Indians. Consequently, the base of United States traditions and world view were essentially English. On the other hand, Mexico is a country entirely mixed, its traditions and way of living derive from a mixture of the indigenous and the Spanish worlds.

The English world of the seventeenth century, the century of origin of the majority of the colonies that would eventually become the United States, was a period of great religious conflict. Many of the founding cities were established by dissident groups of the Church of England. Among them, Massachusetts was the colony that for economic and cultural reasons had an overwhelming Calvinist influence. It was logical that there was a shock between a world impregnated with Calvinism and one substantially Catholic. Thus, a study of the relations between Mexico and the United States is incomplete without a prior understanding of the differences in the mode of thinking of these two worlds.

This study tries to fill a vacuum in the knowledge of the relations between both countries in that while there exists a goodly number of works, some profound and others less so, of the different periods of Mexico and United States relations, none have clearly and chronologically explained what happened between 1821 and 1861 from the beginning of Mexico's independent life until the beginning of the United States' Civil War.

Our distinct forms of viewing reality affect how we state our different opinions, and we need to understand each other's views of reality in order to understand our differing opinions. The guiding thread of my work is making note of the many problems that have been tangled up with and complicated by various methods of approaching these problems. Cultural, religious, and linguistic traditions are what make up a people. Only by mutual knowledge will two countries understand and respect each other. Daniel Cosio Villegas, a great expert on the United States wrote:

One of the most disconcerting facts about the Mexican (the run of the mill who considers himself "educated") is his olympic intellectual disdain for the United States; he libels it, blames it for all his ills, for all his failures and wishes its disappearance from this world; but he has never tried to study or understand it. The Mexican has prejudices... but not judgements or opinions based on study and reflection.*

Of course, with the previous quote I am not trying to say that North Americans do spend their time studying and understanding us, but that it is time that we leave aside the victim complex that has plagued us for so many years, and assume our historic responsibilities. If we committed errors in the past they were usually explainable by the circumstances of the moment. For people, as for countries, one must understand them in their historic timeframe. The main idea that guides this book is to know the beginnings of our relationship with the United States, and that this will clarify our subsequent problems, that plague us to this day.

In my class on the Diplomatic History of Mexico and the United States at the National Autonomous University of Mexico (UNAM), I covered the period from the beginning of diplomatic relations until the presidency of Miguel Aleman. For now, I present to the reader the first part of this relationship until 1861, the year of the liberal triumph, and the year that the United States began the Civil War or the War of Southern Secession which transformed it into a different country, and therefore changed its international political relations. At the same time, Mexico began its phase of European intervention, from which it became a more unified and homogeneous country.

The work I am presenting here is more descriptive than analytic, but I believe that my contribution to the history of the relations between Mexico and the United States, consists, above all, in the combination that I have made of secondary sources and at the same time the primary archives or those of the Secretary of Exterior Relations of Mexico and others located in the Universities of California and New Mexico. From these sources it seems to me that I have been able to bring new information, especially in Chapter 5, where I analyze the various reactions to North America's invasion of various regions of northern Mexico. In addition, the study of some of the most important violations of the Treaty of Guadalupe-Hidalgo on the part of the neighboring country appears to me to be a new contribution to the history of the relations between Mexico and the United States.

I have tried to present a general and sufficiently complete story so that the public can obtain an idea of the origin of the relations noted above.

Ángela Moyano

* Anuario de Estudios Angloamericanos (Anglia), Facultad de Filosofía y Letras, UNAM, México, p. 22

NOTE: Two chapters in this book have been published as articles in specialized journals: "*Violaciones al Tratado: las tribus indígenas*" and "*Modificaciones al Tratado: La Mesilla o compra de Gadsden*"

I. THE UNITED STATES: AN ANGLO-SAXON AND PROTESTANT WORLD

Any attempt to understand the problems arising during a century and a half of diplomatic relations between Mexico and the United States must have a basis upon which to compare these relations. The only way to obtain a more or less clear understanding in this regard is by pointing out the cultural differences between the two countries. For this it is necessary to go back to the beginnings of their colonization, at which history begins to forge two different nations and, as a consequence, faced the same problems from diametrically opposite directions.

The first colony in the territory that would become the United States was founded in 1607 when New Spain had already existed for 80 years, and when its indigenous world began in what would be a long process of hispanisation. On the other hand, the first English colonies in the United States were completely English from their beginnings during which time the indigenous world was completely rejected. The United States established an English environment, and the immigrants who would find a home in this world did so by resorting to a complete adaptation of thought and North American culture characterized by a complete veneration for England including a long list of North American personages who emphasized their English heritage. From the beginning, The United States fought to preserve English political institutions: representative government, common law, jury of their peers, the rule of law, the taxation system, and the subordination of the military to civil authority.[1] At the end of the nineteenth century and despite the intense non-English immigration of the time, this heritage continued to

---

[1] Edward M. Burns, The American Idea of Mission, Rutgers University Press, New Jersey, 1957, pp. 41-42.

1

predominate. Doubtless, this provided a base upon which the United States tried to bring unity out of diversity.

Mexico, to the contrary, cut its ties from the three centuries of its colonial past. As Juan Ortega y Medina said, "this had simply passed us by and not made us who we are".[2] Official thought of Mexican independence was anti-hispanic, and thus destroyed the base upon which to build national unity. The rejection of Spain, being a negative attitude and therefore destructive, did not allow for the formation of a strong national identity, nor did the imitation of new forms of political institutions without deep traditional roots promote the stability necessary for such a development.

Jamestown, Virginia, was founded in 1607, at the beginning of the reign of James I, at a time when the first colonists were Englishmen from the end of the 16th century, the last generation of the great Elizabethan world when the Reformation separated them from Catholic European thought, spurring their end-of-the-century writers with new visions and desires. One needs only to read Elizabethan drama to become aware of the development of a nationalist patriotism that pushed the English to obtain an overseas empire.[3] Numerous pamphlets and plays were written to stimulate the naval calling which fortified the search for new lands. One of the author's favorites was Richard Haklyut, who earned the protection of Queen Elizabeth for his popularity. His writings are interesting for two reasons: his insistence that God predestines the English for greatness, and his hate of Spain.[4]

---

[2] Juan Ortega y Medina, Destino Manifiesto, Sepsetentas, México, D.F., 1973, p.10.

[3] Phillip Powell, El arból del odio, Ed. Jose Porrúa Turanzas, Madrid, 1972, p. 183. Ortega y Medina, op cit.

[4] Ibidem, op cit. p. 107

These are themes that were echoed throughout contemporary England.

This, coupled with incipient English capitalism looking for new forms of investment, promoted the search of new lands, which in time would lead to conflict with another culture with an entirely different historical origin.

After 1580 an intense hatred of Spain began to develop whose seeds were planted at the moment of breaking off from the Catholic church. Phillip Powell, in his book *El arból del odio* (*Tree of hate*), describes the steps that brought England to a violent hispanophobia:

1) In 1580, Drake came back from his trip around the world which had been organized as a challenge to Spain.
2) This same year, the *Apology* of William of Holland was translated into English, where he accused Spain and especially Phillip II of horrendous crimes.
3) This same year, Phillip II claimed and obtained Portugal and its empire, which placed the oldest of English allies into the Spanish world.
4) In 1581, the pretender to the Portuguese throne, don Antonio, fled to England.
5) In 1581, de Las Casas' brief *Relation of the History of New Spain* was published in English.
6) In 1584, William of Holland was assassinated, by Spain of course.
7) In 1584, the passionate Protestant and promoter of English patriotism and expansion, Richard Haklyut, wrote his famous *Discurso sobre la plantación occidental* (*Discourse on the Western Plantation*) a period in which hate of Spain reached its greatest level of hysteria.

3

8) To complete the picture, in the decade of 1580 news began to reach England of the growing naval power of Spain.[5]

With respect to divine predilection, the English did not need to do more than look for proofs to confirm Protestantism and the idea that the English were the new chosen people. From here to racism was no more than a single step in that being Protestant and also Anglo Saxon in themselves gave them the right to conquer the New World in order to redeem it.[6] Pamphlets were published around 1589 that accused the Spanish of being a mixed race: "the perverse race of those half visigoths... those half moors, half jews, and half saracens..."[7]

The English considered the defeat of the Spanish Armada in 1588 was sufficient proof to confirm their superiority. Since that defeat and even now the Spanish world has suffered and suffers the consequences of the Black Legend urged on by both Holland and England. To be able to explain what happened and summarize such a singularly complex theme, we cite professor Powell: "The basic premise of the Black Legend is that the Spanish have been shown throughout history to be singularly cruel, intolerant, tyrannical, obscurantist, lazy, fanatic, greedy and traitorous." [8]

The anti-hispanic attitude that we are referring to appeared at the end of the sixteenth century during the reign of Queen Elizabeth and has continued to our day. Many have examined the problem

---

[5] Ibidem, pp. 105-108

[6] Ortega y Medina, op cit. p. 108

[7] Powell, op cit. p. 108

[8] Ibidem, p.15

4

of the relations between Mexico and the United States, but few have gone back to its English versus Spanish origins. Those who have, have shown how the fundamental problem is mutual preconceptions and misconceptions deeply rooted attitudes in both cultural traditions that, if not possible to destroy, need to be understood. Knowledge of the inherited cultural traditions of nineteenth-century North Americans, the era when our relations began, explains in large part their behavior. The causes of our problems of mutual misunderstanding were profoundly rooted in the past.

From what we have seen, we know that the English who came to found the thirteen colonies brought with them a culture with a strongly anti-hispanic heritage, an attitude of racial superiority and the belief of being selected by God. This sentiment turned into certainty with the arrival of Calvinists to American lands.

Calvinist doctrine penetrated England from the times of Elizabeth I and it gained so many followers that by 1572 a group of reformers in the House of Commons tried to legalize the new religion. The queen was opposed, insisting that the only church in England should be the Anglican church.[9] From this moment, English Calvinists decided to carry out a series of reforms and became the radical wing that tried to suppress everything that had a Catholic flavor within the Church of England. As a result, English Calvinists were called Puritans, and little by little were able to infiltrate many of their doctrines into the heart of the official church. In 1603, with the crowning of James I, the Puritans received royal orders: obey the Anglican hierarchy or leave the country. The king, although born a Puritan preferred to back the church hierarchy which supported the development of royal authority over Puritan democratic impulses. When Calvin

---

[9] Alden T. Vaughan, Ed. The Puritan Tradition in America, Harper and Rowe, New York, 1972, p. 3

abolished the hierarchy in his church it was cause of suspicion and fear on the part of all government leaders. Thus, whoever did not comply with orders had to leave England, while those who stayed continued their infiltration of the Church of England. The Congregation of Leyden among the Puritans who left, moved to Holland, and from there became the first group of Calvinists to reach North America in 1620.

Nine years after the arrival of the pilgrims at Plymouth, a second group, this time Calvinists and not separatists, had to leave England. Since the royal conference of 1604 their ideas had been gaining influence, but the hostility from the Anglican clergy against them had also grown. For 25 years they tried various tactics to weaken Puritanism, but it was all in vain. The Puritans worked in the heart of the House of Commons to obtain the conversion of more members, and eventually, obtain legalization of their sect.[10] The Puritans received the worst blow in 1628 when Charles I decided to abolish parliament when they realized the political persecution would be accompanied by religious persecution. One year later, the archbishop of the Anglican Church, a great friend of the king, began the repression. A severe economic depression ended up causing a Puritan group of lawyers, professors, and rich businessmen who considered themselves chosen by God to create an exemplary community to renew the world to leave England. These were professional and business men, very sure of their mission and accustomed to being in charge.[11] Since success in one's profession was a sign of being chosen by God, their goal was to glorify God through work and living an honest and prosperous life. In March, 1630, the exodus, called the Great Migration, began to the coast of Massachusetts. Before the end of the year more than a thousand

---

[10] Ibidem p. 15

[11] Bernard Bailyn et al., The Great Republic, Little Brown and Co. Boston, 1977, p 52

colonists arrived, and it is estimated that in ten years the population of immigrants reached twenty thousand.[12]

Because of the number, nationality and quality of the Calvinists who reached New England, the Scottish Presbyterians and the Reformed Dutch became the group with the most influence in the formation of the United States. Through a study of their history, it has been shown that the spirit of Puritanism was the most important determinator in North American culture with both admirers and detractors agreeing that the Puritan heritage is the basis of the national character.[13] It is not possible to understand the history of the United States and its relations with other countries without knowing this heritage. There is no truth more evident than the fact of Calvinist influence shaping North-American attitudes towards saving and winning, towards work and overweening pride as examples of this truth.

The Puritan felt chosen by God to transform the world. As such, he must be industrious, for following his ideology this was the way to glorify God and obtain the success indispensable to being considered saved. Luther wrote that to work was to pray, and to this the Calvinists added that their followers must be beneficial to their community, as well.[14] This obsession with work was one of the pillars of the original Puritan community as exemplified b the well-known adage, "An idle mind is the devil's workshop", with their basic principles of work and piety, for their law against laziness was severe, one of the most drastic of their code. Those who spent more than an hour in a tavern during work hours were fined two and a half shillings. Laziness was punished. If one did not change his comportment he was taken, while being flogged,

---

[12] Ibidem, p. 53

[13]Ortega y Medina, op cit. p. 99. Vaughan, op cit., p.XI

[14] Ibidem, pp. 88-89

to the town center where public authorities awaited to continue whipping him until he swore to work.[15]

The belief in the duty of work was a heritage so deeply engrained that observers of the North American character agree that one of the worst faults was wasting time.[16] Time is money, they suggested, and one cannot waste it. The fear of not taking advantage of free time is even today as intense as failing at work. This pushes the Anglo Saxon to fill every little bit of free time with activities that promote personal progress. The average North American does not know the pleasure of leisure for leisure's sake and have little understanding of the saying, "I work to live, not live to work.". Time for the North American means activity and competence. "The average American –man of action– looks with disdain at aimless contemplation."[17] As we will see below, this is one of the reasons for the North American profound disgust with the Hispanic world.

It has been stated that another of the characteristics inherited from the Puritans is the idea of equality. "The Puritan –notes Ortega y Medina– by basing merit in personal success without making distinctions of class or position, supposes that what interests a man is not what he is, but what he knows how to do... definitively breaking with the class hierarchical system."[18] Each congregation was independent and elected its own pastor, named by their own colleagues through an examination. These selective processes, together with the concept of predestination, developed

---

[15] William Woodward, The Way Our People Lived, Washington Square Press, New York, 1965, p. 4.

[16] Agustin Basave, Vision de Estados Unidos, Ed. Diana, México, 1974, p. 280.

[17] Various authors, The United States, Time-Life, Los Angeles

[18] Ortega y Medina, op cit., p.102

modern democracy in the United States.[19] Individual predestination, that manifested itself in efficient personal labor, does not recognize differences of class between men, and rewards the better qualities of the individual. Thus, the anglo-saxon respect for work lies not in the job itself, but in its successful completion.

From its internal theology, Puritanism came up with the ideas of liberty, equality, individualism, governmental convention and conformity, and could thus develop a special class of personal distinction that had nothing to do with the mundane characteristics or privileges of class.[20]

Puritan political radicalism was born from its relationship with society in which the Puritans considered themselves the chosen of God and accompanied by him in all their activities. They thought their enemies were God's enemies. They believed in their right to fight against all those kings or bishops that tried to place limits on them that they did not accept. Morton, an English Marxist, held that the Puritans were people conscious of their mission as a historically progressive class committed to a revolutionary battle.[21] Never was there a people more convinced of possessing the truth: "Our great solace and defense is that we show here the true religion and the holy commandments of Almighty God... thus we do not doubt that God is with us, and if God is with us, who can be our enemy?"[22] Thus they felt they

---

[19] Ibidem p.99.

[20] Ibidem. p. 99

[21] Al Morton, A people's history of England, Lawrence and Wishart, London, 1956, pp.223-225.

[22] Daniel Boorstin, Historia de los norteamericanos: la experiencia colonial, Tipográfica Editora Argentina, Buenos Aires, p. 9.

were elected by God to establish a pure Church. The central reality of their lives was the analogy of their people with the people of Israel[23] with all the answers to all questions found in the Old Testament. They arrived in the New World convinced of being the carriers of the truth and with the mission of renewing the world. "We will be –prophesized Winthrop– as a city erected on a hill; if we betray our Lord in this task he has imposed on us, obliging him to retract the support that he actually offered us, we will be the object of mockery and ridicule in all the world."[24]

The possession of the truth and the mission to regenerate the world with it, became two of the essential characteristics of the founders of the United States. With the passage of time religious truth secularized and became a political truth: the republican system. Consistent with their principles, North Americans dedicated themselves to implanting this system, for good or ill, in all the peoples of the world, thus justifying, at least for themselves, their desire for domination.

Their understanding of riches also constitutes a fundamental difference with the Catholic and Latin world. Calvin was the first of the reformation Protestants to break with the Catholic prohibition of usury as the leader of a bourgeois community that lived by commerce. He justified all economic activity carried out under the Calvinist church. Calvin wrote: "Is there any reason why the profits derived from business not be superior to those derived from ownership of land?" He who could be rich and was not was a sinner.[25] Man must accumulate riches for God, as he was His administrator. Moreover, Calvin was very strict about

---

[23] Ibidem, pp. 26-27

[24] Ibidem, p. 8.

[25] Max Weber, The Protestant Ethic and the Spirit of Capitalism, Chapter V, George Allen Ltd. London, 1976.

the enjoyment of that richness. As man must work, the money earned must remain active through productive investment.[26] Ostentation and superfluous expenditures were prohibited. Poverty, that had been respected and even exalted in medieval Christianity was for the disciples of Calvin despised, and the proof of leisure and vice. The Catholic countries were in Puritan eyes a scandal as much for their ostentation as for their poverty.

Therefore, it is not strange that until the present they continue to be scandalized before our concept of riches and poverty. The average North American does not understand that to a great extent its co-nationals are responsible for the slow economic development of other nations. Within their train of thought the great fortunes of the millionaires are justified for their having the ability and energy to make those fortunes. The duty of the millionaire is to grow his income to help the rest of society by means of job creation.[27] Carnegie justifies his immense fortune in his book *The Gospel of Wealth*: This applies equally to transnationals and countries in general. Thus, they have the right to be rich, like the Puritan of the past, although they had to strip others of what they had to get there.

The Puritans were certain of their right to uncultivated land on their borders because man must glorify God by means of work. As John Winthrop, first governor of Massachusetts, wrote to justify Puritan colonists taking land from the Native Americans:

> That which is abandoned and never occupied nor subdued belongs to whoever occupies and improves it, since God has given to the sons of men a double right to the land, there is a natural and a civil right... and the native Indians of New England did not fence land nor

---

[26] Ortega y Medina, op cit., 96-98.

[27] Burns, op cit.

11

possess fenced houses nor domesticated cattle to improve the soil; thus they only have a limited natural right to these regions. So that if we leave them with sufficient for their uses we can legally take the remainder, and in this way we will have more than enough for them and for us.[28]

Three years after the arrival of the Puritans, their general council decided that the Indians only possessed a natural right to the soil that they had improved or could improve, but that the rest of the country was at the disposition of those who wanted to take it and work it by such things as building fences, grazing cattle and cultivating the soil, like the Anglo Saxons.[29]

These religious commentaries were recognized by later generations, and even John Quincy Adams affirmed that they were their best argument for exploiting the Native Americans and others.[30] The logical conclusion was that they should work the land if the owners did not. It was the perfect justification for their territorial ambitions.The North Americans believed they were undertaking an enterprise that had not been well done, but the majority of the time their exploitation of others was for their own benefit. Ortega y Medina, in his magistral study of Manifest Destiny tells us: "In the case of the Mexicans dispossessed in Texas, New Mexico and California, the cover story to justify the looting was also the traditional: "the Mexicans did not get as much as they should have out of the land."[31] Years later,

---

[28] Albert Weimberg, Destino Manifiesto, Ed. Paidos, Buenos Aires, p. 81.

[29] Ibidem, p. 81.

[30] Ibidem, p. 83

[31] Ortega y Medina, op cit., p. 122

12

President McKinley, undecided over whether to keep the Philippine Islands ended up declaring that he would do "what was best for humanity and civilization." Here we reproduce the report of what occurred after the Spanish-American War in 1898. The government of the United States decided to keep the islands and McKinley explained his decision to a group of Methodist clergy:

> On more than one night I got down on my knees and prayed to Almighty God that he give me a light and guide. And once, at night, it came to me in this form: 1) That we could not turn them over again to Spain, which would have been a cowardly and dishonorable act; 2) That we could not turn them over to France or Germany, our commercial rivals in the Orient as this would have been bad business and dishonorable; 3) That we could not leave them to the Philippinos; 4) and that there was nothing other to do than to take all of them, educate the Philippinos, raise them up, civilize them, and Christianize them, and with the grace of God do all we could for them as our fellow beings, for whom Christ also died. Then I went back to bed, closed my eyes and slept soundly.[32]

Here are, after two centuries, the same ideas and justifications used by the Puritans of Massachusetts were used to take away land from the Philippinos.

The reason that in 1803 was given to the inhabitants of New Orleans to prevent them from voting on their incorporation into the North American nation, was repeated again in 1898: their incapacity to govern themselves. As we will see below, the same

---

[32] Louis Wright, Breve historia de los Estados Unidos, Ed. Limusa, México, 1972, p. 362.

Jefferson who spoke so much about the right of the people to govern themselves, declared, "Our new fellow citizens are still as incapable of governing themselves as children."[33] What he did not say was that among the inhabitants of Louisiana ran a rumor that they preferred Spanish absolutism to the authority of the North Americans. It seems to me this is one of the keys to understanding the United States: the continuous necessity of self-justification that we, with a different cultural tradition, regard as hypocrisy. They use the self-justification to unite their people in search of a common ideal, made up to satisfy their consciences.

The destiny of those first colonists of Massachusetts was to renew the world, not by means of speculative theology, but by example. It was not so important to perfect the enunciation of the truth as to achieve the society established by them to personify the known truth. The New England Puritans made Calvinist theology their point of departure, but not only that. Even as they possessed a theological mentality, their problems revolved around the institutions they had created.[34] The classic example of their Puritanism was obvious in the founding of other colonies in New England. When some Puritan members found themselves at logger heads with their community they simply established another, as happened in the cases of Rhode Island and Connecticut. While their English contemporaries were dedicated to discussing theological differences, those of New England determined the limits of their new towns, enforcing their penal laws, and fighting Indians.[35]

For the new Calvinists, the destiny of the country and the mission of organizing the community were inseparable.

---

[33] Weimberg, op cit. p. 45.

[34] Boorstin, op cit., p. 45.

[35] Ibidem, pp. 12-14.

It appears that the Calvinists and their followers were more interested in making their institutions work than in discussing the finer points of their ideology. For years, when the men of New England spoke of what they had to offer the world, they referred neither to their creed nor to their church, but to their way of life. As we have already explained, two of their main characteristics were to feel themselves owners of the truth and charged with the renewal of the world. This finally led them, first, to a Calvinist view of the gospels, and second, chronologically speaking, to their political and social organization. All who wanted to be saved, not just religiously but also economically, must imitate them. Herman Melville, nineteenth-century man of letters, could announce to the world: "We, the Americans, are a different and elected people, the Israel of our times, we bring the ark of freedom to the world."[36]

In the eighteenth century, barely independent, the founding fathers claimed that the glory of the new country would be better than that of ancient Greece. The great Jefferson was one of the most ardent enthusiasts of the glorious destiny of his country and on the list of famous men who insisted on offering the world the example of their country as a model worthy of imitating. It is enough to cite the phrase of the poet Walt Whitman, who defines the United States as the "guardian of the future of mankind." To the North American people was given the mission to be the school to the world and the privilege to take the knowledge of democracy to all the countries of the world.[37] In 1836, in his farewell speech, President Jackson declared to the nation that God had chosen them to be the guardians of liberty, to preserve it for the benefit of mankind. Remember that it was precisely in this year that Texas became independent from Mexico. The

---

[36] Burns, op cit., p. 2.

[37] Ibidem. pp. 4-8.

North American public interpreted this movement as one more step in the development of liberty. Therefore, the mission was converted into inevitable destiny. As Stewart, Secretary of State, would say, the mission of the North-American revolution could be compared with that of the Christian religion. Even more, the principles of the revolution constituted a new development in the Christian system "by including the golden rule in the science of human government."[38] This new religion, that of Puritan and "scientific" democracy, had to be carried to all the peoples of earth. It was at this point that mission and destiny became one.

The calling to renew the world according to Calvinist protestant doctrine and practice was from the beginning an integral part of the national spirit.[39] Merck explains how this sense of mission changed through time with respect to its ends but has remained faithful to its roots. At the beginning of the history of the 13 colonies, the need was to renew Europe by means of an example of a new life free from corruption. To this idea, the Puritans added the mission to show the purity of their church and the perfection of their way of life by practicing their religion of Manifest Destiny whenever and wherever it could be applied. Later, after independence, the mission changed: from this moment onwards it consisted in making known the superiority of its government by imposing it on other peoples. After the vicissitudes of the Articles of Confederacy period and the new triumph of the Constitution acclaimed as perfect, the mission changed into a need to export that which they considered to be a perfect government "based on the consent of the governed, on a republican system, and free of the abuses of a hereditary aristocracy."

---

[38] Ibidem, pp. 17-18.

[39] Frederick Merck, Manifest Destiny and Mission in American History, Alfred A. Knopf, New York, 19 63, p. 9.

In Jefferson's time, it was imperative to protect states' rights and the security of the rights included in the Bill of Rights. During the Jacksonian period a more profound idea of democracy included more votes for the masses that continued to change over time. It was in this way that Manifest Destiny included a whole series of concepts about natural rights, geographic predestination, land use, the enlargement of freedoms, and the right of self defense.[40] As circumstances and ends changed, new concepts appeared to defend the old calling to renew the world, in the name of the Protestant God..

This sense of calling has been manipulated over the years to include ambitions of domination, expansion and imperialism. To the average North American it has always been presented disguised as mission and as such the North American people have sanctioned, without knowing it, the ambitions of its government and transnationals under the pretext of raising the quality of life of inferior races. The North Americans were certain of having created an ideal way of life and to have discovered great truths that liberate men., and while the original idea of their mission was meant to educate, liberate, and better the world, in many cases this led to abusing that world. Many North Americans, suggested Merck, were impressed by the responsibility and the danger of carrying out this mission, others, the majority, were glad that this mission was converted into Manifest Destiny, which permitted them not only to reach the Pacific, but also to influence world events.[41]

Manifest Destiny, notes Weimberg in his extraordinary study on the theme, "expresses a dogma of supreme self confidence and ambition, the idea that the incorporation into the United States of all the adjacent regions constitutes the virtually inevitable

---

[40] Weimberg, op cit., Index

[41] Merck, op cit. pp. IX, 8.

incorporation of a moral mission assigned to the nation by Providence itself.[42] At the bottom, he continues, it justified an enormous hunger for and thirst for land. Thus, they turned to an infinity of arguments that self justified their conduct. The ideological conduct of the United States government in its relations with other countries does not appear at times to me anything more than a long list of sophisms. The tendency to think that their interests are the interests of the world is an unconscious attitude of the average North American, resulting from the tradition of their educational system, in a word, of their cultural heritage. In the history of its relations with the world we must remember their firm belief that the cause of America is the cause of all mankind.[43]

By considering themselves the chosen people to defend human rights, they acquired the right to judge others. Whatever for them was a benefit, would be the same for all mankind. As Professor Weimberg said: "people who think they are the champion of the freedoms of others, will be led to think that their rights are the rights of humankind.[44]

---

[42] Weimberg, op cit., p. 29.

[43] Ibidem, p. 29.

[44] Ibidem, p. 49-51.

II. FIRST BORDER CONFLICTS WITH NEW SPAIN

At the end of the War for Independence with the signing of the Treaty of Paris in 1783, the United States acquired the much desired Ohio Valley, that bordered the territory of Louisiana. This territory, acquired by France in the seventeenth century had passed into Spanish hands in 1769 and Louisiana was an enormous belt of land that ran from the Canadian border to New Orleans and the Gulf of Mexico. It covered approximately two and a half million square kilometers (965,255 sq. miles) (Figure 1).[45]

By 1790, the North American pioneers colonized the Ohio Valley and began to export their products from the west of the country using the Mississippi River and the port of New Orleans, both in Spanish territory. This caused problems with Spain regarding navigation of the river, given that the newly independent country considered it indispensable for the export of its products. After various years of diplomatic disputes they arrived at an accord in the Treaty of San Lorenzo. Thus, it was agreed that both Spanish and North Americans had free use of the river. Time would reveal that this treaty had opened up Louisiana to the peaceful penetration of North American pioneers.

In 1798, the Spanish governor of the port decided to close Louisiana to North American navigation to lower the amount of smuggling. Already in 1788, the Kentucky Convention had declared that the inhabitants of the Mississippi Valley had the

---

[45] Cesar Sepúlveda, La frontera norte de México, Ed. Porrúa, México, 1977, p. 12.

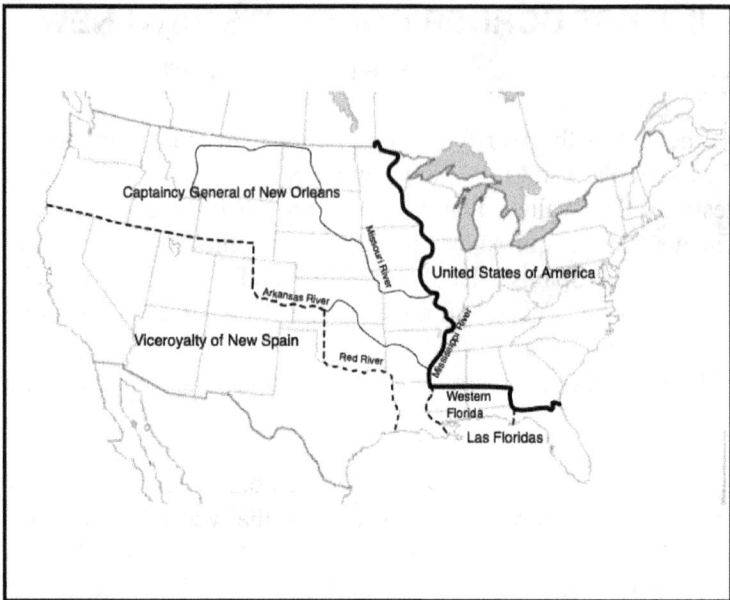

FIGURE 1. SPANISH DOMINIONS IN 1785, CESSIONS
TO THE UNITED STATES

natural right to navigate the river.[46] Based on this antecedent and
without taking its legality into account, the United States
government began to look for justifications to seize such an
important commercial route. Justifications were based, above all,
on the concept of the natural right to security, which arose after
independence and was used for the first time in connection with
Canada. They decided very early in their history, that what they
called the natural right to future security, was superior to the
legal rights of other nations. In the same way, they later argued

---

[46] Albert Weinberg, Manifest Destiny, Ed. Buenas Aires, 1968, p.
36.

their right to the region of Louisiana because it surrounded their possessions. Neighbors must give up their unoccupied regions abutting the United States for the security of the latter.[47]

By the Treaty of San Ildefonso of October 1800, Spain agreed to return Louisiana to France, which seemed to the United States like an aggressive action. They said that Spain should not have returned its possessions without consulting them. They invoked the supposed natural right of security to dislodge the new owners. In 1802, Senator Jackson, the future president, declared before Congress that "God and Nature have decided that New Orleans and Florida belong to this great and growing empire."[48] The neighbor had changed, and the North Americans rapidly began to fabricate the necessary justifications to expel France from the territory. President Jefferson wrote to his envoy in Paris that it was necessary to ally with the British Fleet to attack France.[49] Jefferson, the francophile, was ready to turn against France, because it was in his interest to do so. Surely, he had decided that the loyalty of the western United States depended on his acquisition of the Mississippi, to assure United States' economic prosperity.

In the whole country there arose an obsession to show their right to security. Before France could show its hostility, the North Americans already accused it of wanting to do so. Jefferson thought that a neighbor, for the mere fact of being so, would turn into an enemy sooner or later.[50] The belief in their destiny to

---

[47] Ibidem, pp. 33-35

[48] Albert Weimberg, cited in the *New York Evening Post,* December 30, 1802, p. 55.

[49] Weimberg, op cit., cited the writings of Thomas Jefferson, p. 39.

[50] Ibidem, p.43.

expand across the continent underlay the discussion. An editor of the New York Evening Post expressed it in the following manner:

> It is the right of the United States to control the future destiny of North America. The country is ours; ours the right to all the rivers and all of the sources of opulence, power, and future happiness... and we will be the object of disrespect and taunts in the world if we tolerate being beaten by the intrigues of France. [51]

The problem of French Louisiana in the eyes of the North American government after Napoleon, in one of his rapid decisions, sold it to the United States for 15 million gold francs would not have a chance to deteriorate any further. The interesting thing, for our study, is the spirit that preceded the Louisiana Purchase. Many times it is believed, incorrectly, that North American aggressiveness is directed only towards the Hispanic world.

Only two years after the purchase, President Jefferson sent an expedition to explore the territory. Lewis and Clark reached the Pacific, claiming Oregon. In 1806, another expedition was sent to explore, this time to the northeast of New Spain (Texas region). The leader was Lieutenant Zebulon Pike with orders to study the prospects for business, military forces, and knowledge of the country in general. This was the moment in which the United States discussed the expansion of the territory of Louisiana with Spain. The American president wanted to include Florida in the purchase. He ordered his minister in Spain to threaten them with war if they did not give in. However, it was his own cabinet that did not accept the idea because English

---

[51] Ibidem, p. 42.

embargoes had already begun, and anyway, he would not have had anyone to ally with in a war with Spain. Jefferson, however, pretended to begin war preparations while he secretly planned with Talleyrand to buy Florida. The Napoleonic invasion of Spain frustrated his plans.[52]

It was at this time that Lieutenant Zebulon Pike organized his exploration, a spying expedition that was intended to study the possibility of an invasion of northern New Spain. As a result, the first North American contact in the north of Mexico took place in a context of aggression. His construction of a fort on the Rio Grande (Rio Bravo in Mexico) was interpreted as the beginning of an act of aggression toward Spain.[53] The lieutenant was captured and taken to Chihuahua, headquarters of the Northern Internal Provinces. In his diary, Lieutenant Pike wrote the first report of what was the north of New Spain and what would become for his compatriots the moment when the doors to Mexico opened.

Pike took advantage of his time as a prisoner by writing a detailed description of the route from Santa Fe to Chihuahua, and collecting much information about the geography, politics, and economy of the Mexican border states. He published a list of products and their prices by which he intended to show his compatriots how cheap the border state products were and the high cost of those imported from the center of the country, an economic summary that was fairly complete, especially on New Mexico. The United States frontier at that time was in Missouri with New Mexico as its closest region. His examination, along with that of New Mexican, Pedro Bautista Pino, provided a fairly

---

[52] Samuel Bemis, *A Diplomatic History of the U.S.* Henry Holt and Co., New York, 1942, pp.182-188.

[53] Warren Beck, *New Mexico, a History of Four Centuries*, University of Oklahoma Press, 1962, pp. 101-104.

clear picture of the situation in the province at the beginning of the nineteenth century. Pino, in his account, called *Notícias históricas y estadísticas de la antigua província del Nuevo México*, gave a rather complete view of the internal state of colonialism of the province. The importance of the document comes from the fact that it is based in the socioeconomic context of a region in which the first commercial contacts between the United States and the Mexican border took place.

New Mexico, wrote Pedro Bautista Pino, annually imported merchandise totaling one hundred and twelve thousand pesos, income was sixty thousand pesos, so that it had a deficit of fifty-two thousand pesos. Salaries paid from the capital, Mexico City, to the governor, his aides, and one hundred and twenty soldiers in the garrison maintained cash flow, without which there would have been no money in circulation.[54] Moreover, Pino reports that the New Mexicans lacked the means to extract the natural riches of the area, and he asked for the opening of the ports of San Bernardo and Guaymas because the costs of the Veracruz and Acapulco ports were excessive due to their distance, maintaining that only when the viceregal authorities allowed the free use of what nature provided could the province of New Mexico prosper.

Also, concerning the general state of finances of the province, Pino complained that there were no municipal taxes because no one came to buy, and that New Mexico had no customs offices so that any taxes that could be imposed had to be collected in Chihuahua. There was only one government *estanco*, a store selling tobacco, gunpowder, and playing cards, etc. in the province, which was considered a bureaucratic idiocy since these items could be manufactured in New Mexico. Who would walk

---

[54] Pedro Bautista Pino, Noticias históricas y estadísticas de la antigua provincia de Nuevo México, presentado por su diputado en las Cortes de Cádiz en el año 1812. Imprenta de Lara, México, 1849, p. 14.

800 leagues to buy these items when they could have made them themselves locally.[55]

Pino also felt sorry for his state, as to the administration of justice,. There was no jail to hold delinquents, nor judges who really knew the law. The province constantly suffered the attacks and depredations of the Indians who lived on the other side of the border. The central government maintained a troop of 121 soldiers charged with guarding the entire frontier. This, along with the lack of roads, made it nearly impossible for commerce. On the other hand, products imported from the interior of the Republic cost 300 percent more than their true value.[56] The rest of Pino's work also shows that the viceregal government did not take much care of its border provinces.

Internal Mexican colonialism suffered by New Mexico from its founding would be, with the passage of time, much more damaging than external Spanish colonialism. The Archives of the Secretary of Foreign Relations has an official letter from the governor of Chihuahua in which he complained about the absolute state of abandon in which the government had maintained the borders.[57] With a sole difference, that in Barreiro's time New Mexican markets depended entirely on the United States, the same picture is repeated when Barreiro presented his report 26 years later listing the same abuses and economic abandonment. Despite the monopoly by the central government in Mexico City, local business had developed more in twenty years than in the entire colonial period. The North American attitude was economic and cultural infiltration. As

---

[55] Ibidem. pp. 38-41.

[56] Ibidem, pp. 43-47.

[57] Archivo de la Secretaria de Relaciones Exteriores de México (ASREM) Exp. 17-11-8 f.2

Don Lucas Alamán stated, "...where other countries conquer with their armies, the United States uses its colonists."[58]

The large number of socio-economic observations in the accounts of Pike in 1806 and of San Juan Bautista Pino in 1812 were of enormous importance for knowledge of the frontier. One only needs to point out that the diary of Lieutenant Pike was published in 1810 and was quickly translated into other languages. It became bedside reading for many Anglo merchants who quickly took advantage of the opening of the frontier. However, Pino's account had to wait 27 years to be made public by Barreiro in 1839, and it was only annotated for publication in 1848 by a member of the *Comisión de Estadística Militar*. Pino's report, an important document and the only one to reveal the situation in New Mexico, was published after New Mexico had already become part of the United States. Thus, an account of practical knowledge was converted into a simple list of curiosities. The reading of this document should have been done, at a government level, at least during the organization of the first Mexican Republic.

Thanks to numerous other North American expeditions, the old territory of Louisiana was slowly populated with more colonists. When the United States acquired Louisiana, Jefferson's envoys also claimed Western Florida, which extended to the eastern bank of the Mississippi although it still belonged to Spain. They were not successful, but the envoys kept alleging that the area between the Mississippi and the Rio Perdido belonged to Louisiana. Meanwhile Spain was invaded by Napoleon and the Anglos were advancing towards Western Florida. In 1804, Jefferson, in his characteristic way, asked Congress to pass the Mobile Act which declared that in the Treaty of Louisiana the

---

[58] Valdes Alamán, Jose C., estadista e historiador, Antigua Libreria de Robredo, México, 1938, p. 272.

United States had acquired "all the navigable waters, rivers, bays, in the United States that emptied into the Gulf of Mexico east of the Mississippi River."[59] Throughout his term, Jefferson tried to obtain Western Florida by all means possible. This case is particularly important because it clearly shows the procedures that the United States would follow in its pursuit of territorial expansion. Texas, California, New Mexico, and Hawaii were invaded in a very similar manner.

Let's review the events that established the pattern for future invasions. President Jefferson in his annual message to Congress on December 3, 1805, talked about war with Spain. "Many months have been spent preparing American citizens for war, awakening their anger before the Spanish abuses, real or imagined."[60] On the other hand the whole year of 1806, Jefferson closed his eyes to the English abuses against the merchant marine which was his policy of preventing England from intervening in his plans for Western Florida. Echoing Jefferson's sentiments, voices in Congress began convincing the country of the necessity to take over this Spanish territory. Senator Jackson declared that the natural borders of his country were the Atlantic, the Gulf of Mexico, and the Mississippi. In addition to insisting on the doctrine of natural borders, newspapers explained to their readers how useless it was for Spain to possess these places.[61] Puritan justifications were used to keep the public from feeling guilty over the government's blatant abuse in these matters concerning borders and territorial rights.

---

[59] Weimberg, op cit. p. 36.

[60] McDonald, Decker, The Last Best Hope, Wesley and Goon, Reading, Mass., p308.

[61] Weimberg, op cit., pp. 57-59.

In September, 1806, Napoleon offered to obtain the territory of West Florida, and he ordered that Spain and the United States end discussions of the matter. The following year Napoleon invaded Spain. Taking advantage of the chaos resulting from a civil war against the invader, the United States took the next step, and in 1809, and with the tacit approval of the federal government, thousands of Anglo colonists began to spread out in the region around Baton Rouge on the eastern side of the Mississippi River. The invasion of Western Florida had begun. By the beginning of 1810, the number of Anglos increased and so did the problems for the Spanish. Meanwhile, the list of North American complaints against the Spanish repeated the old prejudices inherited from England. The Spanish authorities were accused of being arbitrary, negligent, cruel, antidemocratic, corrupt, and other familiar calumnies. In July 1810, the mostly Anglo colonists rebelled proclaiming the independence of the Republic of Western Florida. The next step was to ask for annexation by the United States. President Madison declared on October 27, 1810, that the area had been converted into part of the Territory of Orleans.[62]

England, by then an ally of Spain, protested while the North American Congress produced a new proclamation affirming that "the United States cannot watch, without anxiety, that this territory will pass into the hands of a foreign power."[63] In addition, Congress authorized the President to take Eastern Florida under United States' protection, again by any measures necessary, to prevent it from falling into foreign hands, whether French, Spanish or British.

Diplomatic discussions for the purchase of Eastern Florida began in 1817 and ended two years later with the Adams-Onis Treaty

---

[62] McDonald. op cit., pp. 318-320.

[63] Bemis, Samuel op cit., p. 186.

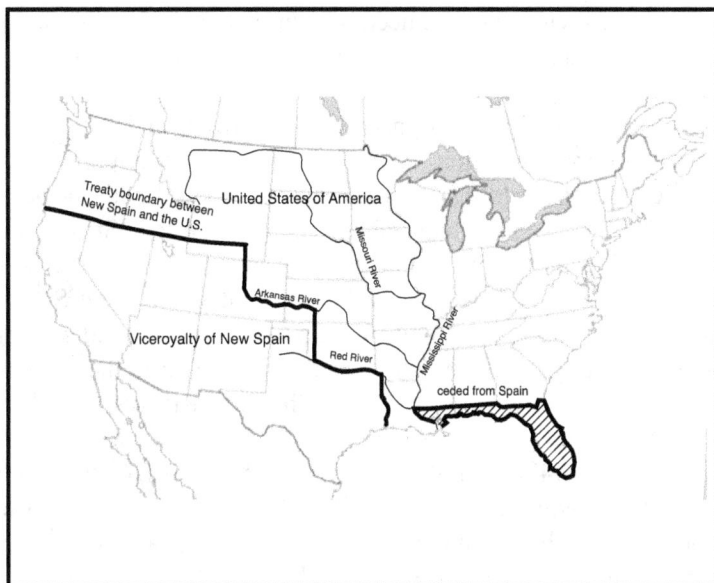

FIGURE 2. ADAMS-ONIS TREATY 1819 (NOT RATIFIED)

(Figure 2), called in North American history the Transcontinental Treaty. Its effects on Mexico will be discussed below. Although the treaty stated that Texas was and would remain part of New Spain[64], the treaty resulted in enormous controversies in the North American Congress and gave rise to a group of politicians who supported that Texas become a part of Louisiana. Senator Benton of Missouri, a border state, went so far as to call Adams inept for having left Texas in Spanish hands. That group of politicians coveted the fertile Texas land and its geographic position, but as President Monroe told General Jackson, "We must content ourselves with Florida for now, and until public

---

[64] Ibidem, pp. 188-196

opinion is convinced of the need of future changes."[65] This same year Moses Austin asked permission to move to Texas.

The Adams-Onis Treaty, signed but not ratified in 1819, was a great triumph for the United States. (Adams-Onis was technically not a treaty but an agreement, since it had not been ratified.) With Spain conceding to the United States the possibility of extending to the Pacific, and fixing for the first time the boundary between the United States and New Spain. The dividing line was established along the 32nd Parallel from the western bank of the mouth of the Sabina River in the Gulf of Mexico in a straight line to where the Red River starts, then along that river to the west until reaching the Arkansas River, then along the 42nd Parallel until it reached the Pacific.[66] The lack of knowledge of the geography of this region was enormous, so that Spain did not realize the great quantity of territory that had been given to the United States. It could not have been otherwise, because the occupants of its empire in America were openly rebelling and one of the clauses in the treaty had been not to give any aid to Hispanic American countries. The United States agreed to pay five million dollars to its own citizens with claims against Spain. The sale on the part of Spain was a desperate measure to save extensive territories and to be able to confront the revolutions in the south of the continent. Nevertheless, it had the merit of keeping Texas in Mexico.

The year of signing the so-called treaty saw two great agreements. One was a bill in Congress prohibiting slavery north of the 32nd parallel, but allowing it south of the 32nd parallel. The second agreement was that Moses Austin was given

---

[65] Baylin, Bernard, et al. The Great Republic, Little Brown and Co. Boston, 1976, p.596.

[66] Ibidem, p. 596

permission to move to Texas which ultimately became the impetus for Anglo control and ultimately the independence of Texas.

We will see in a separate chapter that the case of Texas was of primordial importance for the history of Mexico. It is enough to say that the same method was employed in this future United States state as in Western Florida: it was populated by colonists who began to complain about the political methods of the government that gave them asylum and about economic measures, and finally, as in Florida, a decision on the part of Texans to become independent. It was truly a work of infiltration. The United States never invaded. It was their colonists who carried it out. The idea of separation from Mexico was forged from inside and was the result of the social and economic confrontation between the Anglo-Saxon and Mexican worlds. Following their cultural inheritance, the colonists had a sense of autonomy and anti-Mexicanism that took them first to independence and then to annexation.

It was thought that one of the causes of Mexico's backwardness had been the Spanish policy of prohibiting the outside world from entering its empire. North American merchants, prepared by Pike's account, pushed on to New Mexico. Thus began overland commerce between the two neighboring countries. The first years were characterized by a sincere and mutual sympathy. Josiah Gregg noted in his diary that customs officers only opened certain shipments out of sympathy for the merchants and the desire to help the development of commerce.[67]

Before focusing on Texas, however, it should be noted that contrary to what happened in that future state, in New Mexico

---

[67] Greg, Josiah, Commerce on the Prairies, Norman Press, Oklahoma, 1954, pp. 110-112.

the number of North American colonists was always low. The land was arid and was not welcoming to the typical pioneer. The only ones interested in establishing themselves in Taos and Santa Fe were those who wanted to live by commerce. Professor Weber, an expert on the era, stated that there were fewer than 200 North Americans, while in Texas they were estimated at several thousand.[68] However, there were numerous merchants arriving in wagon trains from Missouri, and even though few wanted to live in New Mexico all wanted a part of its market. From their entrance into the province in 1821, the North American merchants gradually monopolized commerce. Due to the number of habitants, nearly 70,000, it could be said that, "the commerce established between Santa Fe, New Mexico and Saint Louis, Missouri, after the independence of Mexico favored the first commercial and sociocultural relations between the two countries."[69] In 1825, the North American merchants began the march on Chihuahua, Durango, and other productive markets in northern Mexico. In my book, *El comércio de Santa Fe y la guerra del 47*, I explain how this increasingly lucrative commerce did not have fortunate results for diplomatic relations between Mexico and the United States. Through the diaries of merchants like Gregg, Webb, Pattie, and Magoffin it can be seen that the North Americans were convinced of the superiority of their decisions, traditions and customs over the other inhabitants of the new areas. After the first flush of enchantment, they began to ask for the intervention of their government in customs disputes and to complain about Mexican laws along with other grievances.

---

[68] Weber, David H. The Taos Trappers, the fur Trade in the Far Southwest 1540-1846, Norman Press, University of Oklahoma, 1971, p.200.

[69] Moyano Pahissa, Angela, El comercio de Santa Fe y la guerra del 47, Sepsentas, Mexico, 1975, p. 9.

The Mexican government tried to counter these developments with the Immigration Law of 1830. The idea was frankly utopian given the extent of the border, but what interests us here is that the reaction of the merchants, was so violent that it presaged the future invasion. The political instability of Mexico and the disorganization of the customs service, gave a wide field to the reclamations of the Anglos, and these economic complaints were converted into diplomatic disputes. Throughout the decade of the thirties, the Mexican government was preoccupied with the loss of metals and prime materials at the same time as smuggling increased.[70] North Americans have written much in the sense that the Mexican government was not aware of what was occurring. Nothing was further from the truth. Many were the statisticians that expressed their preoccupation over what was happening on the frontier, as much in Texas as in New Mexico.

As already stated, on the Mexican side, in an attempt to stop the commercial monopoly by the neighboring country, the Mexican government began, from the end of the twenties, to establish a long list of commercial restrictions, with the object of restricting the economic invasion of North Americans. All this accomplished was a sentiment of vengeance on the part of the North American merchants. In 1832, the North Americans were convinced that Mexican laws were arbitrary, and the Mexicans were convinced that the North Americans continued to violate them.[71] The first contacts between North Americans and Mexicans in New Mexico was proof that knowing each other does not always mean understanding each other. The same, but on a larger scale, happened in Texas and California, where the large commercial companies soon invaded and as in New Mexico, few of them actually lived there. We can confirm that North American interest in these two provinces, New Mexico

[70] Ibidem, capítulo IV.

[71] Ibidem, pp. 61-66.

and California, was primarily commercial and not colonial as in Texas. Many years passed before the North Americans wanted to colonize them, as much for the distance to California as for the aridness of New Mexico. On the other hand the region of Texas offered colonial potential from the beginning. Therefore, the North American contacts in the north of Mexico varied more in their form than in the final result. In three frontier provinces, a process of infiltration and then domination took place but by different procedures. In California and New Mexico it was merchants, who did not necessarily live there, who were in charge of developing the economic dependence of the two provinces on the United States. Both were invaded from the outside and incorporated by economic conquest, and later by purchase by the United States. In Texas, it was the colonists who rebelled against the Mexican government and nine years later sought annexation, as noted by Lucas Alamán above, "Where other countries send invading armies... the North Americans send their colonists". To summarize, the posture of the United States towards Texas was the same as for West Florida: fill it up with colonists, send in some agitators like Sam Houston, and tie up its economy, all the while professing not to want the territory.

In the following chapters we will see the diplomatic efforts to acquire, first, Texas, then California and New Mexico. Next we will follow a chronological account of the Texas problem until the beginning of the Mexican-American war.

III. FIRST NORTH AMERICAN AMBASSADORS IN MEXICO

Poinsett

With the consummation of Mexican independence, Agustin Iturbide, Mexico's first emperor after Mexico's independence from Spain (1822-1823), asked the world to recognize his government. England was the first country to do so; its desire for markets had converted it into the paladin of liberty, especially when dealing with former Spanish colonies.

The United States recognized the independence, but not Iturbide's empire. They were preparing their famous Monroe Declaration, later known as Doctrine. One of the most important points of this document was its insistence on a republican form of government for countries on the American continent. There were no ties that united the United States and Hispanic America, no language, no religion, no traditions whatsoever. Republicanism was the only thing that could unite them, and naturally, on this point as on so many others, the United States considered itself the example and teacher. They easily claimed the right to teach their political system and insist on its use. By the second decade of the nineteenth century, a group of prominent men in North American public life had proclaimed themselves missionaries of the republican system. Among them was the doctor of laws, Joel Roberts Poinsett.

The personality of this man has been the object of great controversy in our country. He truly had a strange character, as he was as averse to England as he was to Spain, and everything it stood for. Joel Poinsett descended from a long line of French Calvinists that immigrated to South Carolina in the second part of the seventeenth century. By his comportment he demonstrated that he had inherited the well-known Puritan-Calvinist characteristics: a great respect for efficiency and progress, disdain for Catholicism and Spain, and above all, a profound belief of being part of the chosen people, and therefore a missionary of democracy within the republican system. Dr. Ortega y Medina tells us that with the secularization of Puritanism, it was converted into a call to bring republicanism to all nations.[72] North Americans thought that the idea of a free government had been patented by the United States and that to them was reserved the glory and joy of founding this vital principle. It was within this environment of fanaticism that Poinsett moved.

In 1810, he was consul in Buenos Aires as observer of the independence movement, "but in reality he was a confidential agent of his government to spread ideas and collect information."[73] In November, 1811, he was sent to Chile as the first foreign diplomat to be accredited before the Junta of that country. There, demonstrating little diplomacy, he recommended that the Chileans completely gain independence from Spain. Even more, he helped them write a constitution based, naturally, on that of the United States. In October of 1813, the liberal party won, and the triumphant government demanded the withdrawal of Poinsett.[74] Thus, in Buenos Aires, as well as in Santiago, he showed himself to be passionate or even fanatic against

---

[72] Juan Ortega y Medina, Destino Manifiesto, Sepsetentas, México, 1974, p. 100.

[73] Toribio Esquivel Oregon, *Apuntes para la historia del derecho en México*. v. IV (Relaciones Internacionales), Antigua Librería de Robredo, México, 1948, p. 163.

[74] Jose Fuentes Mares, Poinsett, historic de una gran intriga, Ed. Jus, México, 1951, pp.33-37.

monarchy and for republicanism.[75] When he returned to the United States he was elected as the representative of Charleston, S.C., in Congress. It was at this time that the independence of Mexico was recognized. He certainly knew the official envoy of Iturbide, José Manuel Zozaya, who arrived in Washington in December, 1822. The United States government did not send a representative to Iturbide since they were, according to President Monroe, not in agreement with the establishment of a monarchy on the American continent. Zozaya's mission lasted six months. During that time, the Mexican diplomat got wind of the expansionist plans of the United States and the danger this meant for Mexico. In a note sent to Iturbide's government, he expressed his fears:

> The pride of these republicans makes them see us as inferiors rather than equals; their vanity extends, in my judgement, to becoming the capital of all the Americas… with time they will become our sworn enemies.[76]

Therefore, he recommended prudence with commercial ties and made the suggestion of ratifying the Adams-Onis Treaty to avoid the change in borders.

Meantime, President Monroe sent Poinsett to meet with Iturbide to help decide whether the United States should recognize his empire. Poinsett himself declared years later that his report was not favorable as much for the instability of Iturbide's government as because "such a move on our part would discourage the republican party."[77] Iturbide charged Juan

---

[75] Ibidem, p. 22.

[76] Esquivel Oregon, op cit. p. 163.

[77] Fuentes Mares, op cit., p. 81.

Franciso Azcárate to meet Poinsett. At the beginning of the discussions, Azcárate learned that the North American was interested in signing a new border treaty that would give the United States the provinces of New Mexico, California and Texas. Along the same lines, Azcárate answered that Iturbide's government was satisfied with the limits of the so-called Adams-Onis Treaty. A couple of years later, the Republic having been established, Azcárate communicated this to President Guadalupe Victoria when he learned of the impending arrival of Poinsett."[78]

During a short stay in the country, when it was still ruled by Iturbide, Poinsett took advantage of interviewing Santa Anna, Esteban Austin, Zavala, Alpuche, Ramos Arizpe, and other members of the republican party, to whom he communicated his intention to return again only when Mexico had established a republic.

Back in Washington, Poinsett devoted himself to editing his *Notes on Mexico*, a book in which he showed all types of Puritan, republican and Anglo-Saxon prejudices, and that disgracefully, was the mold for North American travelers' writings in the first part of the nineteenth century.[79] It was the first of a long list of diaries by North Americans written after spending a week or two in Mexico, from which their authors felt authorized to opine, based on minimal information, on what they had seen and heard. Poinsett was in the capital 14 days, and it was from there that he wrote about the social and economic world of Mexico.

The first Mexican Republic was established in 1824. It was immediately recognized by the United States, which announced

---

[78] Esquivel Oregon, op cit., p. 31.

[79] Juan Ortega y Medina, *México ante la conciencia anglosajona*, Antigua Librería de Robredo, Mexico, 1958, p. 45.

it was sending an ambassador. President Victoria sent his representative, Colonel Pablo Obregón, to Washington with orders to obtain, among other things, the ratification of the so-called Adams-Onis Treaty. He had already received the report from Azcárate that indicated the United States would ask for border changes. The North American government waited several months before sending an ambassador due to the fact that many of those nominated refused the post. President Monroe's government ended its term, and everyone was involved in the political battle prior to the next elections. The famous diplomat, John Quincy Adams, and the popular hero Andrew Jackson, were the most likely candidates. The post of ambassador was offered to General Jackson to get him out of the election, but he refused. Senator Brown of Mississippi also declined. Similarly, the governor of the state of Illinois and the famous Senator Benton of Missouri did also.[80] Finally, the United States named Joel R. Poinsett as their representative, and Secretary of State, Henry Clay, gave him his instructions.

These included the routine instructions given to ambassadors sent to Hispanic America to counter English activities and explain the Monroe Doctrine. The need to establish new borders especially stood out in the instructions. For this, Poinsett was authorized to utilize three arguments, that navigation of the Red and Arkansas rivers, as authorized in the so-called Adams-Onis Treaty, would only be the cause of future claims; that the frontier change would place Mexico City more in the center of the country; and that the cession would free Mexico from the invasion of the Indians, which would be the charge of the United States. In case Mexico did not want to accept the border change, they would have to ratify the Adams-Onis Treaty of 1819. Two articles to the treaty were proposed:

---

[80] Fuentes Mares, op cit., pp. 90-91.

One- That each government would be responsible for maintaining peace amongst the Indians in their territory.

Two- That the Mexican authorities would return runaway slaves of the United States.[81]

The incursions and devastations of the Comanche, Apache, Lipanes, and other indigenous tribes, was one of the major obstacles in the relations of both countries. Over the years, and almost to the end of the century, both blamed each other for the inability to control the Indian tribes and used them as a pretext for claims and diplomatic complaints. The situation worsened, as Poinsett wrote to the Secretary of State, because Mexico did not consider those Indians in its borders as part of a different nation, as the North Americans did, but rather as citizens.[82] This fact, inherited from Spain, that Mexico considered Indians as citizens occasioned serious conflicts for Mexico since the arbitration of future claims cost a large sum for the Indian incursions into the United States. On the other hand, Mexico could not get paid anything for the devastations on this (Mexican) side of the border as the North American government did not consider the Indians as citizens. The Indian confrontation along the frontier was the result of the politics of expansion at the cost of Indian land and when expelled from their original regions, the tribes had no other choice than to invade the next closest land, starting serious conflicts between tribes north of the border. The Apaches, originally from the Great Lakes, inhabited Texan territory as did the Comanches of Wisconsin. The Indian problem was one of the most thorny issues in the relations between both countries in the nineteenth century. The United

---

[81] Carlos Bosch Garcia, *Material para la historia diplomática de México*, UNAM, Mexico, 1957, pp. 24-28.

[82] Ibidem, p. 75.

States, of course, because of their over-confidence in their military and Puritanical strength, believed they could solve the frontier Indian problem, and for this reason they accepted the obligation to subdue them upon signing the Peace Treaty of 1848. As we will see later, the United States could not pacify the Indians, and five years later in the Treaty of Mesilla (the Gadsden Purchase), they asked to be excused from the obligation. Only by extermination were they able to subdue the Indians at the end of the century.

Poinsett was received by the government of President Victoria on June 1, 1825, and at his presentation of credentials, he declared his pleasure that Mexico had become a federal republic with a constitution similar to the United States. This is an important point. Without a common tradition, language, or religion, he had to emphasize the only thing they had in common to develop a relationship with Hispanic Americans, republicanism. These were the same people, who in Louisiana had denied the inhabitants their democratic rights because they felt that the citizens lacked the necessary tradition to be self governing.[83] On the other hand, in the case of the Hispanic American countries of a similar tradition to Louisiana, they insisted on the adoption of federal republics. Toribio Esquivel Obregón in his book, *Apuntes para la história del derecho en México*, commented, "Did they, in good faith, believe that such a system is good for all peoples, in all climates, with all races, whatever their historic antecedents?", "Or that by eradicating the Latin essence in their social institutions, did they mean to destroy them?"[84]

It appears that President Victoria's reception of Poinsett was cold. Poinsett immediately attributed this to his perception that

---

[83] Albert Weinberg, *Destino Manifiesto*, Ed. Paidós, Buenos Aires, p.45.

[84] Esquivel Obregón, op cit.,, p. 170.

the Mexican president and the secretaries of Foreign Affairs, Interior and Religious Affairs were pro-English. He was preoccupied with measuring English influence and countering it as he had been ordered. It was for this reason that he wrote to his Secretary of State three days after his arrival, adding that there was a respectable group in both houses of Congress in favor of a closer relationship with the United States. This would be the beginning of the political division of Mexicans into two groups, pro-English and pro-North American.

The United States feared the presence of England in Mexico because it was the great power of the moment and would disrupt their plans for expansion. Consequently, one of Poinsett's special instructions was to explain the Monroe Doctrine, one of which's ends was to keep Hispanic American nations away from Europe and especially England, and until, ". . . 1823, the Monroe Declaration (Doctrine) tried to reserve Hispanic America as a field of action for the United States."[85] Initially, Hispanic American governments believed in the good faith of the Monroe Declaration until the facts themselves showed that it had been intended for the sole benefit of the United States.

The declaration, inspired originally by the fear of Russia and its expansion from Alaska, was addressed to his majesty the Tzar of all the Russians, a country that at this time threatened the occupation of the territories obtained by the so-called Adams-Onis Treaty. Russia had been in Alaska since the end of the eighteenth century and had slowly been encircling Spanish California. The government of the United States wanted to make it very clear that they would not accept more Russian expansion. The treaty gave them free rein of the territory north of Spanish California and south of the Russian possession.

---

[85] Carlos Bosch Garcia, *La base de la política exterior estadounidense*, UNAM, México, 1969, p. 19.

The premises of the Monroe Declaration were the following: the isolation of North America from Europe, prevention of exchanges of colonies between European powers, and the firm resolution that these latter would not extend further on the American continent. The most important part of the declaration was, it seems to us, the division of the world into monarchies and republics. Hispanic America should, according to the United States, join the latter.

In 1825, the French invaded Haiti and the United States objected. Spain tried to invade Mexico in 1828; France entered Argentina in 1838 and 1845. England invaded the Malvinas (Falklands) in 1833, Honduras in 1838 and Nicaragua in 1838-1841. Calling on the United States for protection and receiving none, it soon became clear to Latin Americans that the declaration would only be used when United States' interests were affected.[86]

The rivalry with England and the desire to create clearly "American" ties among the Mexicans, however, enabled Poinsett to organize a political group friendly to the United States. He agreed to organize the five lodges of the openly pro-English Yorkish Rite masons in Mexico, with the only lodge organized at that time being the Scottish Rite's. Poinsett wrote on October 14, 1825, "with the goal of countering the actions of the fanatic party in the city, if that was possible, to spread a better level of liberal principles among the leadership of this country, I encouraged and aided a certain number of respectable persons... to form a grand lodge of Yorkish Rite Masons."[87]

---

[86] Dexter Perkins, *Historia de la Doctrina Monroe*, Ed. Universitaria, 1964, pp. 62-68.

[87] Fuentes Mares, op cit., p 111.

The consequences for Mexico of the Yorkish Rite lodges were considerably grave as they provoked a profound battle between the two groups that eventually became two antagonistic political parties. Lorenzo de Zavala states that the Scottish Rite lodges were synonymous with the "Scots Party", and that lodge meetings turned into political meetings to discuss public affairs, the elections and legislative bills, among other issues[88], as the North American party, as Poinsett called the Yorkish Rite group in his reports to the Secretary of State, became more and more important. In July, 1827, two years after his arrival, Poinsett wrote to Clay saying that the reason for the attacks against him in the legislature of Veracruz, was because the legislature had accused him of establishing the Yorkish Rite masonic lodge to divide the Mexican politicians, while Poinsett defended himself with the argument that the Scottish Rite in Mexico had also become a political party. In a later document he explained that the Scottish Rite had come via Spain in colonial times, "where they learned to use this humanitarian institution as a political platform."[89] Poinsett, who lived so long in France, must have known that the Latin masonry was also used as a political instrument. When he was sent to Buenos Aires and Chile he had to have been aware of using apparently non-political organizations to political purposes. It was not without reason that he was known as the North American politician with the best knowledge of Hispanic America. Therefore, his defense against the claim of having promoted the division of the governing class by means of masonry was a great hypocrisy. Just as he knew that anglo masonry did not have political pretensions, he also knew that in Hispanic America it did. The triumph of his instructions was based precisely on the achievement of forming a party in favor of federal republican ideas so appreciated by the North Americans. Through the founding of the Yorkish Rite he

---

[88] Ibidem, p. 150.

[89] Carlos Bosch Garcia, *Material...*, op cit. p. 78.

44

achieved the diminishment of English influence, the change of borders, the sale of Texas, and the opening of the Santa Fe trail from Missouri and New Mexico.

Poinsett said that those who governed the state, and the only ones really organized, were the Sottish Rite masons persons who were the majority centrist members of the high clergy, the aristocracy, centrist republicans and peninsular Spanish. The high clergy did not want a liberal federal regime, and the aristocracy and peninsular Spanish wanted a monarchical regime, regarding republicanism as visionary. In addition, and this is most important, "the scots party had shown themselves to hate the United States, saying in the Mexican Congress that they had considered them the enemy."[90] Naturally, Poinsett searched for a group of politicians that favored the federal republican cause, and thus that of the United States. It was in this way that Poinsett was able to win one of the points on his program, the opening of the Santa Fe trail.

Secretary of State Alamán had refused to give permission time and again until the border was nailed down. The North American ambassador attributed this to pro-English sentiment and had used everything in his power to diminish the influence of the neighboring country in the north of Mexico.[91] Fortunately for Poinsett, Alamán resigned, possibly because of pressure from the Yorkish Rite party, and Sebastian Camacho took the post. On May 13, 1826, at the insistence of the political chief of New Mexico and the government of the United States, Camacho communicated to Poinsett the resolution that the government of New Mexico would permit the preliminary studies for a trail to Santa Fe.

---

[90] Ibidem, p. 78.

[91] Ibidem, pp. 42-43.

The next problem to solve was the border issue. We know the problems that the so-called Adams-Onis Treaty of 1819 and Transcontinentality won by the United States went through to solve this problem, but that was not enough for the United States. In his instructions, Poinsett was ordered to do what was possible to change the border to further the territorial ambitions o the North American government. Two months after arriving and after various meetings with Alamán, Poinsett, however, informed his Secretary of State the oversensitivity that he saw among the Mexicans when he talked about a change of borders. He attributed it to their fear that the United States desired the territory of Mexico north of the Rio Grande. He also noted that Texas was filling up with North American adventurers "and perhaps within some time it would not cost much to take it from them."[92] He was convinced of the aggressiveness of the colonists and could guess that in a few years that what had happened in West Florida would happen in Texas. From the time of Iturbide the Mexican government, totally aware of the threat, had planned to establish colonies along the frontier and tried to populate these regions. Iturbide's minister in Washington was the first to recommend ratifying the Adams-Onis Treaty and not to accept a change of borders as discussions continued and neither country agreeing to cede one centimeter of its territory. In Mexico, they continued to talk about the expansionist designs of the United States, and they sent General Mier y Terán to examine the border situation.

At the same time, new difficulties arose when Mexico decided to institute consular certificates, without which North American merchants could not enter with their merchandise. As the lists became stricter in an attempt by the Mexican government to protect its frontier, Poinsett became indignant and wrote to Henry Clay, "the measures of the Mexican government towards

---

[92] Ibidem. p. 39.

the United States are inspired by a sentiment of jealousy and a fear of evil difficult to define in their personal dealings with us."[93] Despite the complaints, the Mexican government, in a desperate measure to stop smuggling, decided that foreigners needed passports to enter the country, further separating the North Americans from their counterparts south of the border, however tenuous the border tended to be.

In December, 1826, a rebellion in Nacogdoches, Texas, failed, and Mexico asked the United States to publicly declare they had not intervened in the rebellion. This incident was a motive for Mexico to stop discussing new borders and to begin insisting on the ratification of the old treaty of 1819 to maintain the status quo at all costs.

For its part, the United States government continued to be preoccupied by the proximity of New Orleans to the border; and for this reason proposed in March 1827, to modify the dividing line between the city and the neighboring country. They offered two alternatives, one of which was that the Red and Arkansas rivers stay within North American territory, at least the navigable part, with a border near Santa Fe, New Mexico. For this cession they offered one million dollars. The second alternative was that the border would stay very far from Santa Fe, the Red River in North American territory, along with the navigable portion of the Arkansas River. For this cession they offered half a million dollars.[94]

The Mexican government refused to negotiate even before Poinsett made the offer. In July of the same year (1827), attacks against the activities of the North American ambassador began in the Legislature of Veracruz causing Poinsett to again propose a

---

[93] Ibidem, p. 65.

[94] Ibidem, pp. 70-71.

border treaty. It was President Victoria who reopened the idea in August, 1827. The negotiations began to drag on again, and in January, 1828, Poinsett communicated to his government that "the time appears unpropitious for a change in borders." Nothing could be decided without the approval of the legislatures of each state, and Texas could accuse the Mexican central government of dismembering the province. Consequently, it was better to ratify the 1819 treaty as Mexico wanted. According to Poinsett, European agents had convinced the Mexicans that a request for a change in the frontier meant that the United States were their enemies. In addition, the treaty on commerce was stalled in Congress until the treaty on borders was signed.[95]

Finally, in February, 1828, both treaties were signed and sent to the respective Congresses to be ratified. Sepúlveda shows that Mexico had not ratified in the months leading up to the signing because Mexico was trying to extend its territory to the area previously claimed by Spain. He added that the Senate of the United States ratified the treaty in April, 1829, while in Mexico it was allowed to languish. Poinsett attributed the motive of the delay to the laziness of the Mexican Secretary of State. For whatever reason, there was not time for the exchange of ratifications and again the treaty was left dancing on a tightrope. Sepúlveda attributed the failure to exchange ratifications to the fate that seemed to follow Mexico in those years. He is of the opinion that President Adams and the Senate were aware that it was impossible to obtain Texas and they did not insist on ratification. The delay in sending the document, "created a vacuum of authority there (in Texas), opened the doors of temptation to land hungry colonists, and facilitated the

---

[95] Ibidem, p. 83.

penetration of the frontier."[96] And thus it happened. The following year, 1829, General Jackson won the election for President of the United States, and decided to postpone the exchange of ratifications to try to obtain Texas. As a result, on August 25, 1829, Poinsett received instructions from the new Secretary of State, Van Buren, asking him to try to buy Texas. The delay in sending the treaty to Washington definitely opened the way for another attempt at buying territory.

Van Buren employed a new tactic ordering Poinsett to say that the Sabine River was really the one farthest west and thus, Poinsett should insist that the border line be recognized there. Three propositions were made. In the first, the cities of Bahia and Bejar would be left inside United States territory. For this change they offered four million dollars, but if it were necessary they would raise it to five million. The following propositions were each for less land, and consequently, they would pay less. The important thing here is the lack of appreciation that the United States had for the sovereignty of another nation, and the low respect they had for other nationalities. In the proposals, they did not have any trouble declaring that, "there was no difficulty in getting agreement to what was necessary so that the Mexican inhabitants found in the zone along with their cities could join the United States"[97] without ever taking into account the opinion of these inhabitants. As had happened in Louisiana twenty years before, the United States government thought the same way, that the inhabitants were not prepared to decide their own destiny.

---

[96] Sepúlveda, César, Tres ensayos sobre la frontera septentrional de la Nueva España, Ed. Porrúa, México, 1977, pp. 81-83.

[97] Carlos Bosch Garcia, *Material...,* op cit., p. 105.

49

The reasons given by the United States in their request to purchase Texas were patronizing and self serving. Americans had invaded the region against the wishes of the Mexican government and were in effect illegal aliens in Texas, the business spirit of the North Americans was envied in Mexico while also causing resentment, and the North Americans let it be known that they felt that Mexico should have been very happy to see themselves freed of so many problems.[98]

The date of the request to purchase Texas was August 25, 1829. A few days earlier the Barradas expedition, a Spanish attempt to retake Mexico, had arrived in Tampico. But instead of asking for the help offered in the Monroe Declaration of 1823, Poinsett asked that United States ships be sent to the Mexican coast to protect the commerce between both nations and "to inspire respect in Mexicans who would act with more care in their relations with the North Americans."[99] So, instead of offering the help implied in the Monroe Declaration, the ships served as a subtle threat to Mexico to toe the line with no offers of help against Spain.

Four years before, the North American ambassador had given enormous importance to what the Mexican government knew as the Monroe Declaration. Many Mexicans had been led to believe that the declaration contained, implicitly, a message of help if necessary. The Mexican government did not need the Barradas expedition to see the situation clearly. Various incidents had come to pass on the continent to show the lack of interest the United States had to insert itself into others' problems. As Esquivel Obregón said in his study of Mexican international relations, "The Monroe Doctrine is the negation of all rights by Hispanic American countries, forcing upon them a system of

---

[98] Ibidem, pp. 106-107.

[99] Ibidem, p. 103.

government (i.e. republicanism), and that they can do nothing in their internal affairs that the United States considered contrary to its interests."[100]

A few days before he received the orders to purchase Texas, he had written to Washington asking to be allowed to retire. From December, 1827, he had been accused of involvement in Mexican internal politics. For these reasons Poinsett did not present the petition to buy Texas. The Plan of Montaño (December 23, 1827) asked, among other things, for Poinsett's expulsion. Other attacks had followed and created an environment of hostility towards him. On August 22, 1829, he wrote to Washington, informing them that his residency in Mexico had become nearly intolerable. The answer from his government was sympathetic and revealing, the president of the United States and his cabinet believed that the only motive for the hostility was "the argument of those who thought you had used your position to meddle in the internal affairs of this Republic."[101]

The accusation that Poinsett was meddling too much in internal Mexican affairs and which he refused to accept was known by the United States government. Mexico considered that the exit of the ambassador would be beneficial to the interests of the nation. Several days later a formal petition from the Mexican government was received in Washington with respect to the recall, "Things have reached a point that the government of Mexico would be neglecting its most essential duty if it did not ask the United States for the recall of its ambassador." [102]

---

[100] Esquivel Obregón, op cit., p. 169.

[101] Carlos Bosch Garcia, *Material...*, op cit., p. 110.

[102] Carlos Bosch Garcia, *Historia de las Relaciones entre México y los Estados Unidos*, UNAM, México, 1961, p. 44.

Poinsett asked for his passport and the Mexican government fixed the date of his departure at Jan 2, 1830. Thus ended the first diplomatic mission of the United States to Mexico. Mexican historians have been in general agreement over the pernicious influence that he had in the politics of the recently independent nation. He was an example of a man for whom the ends justified the means. His objective was to create a political group favorable to the North American interests, and it did not matter to him that he had divided the country into two antagonistic groups. His legacy was hostility and bitterness between the two nations, and even the United States Secretary of State, Van Buren, wrote that the sentiments of the North American public were profoundly wounded by the acts of the legislatures of Mexico against Poinsett.[103]

Anthony Butler, Ambassador of Claims

A few days before the departure of Poinsett, Anthony Butler, the new North American ambassador, arrived in Mexico, a veteran, and ex-aide de camp of General Jackson, with no other qualification than that he owned land in Texas and had written a memorandum on the necessity of obtaining this province.[104]

Mexican and North America historians have judged him harshly, as ignorant, vulgar, and immoral.[105] Esquivel Obregón quoted Esteban Austin affirming that he had never known a more disgusting man. Everyone agrees that he was the worst choice for the diplomatic post of ambassador to Mexico. After Poinsett,

---

[103] Fuentes Mares, op cit., p. 277.

[104] Karl Schmitt, *México y los Estados Unidos, conflicta y coexistencia*, Ed. LIMUSA, México, 1968, p. 51.

[105] Toribio Esquivel Obregón, op cit., pp. 167-170.

diplomatic relations between the two countries were very tense, but Butler made them worse, and his six years were full of intrigue and poor management, ending in the uprising in Texas.

The Mexican government received him well, hoping to establish better relations with the exchanging of new ministers. Although "his instructions were to lower the tension between the two countries emphasizing the Mexican offenses against the United States."[106] It did not take long to realize that Butler would be as aggressive as his predecessor, but much coarser.

While the animosity of Butler and his ignorance of diplomacy were noted immediately, at the same time, it is curious that they believed that adopting the position of victims would smooth over their differences. Hardly having arrived in January, 1830, Butler sent the Secretary of State a list of the members of President Bustamente's cabinet claiming that all were enemies of the United States.[107] Although he complained that the official newspaper had announced his coming with the intent to buy Texas, this was, in effect, one of his instructions, that he thought was the most important to achieve. Van Buren, Secretary of State, wanted the border settled and for this proposed the three possibilities noted above. The first left the cities of Bahia and Bejar in the North American zone, and, of course, absorbing the inhabitants, the second demanded less territory, and the third, even less.[108] For the first proposal, they offered four million dollars, and for the second and third, proportionally lower quantities. In this same document, Van Buren argued that because the Mexican government no longer trusted the colonists after four rebellions Mexico would be better off with the sale of

---

[106] Carlos Bosch Garcia, *Material...* op cit., p 109.

[107] Ibidem, p. 116.

[108] Ibidem p. 105.

its territory, full of worrisome and bellicose colonists and Indians. As we have seen, the United States from the very beginning insisted that the sale would benefit Mexico, a characteristic argument given the role as defender of human rights that they had given themselves, which at the same time justified the desire to extend their territory at the expense of their neighbor.

A little before Butler arrived in Mexico, the North American newspapers had begun a campaign to convince their fellow citizens of the possibilities the Texas territory would offer. This propaganda put great pressure on Butler, in that he felt destined to be the one to obtain Texas, and had boasted thus to President Jackson. He would obtain that which Poinsett could not and from 1830 to 1836, he tried everything he could think of to obtain this region. Obtaining Texas became a real obsession. His intrigues were sometimes childish and at other times arrogant. His audaciousness was such that he eventually even claimed that Lucas Alamán, Secretary of Exterior Relations, had suggested the possibility of the United States reclaiming territory south to the Rio Grande. Another of his ruses was to revive an old idea of Senator Benton, that Texas was part of old Louisiana. With questionable "facts" Butler decided to ask that Texas be returned to its legitimate owners based on what he called a retrocession.[109]

With the failure of this attempt, he tried to negotiate a loan to Mexico using Texas as collateral; and in case Mexico did not pay up, the territory would peacefully pass to the North Americans. As we shall see desperate in the face of his failures, the march of time, and the slowness of the negotiations, Butler devised the only method he thought could obtain the desired results he wanted in the long term.

---

[109] Ibidem, pp. 140-143.

In his first instructions he had been ordered to insist on the payment of claims that Mexico owed the United States. These were generally economic complaints for damages caused by Mexican citizens on the life or interests of North American citizens in Mexico. He was able to assemble a file so complete and so exaggerated that upon his leaving in 1836, the Mexican government found itself with a debt of an unsuspected sum of money, knowing that this would be a slow but sure process to obtain the desired territory because Mexico would not be able to pay such a large debt and would have to exchange the debt for land. Faced with the impatience of President Jackson, Butler visited Lucas Alamán, Secretary of Exterior Relations, to discuss the existence of a Rio Sabinas different from the one in the Adams-Onis border treaty of 1819, hoping that the visit would facilitate the exchange of territory to realize his objective. This was one of his more infantile schemes because of his insistence that the Rio Sabinas was mistakenly identified in the Treaty when in reality it was the Nueces.[110]

Meanwhile, the United States government kept pressing for the conclusion of a deal. Butler, cornered by the haste of his government then simply recommended the occupation of the territory. A curious result was that several months later the North Americans complained that the Mexicans accused them of fomenting revolutions in Texas.[111]

Butler, desperate before what he considered to be his worst mistake, asked to return to the United States in July, 1834, whether it be for a vacation or to be relieved of his charge. He wanted to talk with President Jackson to decide if he would continue with his mission. Glenn Price, one of the few writers to

---

[110] Ibidem, p. 114.

[111] Ibidem, p. 159.

examine Anthony Butler's documents at the Library of the University of Texas, explains that in this visit to President Jackson, Butler asked for and obtained permission to bribe several Mexican authorities. Even in this he failed, but what we want to underline is the complicity of Jackson in this attempt. Price added that the position of the North American president was clearly to keep Butler in Mexico until the Mexican government requested his withdrawal.[112]

As ridiculous as his invention of the Rio Sabinas, his last intrigue was worse. Butler petitioned Washington for half a million dollars to bribe President Santa Anna, through a fictitious character, President Santa Anna with the story that the fictitious confessor of Santa Anna's sister had promised to use his influence to suborn Santa Anna. The story was so obviously unlikely that even Jackson, upon reading the plot, could only exclaim, "Ah, Butler, what a scamp!".[113] Once back in Mexico in February, 1835, Butler wrote to the president, "I promise you that your administration will not end without the objective in your power."[114]

Butler returned to Mexico, but on the way across Texas, he attended an assembly of rebel Texans, for which the government of Mexico decided to ask for his withdrawal.

The main legacy that Butler left his successors was the use of claims since at that time, they constituted the best pretext not to confront much more important diplomatic tasks. Each time Mexican complaints arose about invasions of its territories,

---

[112] Glenn Price, *Origenes de la guerra con México*, FCE, Mexico. 1967, pp. 40-45.

[113]Ibidem. p. 45

[114] Carlos Bosch Garcia, *Historia...*, op cit., p. 179.

North American ambassadors used the claims as a smoke screen to lower the importance of what had happened and play the role of victim. Thus was formed the myth of a rude and petulant Mexico who did nothing but offend their benevolent neighbor. To this day, this myth is used to justify the aggression of 1846. The average North American sees, in scholarly texts, a history of North American generosity that is invariably responded to with offensive behavior by Mexico. At the taking of territories such as the Mexican Cession, even Polk used the argument that Mexico had stopped paying claims in 1845, as one of the pretexts to declare war in May, 1846.

IV. TEXAS

Much has been written about the Texas conflict in the history of Mexico with most of it being of a passionate character and with a closed, nationalist attitude. There exist, however, a half dozen serious, diligent investigations, some of which have been used here to serve as a basis for understanding the Mexican point of view.[115] In United States' historiography there are also some studies that try to present the information in an unbiased fashion.[116] The authors of both groups think that history is not written to lay blame, but rather to try to explain the why of what has happened. Unfortunately, against these laudable efforts is a much greater number of histories that try to exalt patriotic

---

[115] Among them should be mentioned: Carlos Bosch Garcia's *Material para la historia diplomatically de México, La historia de las relaciones diplomaticas* and *La base de la politics exterior estaunidense*. These three works of Dr. Bosch are, probably, the best that have been written from the Mexican point of view about the diplomatic relations between 1821 and 1846. Also, the work by Toribio Esquivel Obregón, Apuntes para la historia del derecho en México, Vol. IV, dedicated to international relations that cover until 1880, as well as that of Jesús Velasco, *La guerra del 47 y la opinion pública*. Various articles by Dr. Josefina Vázquez on the whole are very useful. She also published an anthology of writings on the theme entitled *Mexicanos y norteamericanos ante la guerra del 47*. Luis G. Zorrilla has two volumes, the only ones covering the colonial period until 1950, under the name *Historia de las relaciones entre México y los Estados Unidos de America*.

[116] For example: James Callahan, American Foreign Policy in Mexican Relations; William Manning, Early Diplomatic Relations Between the U.S. and Mexico; Carey McWilliams, *Al norte de México*; Glenn Price, *Los orígines de la guerra con México*; and Fred J. Rippy, The U.S. and Mexico.

nationalism. It is our opinion that as much in this period of violence and profound hatred as in any other, the professional historian must strive for the clearest, most serious, and most objective writing, possible. There were errors on both sides of the border and the maliciousness that undoubtedly existed was done for the most part not by the people, but by the politicians and the government. President Polk emerges from the account as a villain, but the same is true of Santa Anna. Nevertheless, we have to try to explain the reasons for this behavior at a general level. For this, North American and Mexican publications have been used so that the reader can consult both in libraries to obtain a deeper understanding of the events unfolding in this chapter. The work of Toribio Esquivel Obregón has been especially useful to explain the origins of the colonization of Texas; however, perhaps the best method to penetrate into the causes of the conflict would be to read the letters exchanged between the diplomats at the time and their respective secretaries of state, such as is found in *Material para la historia diplomática* of Carlos Bosch.

In order to understand the complicated Texas affair, it is best to go back to its beginnings. According to trustworthy sources, the coast of Texas was explored by the Spanish from the sixteenth century by various explorers, among them the famous Alvar Nuñez Cabeza de Vaca, as the first to cross and take possession of the Texas territory. Various descriptions of the explorers are conserved in the viceregal archives.[117] There exist as well various *"cedulas reales"* (royal certificates) and agreements that acknowledge Texas as part of New Spain. We also know that, given the bellicosity and nomadism of the indigenous tribes, all

---

[117] Toribio Esquivel Obregón, *Apuntes para la historia del derecho en México*, Vol. IV (Relaciones Internacionales), Antigua Libraría de Robredo, Mexico, 1948, p. 120.

of the attempts to colonize the region in the sixteenth and seventeenth centuries failed.[118]

At the end of the seventeenth century news had arrived in New Spain that the French had a claim on the territory including a French expedition in 1685, under Robert de la Salle, who had supposedly established a fort in northeast Texas, called Saint Louis in the Bay of Corpus Cristi. The governor of Coahuila was immediately ordered to expel the intruders, and several expeditions were sent out but did not find any evidence of the French settlement, "that, following the then international law, was considered a violation."[119] Nevertheless, even the threat of French intrusion impelled the government of New Spain to found missions in Texas, which, however, did not last longer than from 1690-1693 because of the ferocity of the Texan Indians. Twenty-six years would pass to establish these missions and the cause was the same, the French threat complicated by hostile indigenous tribes. It was not a coincidence that the first missions organized were located precisely in the region of the French fort at Natchitoches. One of these missions was San Antonio de Béjar founded in 1718, more than a thousand kilometers (625 miles) from the last Spanish settlement in Coahuila.

These facts will be of great importance later, since the United States over the years, claimed that Texas had been part of French Louisiana, and should thus belong to them, as they had bought the territory in 1803. Incredibly, but true, various present day

---

[118] Luis G. Zorrilla, *História de las relaciones entre México y los Estados Unidos de América*, 2 vols., Ed. Porrua, México, 1965, vol. I, p. 77.

[119] Toribio Esquivel Obregón, op cit., p. 120.

authors continue using such an anachronistic argument to justify the taking of Texas.[120]

It should be added that in 1714, the captain of the presidio of San Juan Bautista, the closest to the province of French Louisiana, arrested a commercial expedition sent by the governor of said province. By express orders of the Consejo de las Indias, the head of the operation was held in confinement.[121] Its Consejo de las Indias wanted to make explicit the Spanish ownership of Texas although Spain was at this time under the government of the Bourbons. From 1714 to 1769, the date France ceded ownership of Louisiana to Spain, Spain had established three more missions and had brought a colony of Spaniards from the Canary Islands. The Marques of Aguayo, as well as of Rubi, reorganized the missions, which show Spanish sovereignty over the Texas lands. As noted above, Louisiana returned to France from 1800-1803, the year in which it was sold to the United States. However, the Spanish government had made it very clear upon its return to Louisiana that Texas had never belonged to Louisiana.[122]

It is a little known story that the insurgent, Berbardo Gutiérrez de Lara, occupied Texas in 1813. When he, with North American help, took control of San Antonio de Béjar, executing Salcedo, the Spanish governor, and declaring the independence of Texas. The territorial constitution published April 17, 1813, says the following, "The province of Texas will be known from henceforth as the State of Texas forming part of the Mexican

---

[120] Seymor Connors, *La intervención norteamericano*, Ed. Diana, México, 1968.

[121] Toribio Esquivel Obregón, op cit., pp. 117-119.

[122] Cesar Sepulveda, *La frontera norte*, Ed. Porrúa, México, 1976, p. 43

Republic, to which it will be permanently united." Gutierrez de Lara, deceiving the North Americans, established the first part of what would become an independent Mexico. The governor of Louisiana was furious and wrote President Madison asking that he take possession of Texas as far as the Rio Grande, initiated a press campaign against Gutierrez de Lara and continued sending North Americans to Texas as hunters.[123] The situation did not last long. In August, 1813, the royalist general Arredondo defeated the rebels and Texas again became part of New Spain.

These events show that the North American interest in Texas dated back a long time. As a result of this interest, in 1819, at the presentation of the Adams-Onis Treaty between Spain and the United States to be ratified by the North American Congress, there arose a group of politicians who accused John Quincy Adams of having ceded Texas to obtain Florida and Transcontinentality. This point of view remained as an antecedent that continued to be invoked to justify the annexation of Texas in 1845. This is what Butler had called a retrocession.[124]

In Mexico, there was never the slightest doubt that the territory had been Spanish since the sixteenth century and thus part of Mexican heritage. A letter from José Maria Morelos (a Mexican founding father) from February 17, 1813, in which he ordered his commissioners to offer to the United States the cession of Texas in exchange for help in the cause of independence proves it.[125] With the revolt by Gutierrez de Lara in 1813, there began to enter into the province a certain number of Anglos "who were staying in Texas and took advantage of the opportunity to

---

[123] Toribio Esquivel Obreón, op cit., p. 130

[124] Connors, op cit.,

[125] Toribio Esquivel Obregón, op cit., p 133. References the letter from Morelos to Marshall Ignacio Ayala.

separate it. Some years later, Don José Manuel Herrera established a small fort on the island of San Luis in Texan territory as a base from which to harass northern New Spain. It was from here that the Mina expedition, which counted in its ranks a large number of North American adventurers, set out in 1817.[126]

The first formal attempt to establish a colony of North Americans in Texas was by Moses Austin, who alleged to have been a Spanish subject in Louisiana. With the help of an influential friend he was able to convince the commandant of the *Provincias Internas de Oriente* (Internal Eastern Provinces) to grant him permission to colonize and was so granted by the viceroy Apodaca on January 17, 1821. After Moses died, it was his son, Stephen, who was in charge of carrying out what the father had been granted.

It is thought that the principal motive for the authorization of the entry of Austin and 300 families was his assertion that having been subjects of the King of Spain in Louisiana, they wanted to become so again. Naturally, the reports from the Minister of Spain in Washington about the expansion attempts by the United States influenced the decision too. The authorities in New Spain thought that a group of people loyal to Spain, would make a good barrier to hold back the Anglo invasion. One more reason for opening the frontier, which had been closed for 300 years, was the influence of liberal doctrines that considered it time to permit the entrance of foreigners. The last legislature of the Spanish Cortes had provided the steps for this liberalization.[127]

---

[126] Ibidem, p. 133.

[127] Carlos Bosch Garcia, *Material para la historia diplomática*, UNAM, México, 1957, pp. 11-19.

The governor of Coahuila and Texas not only authorized that Austin could propose the boundaries of the colony, but also the method of distribution of the land. As a result, 320 hectares (790 acres) were given to each man, 150 (370 acres) to each woman, and 80 (198 acres) for each child, and 40 (99 acres) for each slave. The land gifts were free, despite the fact that at that time within the United States border an acre cost $1.80 and there were limits on the purchase of land. It should be pointed out that the first concession included an area the size of Massachusetts, Connecticut and Rhode Island together. It was thought at that time that the Texas land was not very fertile, and it was not, in comparison to the Bajio of Mexico. The conditions placed on the colonists were: to be Catholic, be good citizens, swear allegiance to the king, and observe the constitution of the Spanish monarchy.[128]

Once Mexico was independent, the reasons that led the Iturbide government to confirm the permission given by the viceroy Apodaca were the same, plus the desire to obtain the military help of the United States in case of a Spanish attack. The Iturbide government wanted to ask for a small loan from the United State and believed that its behavior towards the pioneers would help it obtain one.[129] Equally, they offered a little land and a yoke of oxen to the soldiers that had taken part in the war for independence. In addition, the representatives of the Mexican empire in Europe tried to engage European colonists to come to Texas. The ruling presented to the Governing Council of the Empire (of Mexico), via its Commission of Exterior Relations, emphasized they should search for Irish immigrants, since they were Catholic and did not sympathize with the English nor with the North Americans. The ruling looked to create a barrier to North American expansion with groups of colonists that were

---

[128] Zorrilla, op cit. p. 81.

[129] Bosch, *Material...*, p. 13.

supposedly hostile to the North Americans.[130] It was also necessary to change frontier policies to give more importance to colonization and create more captaincies to guard the new enclave loyal to Spain. It was also thought necessary to populate Coahuila to form a second barrier in case of an invasion from Texas.

In January, 1823, the first law of colonization was handed down. It guaranteed liberty, property, and the nine civil rights of the foreigners, asking in return that they be Catholic, faithful to Mexico, and cultivate their lands and if they did not the land would be taken away. They did not have to pay taxes for six years, during which time they could freely import machinery and farming tools. Iturbide's Congress had the power to grant Mexican citizenship to all colonists who requested it.[131] The only measure that was forbidden to the colonists was that there would be no more trade in slaves and that the children of slaves already purchased would be free at fourteen years of age.[132]

In Mexico, slavery had been prohibited on various occasions, including the constitution of Empire of Iturbide that had forbade it. Instead of appreciating the special case made for them that allowed them to keep their slaves, the North Americans protested because of the clash of institutions and ways of life. Following Anglo-Saxon law, individual property was totally private, and the government had no rights over it. On the other hand, following Roman law, adopted by countries of Latin origin, common well-being lay behind property. The state ceded to its citizens what they needed, but reserved the right to reclaim property when the collective demand required it. Even though

---

[130] Ibidem, p. 17.

[131] Toribio Esquivel Obregón, op cit., p. 137

[132] Zorrilla, op cit., p, 82.

they were allowed to keep their slaves, the Anglo-Saxon colonists considered it an arbitrariness of the Iturbide government to claim to rule about slaves since they considered slaves to be their property. For them it was a matter of principal.

The liberality of the concessions, the fertility of the land, and the law of the United States requiring payment in cash for the lands of the west, motivated hundreds to enter Texas (Figure 3), and in 1824, when the first Mexican Republic confirmed the permission to colonize Texas, the concessions of land continued and increased. Between 1825 and 1831, Stephen Austin, who had sufficient power and authority to grant property titles, brought to the province nearly 1,700 families. The concession granted to Austin was one of twenty five that the Mexican government extended between 1824 and 1834, without counting individual permits.[133]

The Mexican authorities remained firm in their conviction that only by populating Texas could they defend the rest of the country from a North American invasion. Various authors accuse the government of Guadalupe Victoria of being short sighted and the following governments of having been cheated by the Anglo pioneers.[134] Neither one seems to be correct. The first group thought that vacant land would incite the North American government's greed much more than land populated by its fellow citizens. The Mexican governments of the time were accused of a lack of political vision for not realizing what would happen over time. But, placing ourselves in their time and historic circumstances, it becomes easier to understand the past. They knew little, less than today, about North Americans. Even though some politicians knew about the greed of many of them, more had confidence in their honor. They believed in the respectability

[133] Toribio Esquivel Obregón, op cit., pp. 142-153.

[134] Toribio Esquivel Obregón, Carreño, Zorrilla, etc.

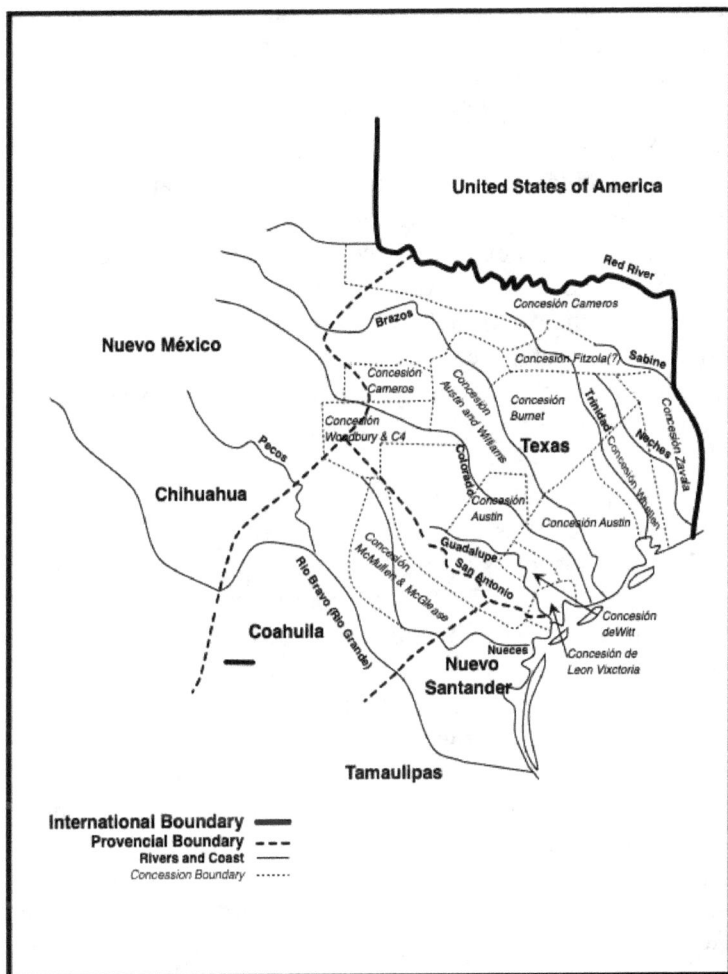

FIGURE 3. CONCESSIONS IN TEXAS, 1835 (BASED
ON LUIS G. ZORILLA, HISTÓRIA DE LAS RELACIONES
ENTRE MÉXICO Y LOS ESTADOS UNIDOS DE
AMÉRICA, ED. PORRÚA, VOL. 1, 1965, P. 80.)

of Austen's original group, those who had been Spanish subjects in Louisiana. They hardly thought they could be converted into traitors. Stephen Austin, personally, gave forceful proof of his desires to become a Mexican citizen. As already pointed out, since 1821, concessions had been given to the colonists on this point, and problems began to surface some years later, especially in reference to slavery. In 1829, President Guerrero declared Anglo slaveholders exempt in the decree that abolished slavery for the fifth time in Mexico.[135] These exemptions had been forced from the Mexican government because of protests and claims from Austin's colonists. We can conclude that for the Texan colonists, the Mexican position against slavery hung like a sword of Damocles over their economy.

The second big difference between the colonists and their adoptive country was their view of the law. "The Anglo Saxons conceived of justice as an expression of popular will, manifested by the popular jury... The Spanish concept of justice had nothing to do with this. It was the application of a pre-established rule, for the common good, that a judge must administer."[136] At the beginning of the colonization, Austin was granted ample political power in his colony, but when in 1826, the Political Constitution of the State of Coahuila-Texas was promulgated, trial by jury ceased. This act seemed arbitrary to the colonists. This combined with the requirement of traveling to Saltillo (in modern Nuevo Leon) to settle legal issues, increased the colonist's exasperation. Following Anglo-Saxon traditions, trial by jury was the only possible choice, and to not have it was cause for a deep concern among the colonists.[137]

---

[135] Toribio Esquivel Obregón, op cit., p. 148; Zorrilla, op cit., p. 87.

[136] Ibidem, p. 152.

[137] Ibidem, p. 153.

The obligation to become Catholics also angered them, equating it with intolerance. They could not and would not accept the fact that where they came from tolerance was only for Protestants. North American historians still today try to justify the colonists, by arguing that while they understood that Catholicism was the official religion, the government should tolerate theirs.[138] Having to pay a tithe to the Church, must have increased their resentment, given that in the Protestant churches such was not the practice. Such animosity against Catholicism was already an old Anglo-Saxon heritage as we have seen in Chapter 1. The oldest North American newspapers in Texas and New Mexico give clear evidence of this position. Catholicism was for them synonymous with servility, superstition, and arbitrariness. The Puritan past of the colonists caused them to rebel against a church that had long been regarded as the enemy. Their attitude was not strictly economic, but in response to historical roots. In summary, the North American colonists in Texas had nothing in common that would unite them with Mexicans: neither customs, nor language, nor race, nor religion, nor economic structures. Why then, we might ask, were they allowed to keep entering the country?

A goodly number of national governors were clearly aware of this clash of cultures. President Guadalupe Victoria affirmed, referring to the Anglos, that they, "were an ambitious people always ready to jump on their neighbors, without a spark of good faith."[139] On the other hand, there was a group of politicians who considered themselves admirers of Anglo institutions, such as Zavala, Gómez Farias, Fagoaga, etc., the nucleus of the friends

---

[138] Karl M. Schmitt, *México y Estados Unidos*, Ed. Limusa, México 1978, p.61.

[139] Vicente Lopez y Rivas, *La guerra del 47*, Ed. ERA, México, 1976, p. 82.

of Poinsett and the founders of the Yorkish Lodge. They determined that the suspicions and opinions of men like Lucas Alamán, José Maria Tomel and General Mier y Terán were unfounded and were due to outdated and intolerant principles.[140]

Mistrust or admiration of the United States became one of the most important points in national politics. Edmundo O'Gorman defined the first conservatives and liberals of our history as: "Politicians of a 'liberal tendency' feel compelled to emulate the United States as the model that should inspire independent New Spain", while those calling themselves conservatives were opposed. "Thus it was that the problem of the identity of the new nation was conceived as a disconnect between being a continuation of the heritage of its colonial past or becoming, by imitation, like the United States."[141] In these words is found, in good measure, the problem of Texas. They probably explained the enormous generosity of the gifts of land and the satisfaction, perhaps unconscious, of thinking that an increasing number of Anglos could live in Mexican territory. The liberal press echoed such a way of thinking and proclaimed that the supposed Anglo virtues only deepened the division between conservatives and liberals about the Texas problem. I cite as an example an article in the Mexico Daily Gazette (*Gaceta Diária de México*) of June 4, 1825, clearly showing a liberal bias:

> The population of the United States is approaching the Mexican frontier. There are already settlements of North American citizens on the banks of the Colorado, Arkansas and Missouri Rivers. The arts, sciences and the benefits of liberty compatible with the nature of man are already spreading out in those

[140] Carlos Bosch, *Material...*, p. 7.

[141] Vicente Lopez y Rivas, *La guerra del 47*, Ed. ERA, México, 1976, p. 82.

directions. The territorial limits are weak barriers to hold back progress. The Mexicans living in abject misery and ignorance on one bank of the river cannot be unaware of the happiness with which the United States citizen lives on the other bank.[142]

These types of articles were written with the intention that Mexicans would become convinced that the proximity of the United States and the imitation of their national model would bring others closer to progress and facilitate the achievement of modernity. It also explains the governmental confusion in its treatment of the North Americans, as Mexican liberals considered themselves carriers of modern ideas of tolerance, liberty, equality and science, while the conservatives saw themselves as the defenders of Spanish traditions.

However, the English ambassador did not stop insisting on the danger of the Anglos to the government of Guadalupe Victoria, and was able to convince the Mexican president, and in 1827, an exploratory commission was sent to verify the borders of the country, as they could not celebrate a treaty to establish the border if they did not know what it was. The commission to Texas left November 10, 1827, commanded by General Mier y Terán. Lieutenant José Maria Sánchez was named official chronicler of the expedition to whom, fortunately, it fell to write a small, but important, diary, that now allows us to appreciate the Texas situation of 1828:

The North Americans have taken possession of nearly all of Eastern Texas; the majority without the knowledge of the authorities, as they are constantly emigrating, without anyone getting in there way,

---

[142] "Comercio", *Gaceta Diaria de México*, 4 de junio de 1825, vol. I. p. 4.

taking possession of the most useful spots, without asking for it, or needing to do more than build a house. So that the majority of the inhabitants in the Department are North Americans, leaving the Mexican population reduced to only Béjar (San Antonio), Nacogdoches and the Bay of Espiritu Santo, miserable towns that between them do not number three thousand inhabitants, with the recently established town of Guadalupe Victoria barely having more than seventy citizens. They have made repeated and energetic declarations of the imminent danger faced by this interesting development of becoming a captive of the ambitious North Americans. Moreover, the Supreme Government of the Federation has never taken steps to save it (Eastern Texas) and has always been occupied in fatal convulsions that have destroyed the Republic, and which, because of secret agents tricking the bureaucrats, made them believe that the risk does not exist and are exaggerations produced by cowards, thus misdirecting the main authorities. Meanwhile the enemies to the north do not miss an opportunity to carry out their perfidious well-known project... Let's move on to something else.[143]

General Mier y Terán sent the following report on the state of Mexican defenses which proved prophetic:

The time has at last arrived that I declare to your lordships the situation that I hold for the defense of this frontier, the resources I have, and the fears I have of seeing myself involved in an incident that I do not believe is far off. The armed forces consist of

---

[143] José María Sánchez, *Viaje a Texas, México, 1829*, p. 31.

one hundred and fifty infantry of the 12th battalion and sixty poorly mounted dragoons. The position is not advantageous; there are no fortifications; the nearest help is distant, as your lordships well know; the withdrawal route is at the mercy of whomever wants to cut it in the enormous and unpopulated distance I find myself. The Mexican inhabitants with whom I can count on are few, spread around the countryside, without arms and fearful, since they know the situation they are in; the Indian tribes serve whomever gives them the most; I am short on all supplies and cannot give them anything; and while it is clear that when they are not enemies they are just indifferent.

It remains to be seen if a force of two hundred poorly equipped men, of whom I am upset to see the abandon with which they are treated, without having any defensive resources; and whose subsistence is at the mercy of the North Americans, is that destined solely to sustain this point. Let me continue.

By news and letters from Orleans and other points and from public papers, I know the preparations of troops that the republic to the north are making on our frontiers, in a fort that is only thirty leagues from here, where there exists today a force of 700 infantry. From the Sabine River to this town there are only North American inhabitants, in my rear are the colonies of Austin and Atascosito, also North American. When they, owners of the provisions, of the river fords, and in the end, the country, take up arms, at any time they want, there are more than 3,000 men. Will it be possible to defend myself? Before now the disaffected colonists to Mexico have shown me, and my suspicions have been confirmed today, that they were going to unite those from Sabine and this town to form a national militia, elect officers, etc., and many fear an attack.

I do not expect the government to the north to invade, but that in agreement with it, the colonists conduct a disturbance/riot, when they see my situation, and are satisfied with the advantage they enjoy.[144]

We have already mentioned the fear of Lucas Alamán and his repeated observations about the North American peril. From his long stays in England he knew enough about the Anglo Saxons to know they would not settle for being Mexican colonists but would try to impose their point of view, establishing their political institutions in a foreign land. The case of Florida was in his mind. When Anastasio Bustamente came to the presidency in 1830, Lucas Alamán became Secretary of Exterior Relations again. This year was key in the Texas problem. The Mexican Senate had turned down the proposal to buy the territory presented by the second North American ambassador in Mexico. In a secret session the Mexican Senate analyzed the Texas situation and had come to the conclusion that the superiority in the numbers of Anglos was already a fact, as well as their disobedience of Mexican laws. They spoke of the expansionist movement in the United States and of the threat of losing the Texas territory.[145] On April 6, 1830, a new law on colonization was passed. Among its numerous provisions was included the creation of commissions that would watch over the entrance of new colonists. Now they would require passports, prohibiting the colonists from settling in areas adjacent to their nation. The law

---

[144] Ibidem, p. 75.

[145] Bosch, *Material…*, p. 121.

was as utopian as the North American government's today to prohibit the passage of Mexican workers. It is known how difficult it is to guard such a long border without any markings and even more in a period when communications were rudimentary. The colonization law also allowed for the sending of Mexican families to the frontier. Governors were urged to each send twenty poor families a year and to give them land and farm tools.[146] This resulted in nothing noteworthy, as the Anglo colonists kept growing such that no Mexicans, even prisoners, were interested in going to their region. Lucas Alamán circulated the law among the governors of the states, accompanied by maps showing how the integrity of the national territory was threatened. He asked them to provide three thousand men to form an army to guard the frontier. His letters were not answered. The recipients clearly considered the Secretary of Exterior Relations' opinion as exaggerated.

The law of 1830 also touched on another difficult theme prohibiting the entrance of more slaves. We have seen that each time the Mexican government repeated its position on slavery, the North American colonists rejected it. The fear of a possible abolition of slavery remained however, since the Texan economy was based entirely on slave labor. Generally, historians do not mention slavery and the North American's persistent insistence on its practice in discussing the Texas problem, but without a doubt it played a very important role. For example, it is worth noting that the annexation of Texas by the United States was delayed nine years by the work of abolitionists. However, the North Americans mainly blamed the conservative party for the discontent of their compatriots in Texas: *La Gaceta Official de Arkansas* published an article which echoed the North American position on the law of 1830:

---

[146] Zorrilla, op cit., p. 80.

> It appears we should not harbor hope of acquiring Texas while there is no government better disposed towards the United States, or while Texas does not throw off the yoke of Mexico, if necessary, which it will no doubt do from the moment it finds what it feels it has a reasonable motive.[147]

The government of Anastasio Bustamente lasted only two years when in 1832, General Santa Anna carried out a coup d'etat. These events caused Butler to write to his government that, "These people will not be prepared to govern themselves within the next fifty years."[148] That same year, Stephen Austin decided to join the liberal party, and taking advantage of the reigning disorder in the Mexican capital to ask Congress for an extension of the customs payments, religious tolerance, and the reopening of immigration.

So far in 1832, a dozen confrontations had taken place between the Mexican authorities and the Anglo colonists, and the discussions were long and heated. On the 22nd of August, the city government of San Felipe convoked a convention that would take place the first of October.[149] In May of the same year, before the convention, seven colonists were arrested without an arrest warrant. The open battle that ensued was of such a nature that the Mexican authorities abandoned the place where the events happened[150] as the contraband activities and clandestine immigration grew by the moment. Glenn Price, in his book on

---

[147] Cited by Orozco Farias Rogelio, *Fuentes histórica de México, 1821-1867*, edición del autor, México, p. 87.

[148] Bosch, *Material ...*, p.147.

[149] Toribio Esquivel Obregón, po cit., p. 192.

[150] Glenn Price, *Los origenes de la guerra con México*, FCE, p. 38.

the origins of the war with Mexico, affirmed that the North Americans always tried to evade customs taxes and to violate immigration laws. He added that the hostility against the Mexican authorities grew during the decade of the thirties when Texas "was converted into a refuge for restless and violent men from the cities of the Mississippi and the Gulf Coast; men who took charge of the resistance to the laws of the 'foreigners' in whose lands they lived."[151]

In the San Felipe convention, the colonists were divided. Some wanted a peaceful solution and some, led by Wharton, demanded the separation of Texas from Coahuila, the free importation of certain necessary articles, and the repeal of the law of 1830. In 1832, when there was an uprising against Bustamente's government, the rebels added to their movement and its triumph with the signing of the conventions of Zavaleta for the time being, ending with suspension of hostilities in Texas. In April, 1833, there was a second convention of Texas colonists, the result of which was the production of a document in which they demanded the independence of Texas from Coahuila, and developed a constitution that would govern the new Mexican state. Among the participants of this second convention was the recently arrived Sam Houston, whose participation in the movement was fundamental.[152] An old friend of President Jackson, he was invited to promote the separation of Texas from Coahuila and to prepare its future annexation by the United States.

Meanwhile, Stephen Austin arrived at a poor time in Mexico with the report written during the second Texas convention. The reformist legislation of Gómez Farias had provoked profound

---

[151] Ibidem, p. 40.

[152] Callahan, James, *American Foreign Policy in Mexican Relations*, Cooper Square, New York, 1967, p. 77.

divisions. As such, Austin prepared to explain his case before Gómez Farias, who received a letter that Austin had sent to the city council of San Antonio. In it, he referred to the disagreements between liberals and conservatives, and recommended that all the city councils organize the government of Texas as a state in the Mexican Confederation in case the Congress turned down its separation from Coahuila. Gómez Farias made out an arrest warrant, and Austin spent eight months in jail until the arrival of Santa Anna to power in 1834. Santa Anna convoked a meeting of ministers who discussed the separation of Coahuila and Texas. A state could not be constituted without the approval of the seventy thousand inhabitants of their region, as required by the Mexican and United States constitutions. However, to demonstrate its good will, the meeting repealed article XI of the 1830 law that prohibited the entrance of Anglos into Texas. Additionally, they gave them new fiscal rights.[153]

Management and paperwork kept Austin in the capital until 1835. In the meantime, a number of Texan colonists who wanted independence began to organize movements hostile to Mexico. Plans were made to hold a third convention in July, 1835, which was put off until October and finally November. The Mexican minister to Washington, Castillo Lanzas, constantly informed his government about "the embarkations of people that were being made to Texas without any respect for the law." He counseled his government that either they sell or impose order and obedience in the region. Meanwhile United States newspapers were writing about the richness of Texas and of the official attempts to purchase it[154], and the famous border treaty (Adams-Onis) still

---

[153] Toribio Esquivel Obregón, op cit., p. 195. Cites file 2, record 5 of the Secretary of Development.

[154] Bosch, *Material…*, p. 172.

78

had not been ratified by Washington increasing the hopes of President Jackson to obtain at least part of Texas.

Then, in the face of the furor of the colonists, General Cos and his troops arrived in Texas. In September, Austin sent a circular to the colonists asking them to organize militias. He was still talking of a union with Mexico and sent a new commission to the capital.[155] The newspapers of Louisiana spoke openly of war and held public meetings with the object of collecting funds and arms to help the Texans. At the end of October, 1835, Mexico made new protests with respect to the boats carrying arms to the North American colonists. A Texas recruiting office was opened on 62nd Street in New York, and in November the newspapers gave out the news of confrontations between the Mexican army and the Texans.[156]

The convention of colonists that took place in November, 1835, supported separation of Texas and Coahuila until the return to a federal system. Santa Anna had established a centralized regime, and the colonists' contract with the federalist government of Guadalupe Victoria had expired with the change in regimes. As we have stated, all of this was just a pretext to justify a rebellion. It is enough to remember that the first contract with the colonists was established by the viceregal government, confirmed by the monarchist regime of Iturbide, and finally by the federal republican regime of Guadalupe Victoria. The rebellion, therefore, lacked a legal basis and except for the apparent affection for federalism, was only a justification to tranquilize the Anglo-Saxon and Puritan conscience. North American

---

[155] Ibidem, pp. 186-187.

[156] Ibidem, pp. 190-195.

historians still today continue to invoke the federalism argument as an explanation of the rebellion.[157]

It should be noted that it was not only Texas that was opposed to the change from federalism to centralism. Zacatecas and Durango, as well as many citizens, did the same. Congress answered them by affirming that the common will wanted to be done with federalism.[158] The uprisings in Zacatecas and Durango could be extinguished, but the ideological division spread to the Mexican-American War of 1846 and served as a pretext for several governors not to intervene in the battle between Mexico and the United States, which, according to the governors, was a fight between centralists and federalists.[159] The attempts to end the Mexican-American conflict continued, since in Texas they had said they would return to be part of the Mexican union when it returned to federalism. In January, 1836, the United States sent a new representative to Mexico, Powhattan Ellis, while Manuel Goroztiza was the Mexican representative in the neighboring country to the north. With the exchange of ambassadors the second major stage of the conflict began. Although they were not really neutral, the United States insisted on its neutrality between federalism and centralism in their petitions with respect to the integrity of its territory. On this pretext, General Edward Gaines and his troops were stationed on the border between Texas and the United States. Ellis, the new ambassador, devoted himself to what Mexico should pay to North American citizens for damages. As we said about Butler, the reclamations file would serve as a distraction from major parts of the problem each time

---

[157] Connors, op cit.

[158] Urbina, Manuel, *Effects of the Independence of Texas on the Government, Politics and Society in Mexico, 1836-1846*, doctoral thesis, University of Texas, Austin, 1976, p. 3.

[159] Zorrilla, op. cit., p. 196.

the situation became very tense. Mexico, in turn, instructed Goroztiza, its minister in Washington, to notify the United States government that the problem of reclamations was due as much to the help that the United States had provided to the Texan rebels.

The Mexican government realized that there was no other solution than to use military force. It also had to subdue Zacatecas, which had rebelled against centralism. The Texas movement was very different because of its Anglo-Saxon culture and its approach to legislation was of a character and tradition unlike that of Mexicans. In addition, the Texan economy gravitated completely towards the United States.

In the March 1st, 1836 convention, the Texans proclaimed their total independence from Mexico without any pretense of being federalist they insisted that their case was the same as that of Mexico when it declared independence from Spain. In addition according to the new constitution, Texas was declared to be a slave nation. On March 6, 1836, the Alamo in San Antonio fell to Santa Anna. The cruelty with which the prisoners were treated has become legend. "Remember the Alamo" continues to be, among Texans, a cry of hate. It has been shown that the colonists, whose warlike actions began with the siege of San Antonio in November, 1835, soon abandoned the site and were replaced by United States citizens. When Santa Anna took the Alamo he found that of the 183 men defending it, only 32 were colonists. The rest were from Tennessee, Kentucky, and Alabama. Minister Goroztiza rightly protested to Washington about United States military recruitment for Texas.[160]

After the fall of the Alamo, General Gaines called upon the governors of neighboring North American states for volunteers. Upon learning of the unexpected triumph of Houston in San

---

[160] Ibidem, p. 107.

Jacinto, he withdrew his request. He helped the Texans by allowing the desertion of his men to join the Texans. More than two thousand North American infantry soldiers wore their uniforms at the Battle of San Jacinto. This was followed by a proclamation of General Gaines pardoning the deserters.

The help of the United States to the Texans was so open that even John Quincy Adams, ex-president and supporter of the Monroe Doctrine, condemned the intervention before the North American Congress, and judged the invasion of Mexican territory as dangerous because it could mire the country in a war with Mexico. Of course, he was not proposing so much to defend our country, but rather to stop the spread of slavery."[161]

On April 21, 1836, Santa Anna was defeated by Sam Houston's army, and he signed the famous so-called Treaties of Velasco, so-called because they were never ratified by the Mexican Congress. In the treaties Santa Anna did not sell the province of Texas, but accepted the defeat of San Jacinto and its consequences. The documents are presented in the book In *México a través de los siglos*.[162] The general accepted to withdraw from the conflict, manage the recognition of the independence of Texas by the Mexican government, and accept the new northern border of the Rio Grande river. The Mexican government nullified all of these dealings and reminded the Texans that the treaties were signed under duress and without the approval of the Mexican Congress, as the United States and Mexican Constitutions required.

The "sale" of Texas is a fabrication of the federalists. It is surprising that it continues to be part of official history (in

---

[161] Ibidem, p. 128.

[162] Enrique Olavarria, *México a través de los siglos*, vol. IV, Ed. Cumbre, Mexico, 1977, pp. 372-380.

schools etc.) when there are documents showing it to be false. In Lucas Alamán's archive at the University of Texas, one can read the account of the return of Santa Anna after San Jacinto. The ex-Secretary of Exterior Relations, referring to the rumor that Santa Anna had sold Texas, said, "the arrival of Santa Anna has been like a ray of light that happily dissipated the obscurity. We now know with certainty that there was no sale of Texas."[163] It was an unconditional surrendering of territory and an unconditional acceptance of the so-called Treaties of Velasco. Texas acquired its independence by right of conquest. After the defeat of San Jacinto, the centralist government, with José Justo Corro as interim president, began to think about how to reconquer the Texan territory. The project was not completed for two reasons: the lack of economic resources, and the great rivalry that existed between the federalists and the centralists, a hostility that we have seen was due to ideological differences. Conservative elements sided with centralism, and the liberals with federalism. They accused the central government of having provoked the rebellion with the change in government from federalism to centralism.

The revolutionary movements supported by the federalists began while the centralist Congress was discussing plans for the reconquest of the territory. "It was written without doubt that Texas was lost to Mexico, and the lack of unity of the Mexicans to fight against such looting, was perhaps a major reason influencing the conduct by the United States to take over said territory."[164] The federalists took advantage of the general disgrace occasioned by the Texas campaign to discredit the government in office. The Texas question served them as a plank of support to retake political power. Thus they saw the Texas

---

[163] Urbina, op cit., p. 67. the Alamán Papers, Document A-227, f. 564.

[164] Olavarria, op cit., p. 381.

question as purely political and championed the restoration of federalism to open the door to negotiations with the Texas colonists, since they would never do so with the centralists for ideological reasons.[165] According to the federalists, their system was the only solution to obtain the restoration of territorial integrity.

The centralists, naturally, did not want to give up power, by declaring that this was the worst time to change governments. They defended themselves against federalist accusations by arguing that the Texas rebellion had begun before the promulgation of the centralist constitution of 1836. The controversy continued, but underlying the conflict was the ambition for power on both sides, economic poverty, and political polarization. If two people agreed on the same goals, they totally disagreed on the means of reaching it. The best way to appreciate the confusion of the times is to read the newspapers. Through them one can see that the political groups dedicated themselves to mutually blaming each other for what happened in Texas. There existed, in addition, a deafening battle between the executive and the legislative branches that ended with the triumph of the former, but that contributed to complicating the situation even more. Federalist newspapers took advantage of the situation to accuse the centralist politicians of a lack of honesty. Even when a small group of moralists pushed for the cessation of hostilities, the great majority of patriots agree with what General Mier y Terán declared, "whoever consented to the loss of Texas without offering resistance is a vile traitor."[166] If given the opportunity, both sides would be willing to work together to preserve national integrity.

---

[165] Urbina, op cit., pp. 12-16.

[166] Ibidem, pp. 27-39.

Texas became an independent country, recognized by the United States, England, and France, for nine years (1836-1845). During this time battles along the border continued, as did United States' aid to the Texans. General Gaines and his troops were stationed in Texas from 1835 onwards with the pretext of preventing the fight from spilling over into North American territory. After the declaration of Texan independence General Gaines was commissioned to guard the border between Texas and Mexico. Naturally, the Mexican government protested, since they still considered Texas a rebel province within Mexican territory. The United States held a different point of view, and insisted on its neutrality. Diplomatic discussions about the legitimacy of the Texas government lasted nine years.

In the meantime, there were new events that only made the situation worse. The first was a diplomatic dispute. Mexico had sent Manuel Goroztiza as minister extraordinary in Washington with the order to watch North American movements with regard to Texas (Castillo y Lanzas was the ordinary minister). Given that the activities of General Gaines were in territory Mexico considered its own, Goroztiza jealously dedicated himself to observe Gaines activities. Time and again he presented complaints about raids within Mexican territory, and time and again their answer was that Gaines was only protecting the border against Indian raids that Mexico should have put down, and for which Mexico should thank the United States.[167] From October, 1836, what would become the basis of North American policy began to be employed: "Mexico should be thankful instead of complaining, as the United States carried out an obligation that the Mexican nation could not accomplish."[168] When he received the news that Gaines had the United States' authority to enter Mexican territory, Goroztiza demanded his

[167] Bosch, *Material...*, pp. 240-251.

[168] Ibidem, p. 257.

passports, putting an end to his mission. Before leaving he published a pamphlet in which Goroztiza recounted the North American expansionist policy and its disrespect for Mexican sovereignty.

Andrew Jackson, then President of the United States, called the pamphlet the greatest insult in the history of diplomacy"[169] and made the first threat of war against Mexico. Later, the North American government asked that the pamphlet be refuted or else it would recall its ambassador in Mexico, but the Mexican government backed Goroztiza, blaming the North American bureaucrats who had not wanted to give satisfactory explanations to Goroztiza's complaints.

Jackson's ambition to acquire Texas was well known, as was his hypocrisy in denying it in public. He ordered his ambassador in Mexico, Powhattan Ellis, to insist that Mexico had not paid its debts to the United States, and therefore ended his mission five days after Goroztiza had left the United States. It was another example of the characteristic way the United States government handled such matters by always finding a way to blame the victim. Let's review the case: Goroztiza withdrew because of the invasion of Mexican territory by the United States, while Ellis threatened to withdraw because of Mexico's lack of attention to North American claims. It is clear that their reasons were not of equal weight. Ortiz Monasterio, the Secretary of Exterior Relations had sent Ellis a long document in which he specified the nullity of various of the claims and asked more precision from his North American colleague. Ortiz Monasterio complained that the Mexican government was accused of many things for which they were not responsible. In addition, he did not understand why so much importance was given to colonists'

---

[169] Ibidem, p. 270.

claims, when Mexico wanted answers to serious affairs.[170] Monasterio was referring to the invasion of Mexican territory and the North American aide openly given to the Texans. Ellis did not find the answer he received from Monasterio satisfactory and asked for his passport, withdrawing from his mission. To try to balance the scale that was objectively inclining in favor of the Mexicans (invasion of territory and aide to Texans, versus a long list of claims), the United States countered with the enormous offense, according to them, the pamphlet published by Goroztiza.[171]

On March 7, 1837, during the five months following the mutual withdrawal by Mexico and United States of their ambassadors, the United States recognized the independence of Texas, which Mexico judged as hypocritical, since in all the communications between the two countries the United States had continually specified that they would not recognize the new country. The reason given for the recognition was that the United States had been guided by sentiments of friendship to a bordering country.[172] Diplomatic relations were reestablished in 1838, with the pretext of preparing a conference on colonists' claims. England offered to act as mediator as long as Mexico recognized Texas as an independent country. English interest was stimulated by the abundant harvests of cotton in Texas, and had a great determination to prevent, for mercantile reasons, that Texas be annexed by the United States. Martin Van Buren, the president who succeeded Jackson, also wanted to incorporate Texas into the United States, but without provoking a conflagration, as the struggle between slave and free states was already a fact. Therefore, the North American president opted to leave the

---

[170] Ibidem, pp. 262-263.

[171] Ibidem, p. 276.

[172] Ibidem, p. 283.

decision to his successor since the north had come out against annexation.

During Van Buren's term the avalanche of complaints against the Mexican government never ceased. Along the border the skirmishes between Texans and Mexicans continued, and as a result, Mexico and the United States lived in a state of constant tension with the North American citizens never losing a chance to maltreat Mexico or Mexicans.[173]

Meanwhile the federalists continued their battle for power taking advantage of the problems created by the Texas question. On December 30, 1836, the centralist constitution decreed by Congress as the "Seven Laws" was published. According to the "Seven Laws", the states would be converted into departments, their legislatures into departmental assemblies, and their taxes would be at the disposition of the central government.[174] Congress determined that half the taxes would be used to continue the war with Texas. Three months later a revolt against this decision erupted. In April, 1837, Colonel Ramón Ugarte spoke forth in San Luis Potosi, proclaiming a federalist constitution. In August, the federalists of New Mexico rose up and assassinated the governor. This second revolt caused innumerable problems for Mexico and the United States, since our government accused the Anglo merchants of fomenting the revolt. Hubert Bancroft, in his *History of Arizona and New Mexico*, blamed his compatriots of having instigated the rebellion with the idea of fomenting discontent. "The Mexicans believed, and not without reason, that the rebellion was another

---

[173] Carlos Bosch Garcia, *Historia de las relaciones diplomáticas entre México y los Estados Unidos*, UNAM, México, 1961, pp. 202-203.

[174] José Bravo Ugarte, *Compendio de historia de México*, Ed. Jus, México, 1973, p. 173.

issue "a la Texas" influenced directly or indirectly by North American merchants to foment discontent among the New Mexicans with the new policies of their government."[175] Among contemporary Mexican historians, Carlos Maria Bustamente, opined that the rebellion had been instigated by the North American merchants who did not want to pay taxes and wanted to take over the territory.[176] The archives of Exterior Relations contains a communication from the priest of Santa Fe, in which he affirms that the rebellion had been fomented by North Americans who had received aide from Texas.[177] At the same time the Anglo merchants of New Mexico proceeded to send complaints and economic claims to Ambassador Ellis, heavily augmenting the Mexican debt. On the Mexican side suspicion and hostility grew. As a result of the rebellion, new commercial restrictions and additional contributions were reestablished. In 1839, the North American consul in Santa Fe informed the Secretary of State that the recent taxes and restrictions were a deliberate attempt to kick out the United States merchants from Santa Fe.[178] The cold war was becoming increasingly violent.

During the last months of 1838, both countries attention was distracted from the Texas problem to confront the French intervention, called the "Pastry War", which became another controversy between the federalists and centralists. The federalists were accused of provoking the anger of the French to

---

[175] Bancroft, Hubert Howe, *History of Arizona and New Mexico*, the History Co. San Francisco, 1889, p. 317.

[176] Carlos Maria Bustamente, *Gabinete mexicano*, Ed. José Maria Lara, México,1842, vol. II.

[177] "Ministro del Interior al Ministro de Relaciones Exteriores", *Archivo de la Secretaría de Relaciones Exteriores de México* (ASREM) LE-1081-f.21.

[178] Bancroft, op cit., p. 328.

get an intervention that would permit the consolidation of the power they had nearly lost. Conservative newspapers accused the federalists of cooperating with the French.[179]

However, a peace treaty with France was signed on March 9, 1839, and with it the attention of both parties returned to the Texas problem. In June, it was learned that the ex-governor of Coahuila-Texas, General Francisco Vidaurri, had looked for North American support for the federalist cause, soliciting an alliance among Texas, Nuevo Leon, Tamaulipas, Chihuahua, Nuevo México, Durango, and Upper and Lower California, with the goal of establishing an independent republic. Upon learning of this, a new journalistic controversy began: the conservatives called the attempt to form an alliance with France treason, while the federalists said that to defeat the centralists they had the right to ally themselves with anyone, even the Chinese.[180] El Mosquito declared it was necessary that "all Mexicans learn to distinguish between an internal political fight and a foreign invasion."[181]

In the midst of all this chaos and confusion, Yucatán declared independence from Mexico on February 18, 1840. Historians think that the independence movement was provoked by the imposition of new taxes, producing expropriations in April, 1837, under the pretext that they were necessary to conduct the war in Texas.[182] The Yucatecan rebellion lasted until the 15th of December, 1843, when the province was reincorporated into the nation. It was, however, a sad episode which only dispersed the

---

[179] Urbina, op cit., p. 65.

[180] Ibidem, pp. 75-76

[181] Ibidem, p. 76.

[182] Ibidem, p. 76.

national forces and prevented the Mexican government from concentrating in the north.

This same year, José María Gutierrez Estrada published his letter on the necessity of establishing a foreign monarchy in Mexico. The republicans, as much centralists as federalists, were alarmed and spent their time in byzantine debates. Meanwhile, the Texans kept asking Mexico for the recognition of their independence.

In May, 1841, the Texan president, Mirabeau Bonaparte Lamar, asked for permission of the Mexican government to send a scientific and commercial expedition to Santa Fe, New Mexico. In this same month, however, Mexican residents in the area reported that the expedition was making military preparations and was not entirely commercial or scientific. Worried, the Mexican government sent reinforcements with orders to watch the Texan convoy. General Arista sent troops from Matamoros to reinforce the defense in Santa Fe, and a newspaper in Mexico City published the news that a Texan military expedition had left for New Mexico with the object of uniting it with Texas.[183]

In Santa Fe the authorities arrested various North American merchants under suspicion of complicity with the Texan expedition. General Armijo, governor of the province, sent a note to the United States' consul which said, "I warn you as consul of the United States that neither you nor foreign inhabitants of this capital (Santa Fe) will be separated from it under any circumstances until my return from seeing to the expedition.[184]

---

[183] Nance, Joseph Milton, *After San Jacinto, the Texas-Mexican Frontier, 1836-1841*, University of Texas Press, Austin, 1964, p. 437.

[184] Moyano Pahissa, El comercio de Santa Fe y la guerra del 47, Sepsetentas, México, 1975, p. 139.

Meanwhile, the president of Texas, Mirabeau Bonaparte Lamar, conceived a grand plan to save Texan finances from bankruptcy. With the support of old geographic claims, the Texan government built a military road from the Red River to the riverbed of the fort of Nueces, and another from Austin to Santa Fe, and exaggerated the economic importance of the commerce between Santa Fe and Missouri. From the time of Moses and Stephen Austin there had been talk about the possibility that this commercial trade would pass directly to the Gulf rather than through Missouri. Stephen Austin felt that geography indicated that the Texas ports and not the river ports of Missouri would be logical bases for commerce with Santa Fe. In 1824, a group of Texans made a first commercial attempt resulting in considerable profits, but the fear of the Comanches and the competition from the Missouri merchants made them give up on that enterprise.[185]

When Texas declared its independence from Mexico the Texan newspapers began to talk up the possibility of Texan participation in the Santa Fe trade. In 1839, a caravan of merchants bringing with them a half million pesos of silver from Chihuahua crossed Texas to Louisiana. Considering this events economic importance, the newspapers renewed their plea for Texan involvement in the Santa Fe trade. In 1840, a sensational article appeared which emphasized that the distance between Austin and Santa Fe was only 450 miles across rich plains with abundant water adding to the Anglo perception of the region as a commercial fruit to be plucked. The author spiced up the profits to be made and the geographic advantages that Texan merchants would have in the new region over those of Missouri. In April 1841, the Austin City Gazette announced that two envoys from northern Mexico had arrived to negotiate the establishment of commercial ties. They projected that the route from Zacatecas,

---

[185] Ibidem, p. 109.

Durango, and Chihuahua would one day reach the Colorado River in Texas, and from there by river to the gulf.[186]

Texas' President Lamar decided to take commercial control of this jurisdiction, and at the same time push Texan claims regarding portions of New Mexico. Consequently, in 1839, he informed the Texas legislature about his project to place agents in Santa Fe, who, according to him, were North Americans naturalized as Mexicans and who were preparing New Mexican citizens for a change of government. His idea was to establish a commercial route from Santa Fe to Habana, Cuba, without passing through North American customs. Texas was bankrupt, and the government wanted to revitalize the economy as an independent country. On February 27, 1841, the Texan consul in Washington wrote to the Spanish minister asking to begin a commercial interchange. Among other things he said, "The Santa Fe commerce that is now going through the United States by Missouri could be diverted to the Texas ports via a cheaper, more direct and faster route. For the rapid implementation of this objective Cuban products are necessary." In January, 1842, the ministers' answer came back that even though the Spanish government did not want a treaty, the commander of Habana agreed to open commerce between Cuba and Texas. Spain did not recognize Texas independence, but it did accept the establishment of commercial relations.[187]

On January 20, 1841, the fifth Texas Congress proposed the creation of a company that would take charge of commerce with Santa Fe and discussed the possibility of sending an expedition

---

[186] Marshall, Thomas Maitland, "Commercial Aspects of the Texan Santa Fe Expedition", *The Southwestern Historical Quarterly*, University of Texas Press, Austin, 1917, vol. II, pp. 246-248.

[187] Ibidem. pp. 249-250

to Santa Fe was also discussed. A resolution was presented asking that a law be passed that would inform the inhabitants of Santa Fe of the rights they would enjoy as citizens of the Republic of Texas. Finally, a bill was written to protect militarily communications with Santa Fe and another bill was accepted by the Texas House of Representatives that authorized a levy of volunteers to organize an expedition to that city. However, because of discussions about war with Mexico, the Texas Congress ended its sessions without clearly stating the legal basis for such an expedition.[188] In spite of this, President Lamar proceeded to organize the expedition and asked the treasury for eighty thousand pesos to equip it. With these two measures he exceeded his constitutional powers, so that the Texas Congress could later deny responsibility for the project. The president organized the project with the declared purpose of promoting commerce, but in reality with the intention of inviting the New Mexicans to participate in the "blessings of Texas liberty."[189] With the pretext of establishing commercial treaties, the objective was the annexation of New Mexico enriched by commerce with the United States.

Such were the events that resulted in a group of 321 men leaving Fort Kenney, 22 miles (35 kilometers) from Austin on the 19th of July, 1841. The non-Texan members of the expedition had a double objective: to open direct commerce between Santa Fe and Texas by a route shorter than the Missouri Trail and to peacefully establish Texan jurisdiction over a territory that they considered theirs since Santa Anna had included it in the so-called Treaty of

---

[188] Ibidem, pp. 254-257.

[189] Moorhead, Max, *New Mexico's Royal Road*, Norman Press, Oklahoma, 1958, p. 72.

Velasco in 1836.[190] It was never mentioned that in this same year the Mexican Congress rejected Santa Anna's treaty, declaring it null and void.

The majority of the members of the expedition were botanists, journalists, and North American voyagers interested in exploring a new territory, without knowing, as they later claimed, the bellicose intentions of the expedition. Upon being notified of the expedition, the government of New Mexico prepared its defenses, and spread the word that the Texans were coming to rob and sack Santa Fe. In the current state archives of New Mexico, a letter exists from a prominent citizen of Santa Fe to the Secretary of Interior in which he communicated that the public was ready "to spend the last drop of blood in defense of the fatherland."[191] The very same day, the United States residents in Santa Fe, wrote to the United States Secretary of State complaining of their mistreatment because of the Texan expedition, "Officers publicly stated in the presence of a large number of citizens, that after they had defeated the Texans, they would come back with their troops and destroy all the foreigners."[192]

General Armijo, governor of New Mexico, left with his troops to capture the Texans, with all the members of the expedition taken prisoner and sent to Mexico City. Proclamations, other documents including the names of governors, heads of internal revenue, tax collectors, and other posts, and lists were

---

[190] Beck, Warren A., *New Mexico, a History of Four Centuries*, University of Oklahoma, 1962, p. 213.

[191] Moyano, op cit. p. 113.

[192] Carta de los ciudadanos norteamericanos en Santa Fe a Daniel Webster, secretary de Estado, Archive de la Universidad de Nuevo México, Albuquerque, Colección Read, Rollo 49.

confiscated from the prisoners in which many foreign residents in Chihuahua were shown to have been complicit in the expedition by being promised public positions in the new government that would be established by President Lamar.[193]

The most important document found was a Lamar proclamation to the New Mexicans one year before, in which he invited New Mexican citizens to a closer union and political cooperation with the Republic of Texas, offering them the security of all the civic rights that Texans enjoyed. This letter, dated April 14, 1840, was signed by the governor of the Republic of Texas, and is not mentioned in North American books dealing with the expedition of 1841. The original letter is certainly lost, so we do not know if the citizens of Santa Fe were aware of it. There were no newspaper reports, except for those done clandestinely.

The personal proclamation of President Lamar was published in the newspaper El Siglo XIX in October, 1841. His thesis was that he had been aware that the New Mexicans had sympathized with the Texan conflict against Mexico, and that they had not joined him solely because of geographic constraints. Lamar also stated that while Texas territory included the area from the Sabine to the Rio Bravo and from the Gulf of Mexico to the Pacific, "Texas, however, would not do anything to extend our government's jurisdiction in opposition to your (New Mexico's) wishes." After enumerating a long list of grievances that Mexico ("monstrous mother") had imposed, Lamar boasted that the Texan forces would be at the service of New Mexico in case it ever decided to fight to join Texas. He ended his proclamation by presenting the members of the expedition as having been commissioned by the Texas government to be friends with the

---

[193] Moyano, op. cit., p. 112. Cita la proclamación del presidente de Texas publicada en El silo XIX, México, 21 Octubre de 1842, pp. 1-3.

citizens of New Mexico.[194] After reading the proclamation it is interesting to note that so many North American historians insist in making it seem that the expedition was a simple and scientific commercial venture.

Even when the Texan expedition of 1841 ended in disaster, the company of "silly ducks", as they were called by President Andrew Jackson, had a large impact on Mexico-United States relations. Joseph Milton Nance, in his book, *After San Jacinto*, said, "The expedition to Santa Fe served to maintain the animosity between Texas and Mexico."[195] There were violent reactions on both sides of the frontier. The Mexicans were furious at learning that, according to the North Americans in Santa Fe, the New Mexicans were only awaiting the opportunity to rise up and declare their independence. Carlos Maria Bustamente wrote, "New Mexico, from a political stand point, would have to suffer further invasions, given that they were the main cause of the invasion (Texan expedition), and their agents in New Mexico as shown in a report sent from Santa Fe."[196] In July, and again in August, 1841, the Mexican minister in Washington accused the Department of State of having intervened in the expedition, an accusation that was, of course, denied. The Mexican suspicions and resentments continued to grow. New laws appeared restricting commerce, and the desire to kick out the North Americans from Santa Fe became even more vigorous.

The North American merchants of Santa Fe did not just keep asking Washington for protection, they began to demand it. Nance, in his *After San Jacinto*, emphasized that the news about

---

[194] Ibidem, p. 112.

[195] Nance, Milton, op. cit. p. 437.

[196] Bustamente, op. cit. p. 216.

the Mexican cruelties to the expeditionaries ended with the opposition of many Texans to annexation of their country by the United States, since they perceived independence as a better choice. The wave of sympathy for the Texans for having been punished unnecessarily —according to the particular point of view of the North Americans—, ended major opposition to its entry into the Union. For months, North American newspapers gave ample space to the plight of the prisoners and the news of their imprisonment in Mexico City. It was obvious that they had taken part in a war described "as the battle between liberty, the light and civilization against despotism and barbarism."[197] There were many meetings in various states of the Union, in which it was agreed to demand retribution for the bad treatment to which the expeditionaries were subjected. They wanted to show, as much to Mexico, as to the world, that the North American citizenry was a shield against abuse and arbitrariness. On February 4, 1842, five thousand people demonstrated in Austin to condemn the treatment of the expeditionaries by the Mexican government.[198]

In the United States Congressional records there are lists of letters soliciting official intervention to liberate the expeditionaries. However, Powhattan Ellis, ambassador in Mexico, was of the opinion that nothing should be done to intervene since they (expeditionaries) were Texan troops (not United States troops).[199] There was also a group, led by ex-president John Quincy Adams, who considered that the expedition had been organized by the United States government with the objective of provoking a war with Mexico and the annexation of Texas, who accused President Taylor of having

---

[197] Nance, Milton, op. cit. pp. 145-148.

[198] Moyano, op. cit. p. 117.

[199] Bosch, *Material…*, p. 332.

encouraged the idea of the expedition, and who were against granting the protection demanded by the expeditionaries.[200]

With the insistence of the Mexican government to the effect that all of the expeditionaries were armed, the North American Secretary of State recognized that there had been a military deployment, and therefore, the United States citizens could not be involved without violating the law and losing the right to the protection of their government."[201]

However, the United States government continued to insist on the release of the non-Texans and that they be treated as prisoners of war. Mexico could not accept the latter which would mean admitting that Texas was an independent country. Diplomatic discussions were drawn out, and Mexico was threatened with suspension of relations. Santa Anna, again president of Mexico, promised to free the North Americans as soon as the United States warships sent to back up the threat were removed from Veracruz. Finally, Santa Anna agreed to liberate the North American prisoners, and a few months later the Texans. At the end of 1842, the last prisoners returned. President Lamar's expedition, disorganized and poorly equipped, had failed completely, but we have seen the chain of events it caused. The year 1842 was definitely the most crucial in Mexico

----

[200] Moyano, op. cit. p. 119.

[201] Ibidem, p. 120.

and Texas relations.[202] On April 14, Houston, who had just won the presidency, gave a long speech to his people. In it he spoke of the repeated aggressions that they had suffered and the perfidy and Mexican cruelty towards the expeditionaries. According to Houston, Texas had tried to obtain a reasonable peace, but as Mexico refused to do so, war was the only option.[203] In May, Bocanegra, Secretary of Exterior Relations, sent a circular to the diplomatic corps bringing them up to date on the status between Mexico and the United States. Mexico had not been able to recuperate the rebellious province because the North Americans had impeded them with their growing help to Texas. Bocanegra added that the United States had openly talked of making war on Mexico and helping Texas.[204]

History will show that Bocanegra was right. Nance, in his book *Attack and Counterattack*, includes a list of cities in the southern United States that collected funds and sent volunteers to help Texas. In Memphis, Tennessee, a company of volunteers was formed, the Tennessee Wolf Hunters, with the object of hunting "Mexican wolves" who had invaded Texas. In Mobile, Alabama, they collected ten thousand dollars in less than two weeks and offered one hundred volunteers to defend Texas from the Mexican aggression. The Philadelphia Public Ledger announced that New Orleans offered to contribute fourteen thousand dollars and 1,000 men. Mobile with fourteen thousand dollars and 500 men, Tuscaloosa with four thousand dollars and 100 men, Natchez with six thousand dollars and 225 men, and Columbus, Georgia with $885 dollars. The Texan consul in New York received enough donations to buy several cannon. Even in peace

---

[202] Ibidem, p. 127.

[203] Nance, op. cit. pp. 134-138.

[204] Bosch, *Material…*, p. 343.

loving Philadelphia there was heard the bellicose clamor against Mexico.[205]

On July 18, 1842, the sixth Texas Congress approved a resolution to initiate hostilities against Mexico. And to that end, authorized the president to ask for volunteers to form an army. All volunteers who served for six months would receive 640 acres of land.[206] The reasons given were the Mexican rejection of Texan independence and their constant hostile actions on the border. The last reason cited in the declaration was "keeping our citizens of the Santa Fe expedition in abject captivity, contrary to the rules of war between civilized nations."[207] When the members of the failed expedition returned to Texas they began to organize reprisals against what they called the treason and cruelty of the New Mexicans. They were convinced that the defeat had been caused by geography and treason, not the military superiority of the New Mexicans. Thus, the Texan legislation provided a legal basis to annex New Mexico and California and parts of other Mexican frontier states. Sam Houston vetoed the resolution knowing that they lacked the resources to carry it out. However, the legislators commissioned Charles A. Warfield to organize an expedition. He was authorized, in the name of Texas, to appropriate Mexican properties on the condition that half of the proceeds obtained would go to the Texan government. In addition, he was allowed to cross the Rio Bravo and retaliate. Once in Mexican territory he should wait until Mexico recognized Texan independence.[208]

---

[205] Nance, op. cit. pp. 147-151.

[206] Ibidem, p. 261.

[207] Nance, *Attack and Counterattack, the Texas-Mexican Frontier, 1834-1836*, p. 256.

[208] Ibidem, pp. 288-290.

On the 20th of August, 1842, while they were making preparations for the offensive, the commercial officer of the United States in Texas communicated to the Texan Congress that his government asked for the suspension of military operations until they knew the results of the negotiations of the new ambassador in Mexico.[209] General Waddey Thompson had been sent to try to get Mexico to accept Texan independence as an accomplished fact after six years of effective independence. North American interests demanded peace, because without it the effects on commerce would be felt in the Gulf of Mexico and North American citizens would see their land communications with Mexico disrupted.[210]

In July of the same year, Thompson reported back to his government that Mexico tried to mortgage California to England for a loan of fifteen million pesos. Thompson, a fervent expansionist, reminded his Secretary of State of the importance of this territory and the loss the nation would suffer if California passed into English hands. According to him, the English would loan money to subdue Yucatan as well as Texas[211] Since April, Thompson looked for a way to buy California. President Taylor had written to him, "The acquisition of California is a matter of utmost importance in public opinion". During all of his stay in Mexico, Thompson tried to find a way to obtain California. He had been told that if he could find a way to obtain or buy this region he would be crowned with glory and the country would be doubly thankful.[212] Around September, the Mexican General

---

[209] Ibidem, p. 293.

[210] Bosch, *Material…*, p. 348.

[211] Ibidem, P. 350.

[212] Price, op. cit. pp. 50-52.

Adrian Wall took control of San Antonio and captured 53 prisoners and took them to Mexico City. Among them were a great number of prominent figures of the district, such as judges Anderson and Robinson, the attorney for the fourth district and his assistant, a member of Congress, and many lawyers, doctors and businessmen. His capture interrupted government functions in Texas for 18 months.[213]

The Texan response did not take long. They asked the United States and England to convince Mexico that they should make peace or conduct war following international rules. By the time, Webster, Secretary of State, instructed his ambassador in Mexico to present this petition, relations had become even more complicated, as the North Americans had taken control of Monterrey, California. The case was perhaps the funniest in those years of crisis. Commodore Jones had arrived in El Callao, Peru, in the spring of 1842 to take charge of the North American fleet of the Pacific. The tension between his country and Mexico was already so intense that Jones was very occupied with the idea that a third power could take control of California. When the French fleet of the Pacific suddenly left El Callao, Jones figured it was headed to California. A few months later the British fleet also suddenly left El Callao, and Jones, convinced that this meant the invasion of California, followed them. It is said that Jones supposed that war had broken out between Mexico and the United States. North American historians excuse his rashness by putting forward motives of patriotism on his part. It is implausible, however, that a commander in chief of a fleet far from his base would decide on his own to occupy a foreign port. Jones must have left his country with secret instructions to attack Mexican territory as soon as he knew that war had broken out. His error consisted in supposing that war had broken out.

---

[213] Nance, *Attack...*, op. cit. p. 323.

What is important to note is that it was the environment of bellicosity that motived him to invade Monterrey. The Mexican government correctly protested over this new violation of its territory, and the Secretary of Exterior Relations, José María Bocanegra, sent to Ambassador Thompson an energetic note demanding an explanation. Following his custom that the best defense was a strong offensive, Thompson accused him of indirectly causing the incident by the recent publication of a hard reproach of the United States. The North American government presented official apologies, making assurances that Jones had proceeded without authorization.

In Mexico, the event provoked enormous indignation. The newspapers never accepted the explanation that Jones had acted alone, since it was thought, correctly, that an officer could not take such a decision on his own. The invasion had been an injury to which was added Jones' proclamation in which he announced at different places in the area that they were now lucky to be North American citizens. In 1844, the press was still publishing news of the incident. It was then that letters to the editor began to demand a declaration of war against the United States.[214] The Mexican public began to be aware that the danger of North American expansion was already at its frontier and that California was repeating the Texan situation. And the old conservative-liberal dispute began again. Jesús Velasco Márquez, in his study of the period, shows that journalists were those who were most interested in explaining to their readers the causes of the North American expansionism in order to find the means to stop it. Newspapers brought their point of view of the battle between conservatives and liberals to an international level, thus the North American expansionism had two interpretations.

---

[214] Knapp, Jr., Frank A. "Preludios de la perdida de California", en *Historia Mexicana*, IV:2 (14), El Colegio de México, México, 1956, pp. 235-249.

Conservative newspapers explained it as the need for unity in a country of adventurers and thieves with no other ties of unity than avarice. "Despite the fact that their current territory could contain a hundred times more population than they have, their greed is not satisfied." The expansionism was, according to conservatives, an escape valve, but there was nothing to worry about as it would lead to North American destruction.[215]

The liberals saw it as the natural result of the manner in which the United States was organized. Innumerable articles in the liberal press emphasized the pragmatic character, the entrepreneurial spirit, and the natural greed of immigrants which pushed them to constantly look for new territories. "Because the geographical mobility of North American society was uncontrollable." In sum, explained the liberal journalists, the expansionism was a tie that unified the nation as shown in the presidential election of 1844. In his study of the press in the decade of the forties, Jesús Velasco concluded, "There is no doubt that for the liberal press, economic progress, political stability, and even North American expansionism were to be admired.[216]

The election of 1844 was one of the most important in United States history. It changed the course of its history with the incorporation of vast new territories. This fact allowed the North American public to occupy territories from New England to the Pacific and the much desired acquisition of California and Texas. The pressure of the expansionist movement, developed in innumerable publications had reached its climax. The north of the country, which had opposed the annexation of Texas over the slavery question, compromised by accepting Oregon.

---

[215] Jesús Velasco Marqués, *La guerra del 47 y la opinion pública, (1845-1848)* Sepsetentas, México, 1975, p. 59.

[216] ibidem, p. 56.

So it was that the Democratic Party declared in favor of the "re-annexation of Texas and the re-occupation of Oregon" in the campaign of James E. Polk. The territory of Oregon was, like Texas, a legendary land. Disputed by Russia and Spain at the beginning of the nineteenth century it was delimited by a Russo-North American-English treaty signed in 1829. From that time the dispute over the territory had been between England and the United States. Not being able to reach an agreement, the two countries signed a treaty of joint occupation. In the following years there was heavy publicity in the United States to bring colonists to the region. President Jackson supported the publication of various travelers' reports as publicity for the territory. "Oregon fever" did not take long to arrive in the east of the country. English colonists became a minority as the North Americans surpassed them in numbers, and in 1844 there were five thousand of them asking for annexation by the United States. The hostility that reigned between them and the English caused fear of a third war with Great Britain. In this moment, Oregon took on great importance in the eyes of Mexico. Our government had hopes that an anglo-american conflict would solve the problem of Texas. England and Mexico could easily defeat the United States and recuperate the lost territories.

Since the Texans proclaimed independence in 1836, Mexico had looked to an alliance with England to get back Texas and for four years was able to keep England from recognizing the independence movement. England did not recognize Texas until 1840, so as not to wound Mexico's feelings, since it totally dominated commerce in the country. It took four years for Mexico to realize that it would not get the lost province back, and that to recognize Texan independence would give it many advantages. The United States had not completed its industrial revolution so that England could control the Texan market and could take more advantage of the southern states by having a representative in Texas. In addition, English bureaucrats had come to the conclusion that Texas would be where they could obtain the cotton necessary for its textile industry without paying the high North American taxes. Therefore, they decided to recognize Texan independence and began a campaign to get the Mexican government to recognize it in the near future. For four years they had insisted to the governments of Bustamente, Herrera and Santa Anna to do so. The advantages to Mexico, they affirmed, would be immense, since Texas would be a wall to the United States expansion, while the United States would impede the encroachment of Texas into Mexico to prevent North American commercial development that could cause them problems. In exchange, the hostile attitude of Mexico would end up provoking the southern states to join Texas in its war with Mexico and end with it being annexed by the United States. Various Secretaries of Foreign Affairs understood the logic of the suggestion, but Texas had become a question of national honor, and the government that recognized Texan independence would inevitably fall.[217] Additionally, as we have said, Mexico had hopes of starting a conflict between England and the United States over Oregon.

The English position that Mexico should recognize the independence of Texas not only did not vary, but intensified between 1840 and 1845. By means of their envoy they were at the point of accomplishing a solution to the conflict. The envoy of the United States in Texas was effectively working in the contrary direction. The northern states feared the English presence in the territory of the conflict because they would snatch away the markets in the south of the country. The southerners feared that England would be able to convince Texas to abolish slavery. "The North American nervousness grew with the speculation of how England would put to use its influence in

---

[217] Toribio Esquivel Obregón, op. cit. pp. 252-258.

Texas." The fear was that the English would accomplish an agreement between Texas and Mexico that would enhance English influence in the region. The North Americans finally were afraid that Mexico, even in peace with Texas, would sell the province to England.[218] The United States suspected that the British would declare war, because they wanted Texas as much as they did Oregon. Nothing could have been more wrong, as history demonstrates. But it was this fear of English intervention that provoked a strong campaign by Tyler's government to accelerate annexation. As we have said, the electoral campaign of James Polk had as one of its main planks the annexation of Texas and the obtaining of Oregon. Tyler, however, wanted to take the glory of being the one to accomplish the annexation. Therefore during all of 1844, the last year of his term, Tyler tried to obtain the ratification of the treaty signed by the representatives of Texas on April 12, 1844. A good number of northern senators were opposed until the election of Polk confirmed public support. To be sure about the ratification, Tyler convoked both houses of Congress to decide together. The 27 of February, 1845, when he only had three days left in his term, Tyler won the ratification of the treaty of annexation, that in reality had been won in the election of 1844.[219]

The reaction of Mexico was immediate. Bocanegra had repeatedly declared that the annexation would be interpreted as a declaration of war. Crescencio Rejón, his successor as Secretary of State also declared that the United States violated international law with the treaty of annexation. The period from April 1844 to the end of February, 1845, was interesting in that the differences between the two cultures were demonstrated one more time. It is curious to observe how the Mexican government proposed a list of justifications in place of openly declaring war.

[218] Bosch, *Material..*, pp. 218-222.

[219] Price, op. cit. pp. 60-62.

The first argument was that they had the right to the Texas territory since the Louisiana Purchase. The North Americans compared it with the case of New Spain adducing that both had a right to independence. They spoke of the cultural differences that had impeded the independence of the people of Texas. They blamed Mexico for getting in the way of developing an independent Texas. Finally, they said that Mexico had put Texans in danger of falling into the hands of England. They even proposed Mexico pay a compensation for the costs. Before the Mexican protests, the United States decided that they would provide an explanation of their motives for annexation as a courtesy, since they did not recognize Mexico as possessor of Texas. The communications between the Secretary of Exterior Relations and the North American envoys give ample evidence of the chain of explanations to justify the United States position.[220] Mexico, for its part, constantly defended its right over Texas and accused the North Americans, time and again, of malevolence and greed. On March 13, 1845, J.N. Almonte, Mexican minister in Washington, asked for his passport and ended his mission. This, of course, signified the breaking of relations with the United States. However, the Mexican government held some hope that the Texan legislature would not ratify the treaty of annexation. It was rumored that the candidate for president of Texas, Ashbel Smith was against the annexation since he wanted to be elected president. If Texas joined the Union, this position would no longer exist. Meanwhile, the Mexican government gave Shannon, the North American ambassador, his passport, ending relations between both countries at the end of March, 1845. It was then that the Mexican consul in New Orleans wrote to his government to inform them that France and England had decided not to allow the annexation, convincing Mexico that they should recognize Texas independence if they rejected annexation by the United States.

---

[220] Bosch, *Material…*, pp. 390-450.

The consul added that he doubted the success of this undertaking since the "Texan public, who do not take into consideration the opinions of their own government, supported the North American decision in favor of annexation."[221]

Discussions about the possible ratification or rejection of the treaty of annexation by the Texan Congress took four months. The United States ratification was on February 27, 1845, and Texas did not ratify until July 16, the same year. During this time, England was able to persuade Mexico to recognize the independence of Texas with the sole condition being that it would not be annexed by the United States. Jones, the Texan president decreed an amnesty with Mexico. On March 29, 1845, he agreed to wait 90 days before convoking Congress to discuss the union issue, meanwhile entertaining Mexican offers; and on June 4, after receiving them, he announced in a proclamation to the Texan public that they would decide to take the offer of peace and independence made by Mexico or that of annexation by the United States.[222]

He had to confront, however, the powerful group of Sam Houston, the efforts of President James Polk, and of his attache, Commodore Stockton, who together mounted such a strong publicity campaign that the Mexican consul in New Orleans wrote to his government, "In case the Texan Congress does not decree annexation, the North American forces will go help the public proclaim it."[223] In the second half of June, the North American government ordered General Gaines and his forces to station themselves along the coast of Texas. At the beginning of July, as the meeting of the Congress approached, Lord Aberdeen,

---

[221] Ibidem, p. 488.

[222] Price, op. cit. p. 213.

[223] Bosch, *Material...*, p. 497.

110

British minister of foreign relations, openly expressed that Mexican management of the land had begun too late.[224] Meanwhile, North American soldiers kept arriving in Texan lands. Finally, On July 4, 1845, Congress ratified the treaty of annexation to the United States and Texas became a state of the Union.

When the news reached Mexico, the government was accused of being duped by the Texans with their proposals of treaties and of having lost too much time instead of declaring war. The government of José Joaquín Herrera answered that to not have negotiated would have meant nothing less than aggression and going down a road to an uncertain battle. England had recommended that the government limit itself to a break of relations since in the case of a war Mexico would be invaded, its ports would be blocked, and commerce interrupted, which would mean the ruin of the Mexican economy. In addition, explained Lord Aberdeen, the United States would have no right to invade Mexico if there were no declaration of war. However, and despite his councils, the English ambassador offered no help.[225]

On September 15, 1845, José Joaquín Herrera was declared president, and he issued a law that authorized a request for a loan of 15 million pesos to catty out the war with Texas. Despite this, his cabinet was pacifist, the Secretary of Exterior Relations, Manuel de la Peña y Peña, agreed to send an extraordinary commission on condition that the North Americans withdraw their ships blockading Veracruz. The North American government gave instructions to John Slidell to settle the new frontiers leaving New Mexico and California on its side. In exchange, they offered to pay the claims of their citizens and

[224] Ibidem, p. 511.

[225] Ibidem, p. 522.

would give Mexico 5 million dollars.[226] When he arrived in November, President Herrera asked him to stay in Veracruz, explaining that his presence in the capital could bring down his government. The idea of peace was not popular and the president and his ministers were denounced as traitors. Slidell did not heed the warning and headed to the capital.

Mexican newspapers demanded war from the beginning of 1845, alleging a thousand and one reasons, but especially the defense of national territory. On December 3 of that year, *La Voz del Pueblo* announced the arrival of Slidell. An anti-Herrera newspaper, *La Voz* had, since its beginning, been for federalism and the re-establishment of the Constitution of 1824.[227] It was also what various states of the Republic had asked for and whose leaders thought; that only a change to federalism could fix the situation.[228] They clearly knew that the North Americans had set their sights on taking California and New Mexico, but tried to avoid a conflagration. For this reason they accepted a dialogue with Polk's emissary.

However, Slidell had other goals. After the fracas of the intrigue to push Texas into a war with Mexico, they looked for other peaceful ways to change the frontier. Polk had promised to obtain California for the United States and was ready to do so. The last Texan president had accused him of looking for a war with Mexico at the moment of the annexation of Texas to relieve himself of the responsibility of starting an aggressive war for the sole purpose of taking California and New Mexico.[229] Therefore,

---

[226] Ibidem, pp. 533-539.

[227] Velasco, op. cit., p. 16.

[228] Bosch, *Material...*, pp. 528-529.

[229] Price, op. cit. p. 9.

Slidell had instructions to pressure Mexico with the United States' debt claims, and to get the Mexicans to agree that the border with Texas was the Rio Bravo (Rio Grande), as well as to purchase California and New Mexico.

It is hard to believe that the proposal was done in good faith. After the problems of independence and annexation of Texas, anything was possible, except a peace offering, considering the extra demand to purchase California and New Mexico. In the middle of the media furor against the United States and the bellicose environment that had existed in Mexico since the beginning of 1845, it was illogical and insulting to solicit this sale. The petition was definitely one more step towards war. The document of the Secretary of State Buchanan with the instructions to Slidell seem to us denigrating. In Poinsett's time, Mexico was offered different options for the sale of its territories. The monetary proposals were from five to 25 million pesos if California was included in the sale.[230]

One sentence in the document was particularly insulting, "The sums offered were considered as maximums and the government would be happy if the money were less."[231] A later letter urged Slidell to hurry up to get the treaty of sale. The major explanation of the reason why the key North American documents in the relations were always impertinent can be found in the study of Glenn Price. He claims that it is impossible to find any direction in the North American diplomatic missives of the period unless you remember that, "the North American diplomacy with Mexico reveals the common judgement of the North American public towards Mexicans. This attitude indicates that in reality there was little difference between an Indian and a Mexican. Therefore, in this case the need of a serious and

---

[230] Bosch, *Material...*, pp. 528-529.

[231] Ibidem, p. 541.

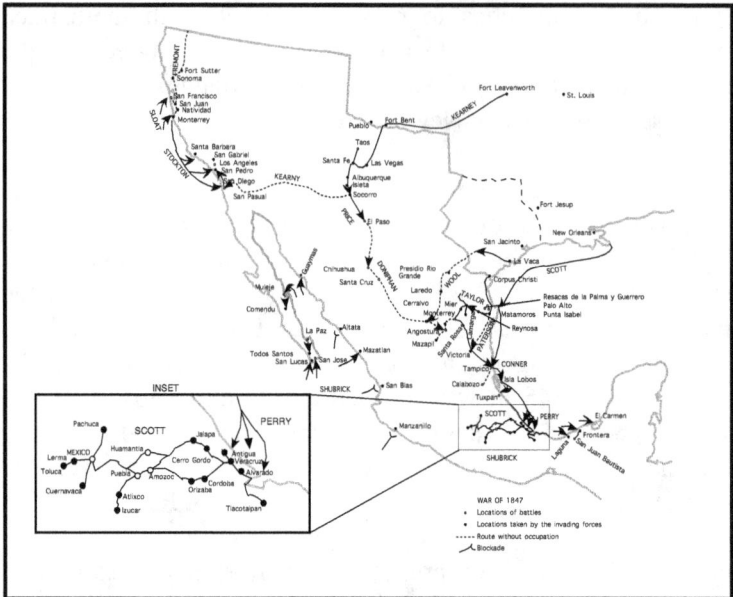

FIGURE 4. WAR OF 1847, TAKEN FROM LUIS G. ZORILLA, HISTÓRIA DE LAS RELACIONES ENTRE MÉXICO Y LOS ESTAOS UNIDOS DE AMÉRICA, ED. PORRÚA, VOL. 1, 1965, P. 192

respectful diplomacy was tossed aside."[232] From the first attempt to buy the territory, with the argument that selling Texas would put Mexico more in the geographic center of the country, to the last just discussed, Price's opinion is confirmed.

We know that the conflict began on a futile pretext. Polk wanted war and worked to get it. With the failure of all his intrigues he chose the only incident that had worked on the frontier, the

---

[232] Price, op. cit. p 36.

encounter between the forces of General Taylor and General Arista (Figure 4). This encounter was trivial because the territory officially had no owner. The area between the Rio Nueces and the Rio Bravo had been in dispute between Coahuila and Texas since Mexican independence. Therefore, before declaring war ownership of the territory should have been determined. Polk, knowing this, dismissed it and asked Congress to declare war on May 13, 1846, "for shedding American blood on American soil."[233] Paredes Arrillaga, at that time president, declared war on the 23rd of April. The Mexican Congress did so on July 2. Mexico lost the war, in large part because of internal political divisions. The first step towards disaster belonged to Paredes.

The forces of the United States threatened from Texas and the government of Herrera commissioned General Paredes to support General Arista. Then General Paredes decided to revolt against the government, which he considered weak, at the end of December, 1845. In Mexico City, General Valencia seconded him. In the moment that the country should have been preparing for defense, one again sees it occupied by the quarrel between liberals and conservatives. These latter, since the proclamation of Gutierrez Estrada in 1840, had declared themselves monarchists. The first rebellion of Paredes against the centralized government took place when war was declared. Stalled in Guadalajara, he asked for the re-establishment of federalism. Paredes sortied to confront General Salas' force, and General Salas on June 27, 1846, took advantage to conduct a coup d'etat, demanding the return of Santa Anna who had been exiled to Cuba. Santa Anna was named president and Valentine Gómez Farias vice president.

During General Paredes' time in the war, May 13 to July 27, Mexico disintegrated. Zorrilla notes, "the majority of states did

---

[233] César Sepúlveda, *La frontera norte de México*, Ed. Porrúa, Mexico, 1977, p. 53.

not send men or supplies or they openly rejected doing so, with some in open rebellion against the central government, or divided into local bands as occurred in California, Tabasco, Chihuahua, etc., since they considered the foreign war as a war against centralization, or pretended to, for their own ends." This was the great tragedy of the war. It was not a national war but only one by the government in power and those few states that had been invaded. Puebla did not take part, and even the state of Mexico, through which the invading troops had to pass to get to Mexico City, declared itself neutral. Yucatan did the same. The North American government astutely took advantage of the Mexican division. President Polk asked the North American Catholic bishops to communicate to their Mexican counterparts assuring them that the Unites States army would respect and help the Mexican Catholic Church at all times. [234] This idea was incorporated into the proclamations of General Taylor and later General Scott when taking Mexican cities. The proclamations of Scott, from his arrival in Veracruz, were used to politically divide the public, showing that one of his ends was to combat the monarchist party as an enemy of national interests. Even more, he declared that they had the right to conserve and protect Mexican liberty and its republican system. Zorrilla says that Scott's words created a group, "of naifs who believed him or appeared to do so." For this reason various states declined to cooperate in a war that, according to them, was against federal and republican interests given that a Santa Anna government could not convince them to become liberal.[235] Thus, the city of Puebla received Scott with peeling church bells.

In full battle against Taylor, Santa Anna had to return to the capital to restore order. The famous liberal, Valentin Gómez Farias, had instigated a rebellion by applying the law of January

---

[234] Zorrilla, op. cit. p.198.

[235] Ibidem, p. 203.

1847. This law authorized the government to dispose of church assets to obtain money for the resistance. The church protested which allowed the uprising of the *"polkos"*, rich young military men from elite conservative families who were known for dancing the polka. Even with the enemy present in the country the differences in philosophy continued to prevent a united front. From the first revolt in Guadalajara against Paredes (who like Santa Anna, moved back and forth between the liberals and conservatives), the conservative press accused liberals of being traitors. Naturally, the behavior of Santa Anna only reinforced the accusation. Until today it has not been possible to document Santa Anna's treason. His attitude is made clearer by studying his defense of the country: the abandonment of Tampico; his inactivity in San Luis Potosi; his withdrawal from the field of battle at Angostura; his repeated declarations about the impossibility of crossing the Sierra Gorda; the strategic error of not realizing from which direction Scott would attack the center of Mexico City, that culminated with the disaster of Chapultepec. Finally, the cusp of the errors was the abandonment of the center of the city upon hearing of the defeat at Chapultepec. The historic documents need to be found that prove, once and for all, Santa Anna's treason from the beginning to the end of the war.

However, we should not minimize the role of technical progress in the war. Mexican artillery was inferior to that of the North American's. While Mexico used 18 pound cannon maximum, the enemy had artillery of 30 pounds. The battle of Palo Alto, which began the war, was an artillery duel that showed the North American superiority. The Mexicans made 650 shots to the enemy's 3,000.[236]

---

[236] Manuel Cazadero, "¿Pudo México ganar la guerra contra los Estados Unidos?" en *Anglia*, num 5, Facultad de Filosofía y Letras, UNAM< México, 1973, p. 115.

Fortunately, while the Mexican fortresses were falling one by one, the North American government was also the victim of dissension. Otherwise, they would have conquered the whole of Mexico. In the country to the north there were objections to the war from abolitionists and members of the Whig party. They accused Polk and his friends of wanting more slave territory and of having declared war without the permission of Congress. Also, the voices of prominent writers such as James Russell Lowell and Henry David Thoreau accused their government of wanting to take Mexico. Little by little opposition to the war grew, and "at the beginning of 1847, the United States was almost as divided as Mexico." Since this was the year before elections, Polk and the Democratic Party wanted to end the war. The Whigs had mounted a campaign against it and nominated as candidates the two most popular generals, Taylor and Scott.[237]

For all these reasons Polk and Congress, finally, accepted a treaty sent by Trist. The arguments in Congress about the extension into Mexican territory took place daily. The historian Josefina Vázquez examines the situation in a brilliant article entitled, *"El Congreso de los Estates Unidos ante la guerra de 47"*. The real reason for the disputes was the fear in the north of the extension of slavery. Abolitionism was already as strong in some parts of the country as the desire for expansion. However, Josefina Vázquez thinks that what saved Mexico from being absorbed by the neighboring country was, in addition to anti-slavery and economic factors, "the repugnance of expanding and thus absorbing people of other races."

At first glance this statement does not appear to be well-founded. After all, the United States is a country made up of many races and creeds. How is it possible that Congress would refuse taking more territory so as not to absorb different people? Upon

_____

[237] Connors, op. cit. pp. 157-172.

investigation we note that, during the war with Mexico, a great migration had taken place, especially in the case of the Irish, who were forced to migrate because of the famous famine that decimated its population. The same happened to the Germans for other reasons, but mainly like the Irish, for economic ones. It was at this moment and in these circumstances that the nativist Know-Nothing Party appeared. In 1844 and 1845, respectively, the two cities most affected by immigration, Boston and New York, elected nativist mayors. The following year, 1846, six nativist representatives were elected to Congress.

Members of the party swore to elect only men born in the United States and Protestants. Their slogan was Keep America American. And as the majority of immigrants were Catholic, the party was also against this religion. Their principles and life style were seen as a threat to the ordered and Anglo-Saxon vision of society, as exemplified by the violent riot in Philadelphia in 1844.[238]

Fortunately for Mexico, these happenings greatly impressed Congress. Using the harshest terms inherited from the "black legend", Whigs, like Democrats, and even pro-slavery members united in the rejection of immigrants behind their fear off taking over our country (Mexico). They called us a semi-barbaric, uncultured, superstitious, and mixed race. Thus, the absorption would be a great danger to the stability of a country conceived, as the politician John Calhoun said, by the white race. "…We never dreamed of incorporating into our Union anyone other than the Caucasian race, the free white race." The already

---

[238] Bailyn, Bernard, *The Great Republic*, Little Brown and Company, Boston, 1977, p. 491.

annexed areas did not bother them since they were hardly populated.[239]

This sentiment brought agreement between senators and representatives in their opposition to the absorption of all of Mexico. It was the old Anglo-Saxon belief in the superiority of a pure race over a mixed one and its institutions over those inherited from Spain. In the chapter about the "black legend" we mention that one of the reasons for the rejection of all that is Spanish was that the Spanish would accept being mixed with other races considered inferior by the Anglo Saxons. This belief had so much force that it united abolitionists and pro-slavers in a common vision for the country, and as we have noted, with the political events provoked by the Know-Nothings. "Mexico was saved thanks to Trist's disobedience and to the racism, open or hidden, of many Congressmen,"[240].

Trist disobeyed the orders to await new instructions to tackle a treaty. The approbation of the Mexican government made him think that he needed to grab the opportunity before there was another coup d'etat. However, Mexico had rejected him as he had asked since the beginning, not only for the cession of Upper California and New Mexico, but of the peninsula of Baja California, and the right of passage across the Isthmus of Tehuantepec, and he had declared that "the United States had to go along with the cession that Mexico would be disposed to make."[241] In answer, President Polk let it be known the possibility of occupying the entire Mexican Republic to demand

---

[239] Josefina Vázquez de Kanuth, "El congresso de los estados unidos y la guerra del 47", en *Anglia*, num. 5, Facultad de Filosofia y Letras, México, 1973, pp. 39-92.

[240] Ibidem, p. 92.

[241] Zorrilla, op. cit. p. 208.

a larger cession of territory. Even the United States press, always a loyal voice of the government, had begun to discuss the annexation of the frontier states in a block. "During the war the press spoke unceasingly that God had chosen the United States to regenerate the decadent population of Mexico."[242] The discussions in the North American Congress, that we have already examined, however, avoided the option to take of Mexico.

At the same time the Mexican government became aware that their political situation did not lend itself to a strong resistance as the proclamations of the "Puros"(conservatives) and of the "*Polkos*" they began to see would only lead to the annexation of the whole country. Therefore, on December 30, 1847, Mexico decided to discuss a peace treaty written by the North American Secretary of State in which the modifications were in reality secondary. The peace treaty, called Guadalupe-Hidalgo for the place where it was signed, was finally accepted by both delegations in January 1848. The United States insisted on paying fifteen million dollars for the ceded territory. This was a measure to justify the taking of the territories which by right of conquest they could have taken without paying anything. Also in this way they took away Mexico's right to reconquer the territory, as on a sold property all rights are removed. We should note that in the discussions prior to the treaty, the Mexican delegates fought to defend the rights of their resident compatriots in the purchased territories. Even North American historians state that the delegates were more preoccupied by the people they were selling to than for the limits or indemnifications involved."[243]

---

[242] Ibidem, p. 215.

[243] Carey MacWilliams, *Al norte de México*, Ed. Siglo XXI, México,1972, 1972, p. 11.

The Treaty of Guadalupe-Hidalgo was not simply an accord to end the war. With its twenty-three articles it was an attempt to modify subsequent relations between the two countries despite the fact it contained various errors. For the lack of review about what can be called geographic problems, the quarrels about the frontier did not cease until a century later, when the dispute of the Chamizal was resolved. The lack of precision in many of the articles caused innumerable diplomatic problems that almost reached the point of war in the following decade (1850-1860). In the next chapters we will try to point out the failures and violations of the treaty on the part of the United States. The Treaty of Eighteenth is still in force, and thus it remains important. It is a document with meaning for a great number of inhabitants living along the border who still invoke its articles to demand its enforcement by the North American government. We have chosen diverse articles of the treaty that, according to the documents, were the least respected, to see the imprecisions, failures, and misunderstandings caused. If today it is so difficult to resolve the problems of "illegal aliens", of the *braceros*, and even of the Chicanos, it is because their roots can be found in the treaty. Articles eight, nine, and eleven were the ones most often broken.

The curious part of all this is that the treaty satisfied no one. Mexicans consider it one of the harshest in history for the enormous territory we lost. The North Americans suggest it is a treaty that is not very advantageous for them, who wanted to reach the South Pole if they could. The signers of the treaty, and especially Trist, were for many years called traitors in their respective countries. However, the treaty was a lesser evil, because Mexico was on the point of disappearing as an independent nation, at least for a while. Instead of remembering what we have lost, we need to emphasize what we have defended and been able to conserve until today.

The treaty put an end to the war, but did not achieve peace. In the following chapters we will see how its own provisions were the cause for a continuous diplomatic battle and innumerable armed encounters along the frontier. The desire to obtain more Mexican territory continued for many years. For example, the North Americans always wanted Baja California and Tehuantepec, but never got them. In the following pages we will see these attempts at invasion and the response of the Mexican government and people. The effort to maintain territorial integrity is one of the most honest and dynamic chapters of our history, which while lacking brilliance, is little known, yet deserves to be. Witness once again that the defense of the country was done by diplomats and not politicians or the military.

V. RESISTANCE TO THE NORTH AMERICAN INVASION OF NEW MEXICO

The resistance to the invasion of California and New Mexico (which at that time included Arizona), holds enormous importance in the history of Mexico. Since the conquest of the two frontier provinces, North American historians have decided to ignore the rebellion of thousands of Mexicans who rose up in arms against the invading army in these regions. For these authors, the period 1821-1846 was nothing more than the period of cultural penetration prior to the invasion. By virtue of the stereotype of many historic works about the frontier, the theme seems to stay the same: North American cultural penetration and the superiority of its institutions conquered the frontier regions before military occupation. According to this thesis, the so-called peaceful conquest or "bloodless" conquest in which New Mexico and California surrendered unconditionally, took place because the population had already accepted the United States ideology and felt closer to the country to the north than to Mexico.

These writers cite as an argument to sustain their thesis, the diaries of merchants in Santa Fe. Their opinions, expressed in different ways, agreed on various points: the inferiority of Mexican institutions, the commercial exploitation they experienced due to the arbitrariness of the roadblocks presented, and their admiration for the United States. It is not unusual that the merchants and soldiers of this time felt sure of having obtained a cultural, economic and political triumph. At that time, all North Americans believed that they had the obligation to share their blessings with what they considered to be inferior peoples. However, generations later, historians continue to hold to what is expressed in those diaries. Moreover, they ignored and continue to ignore the documents of the United States military commanders in the recently conquered New Mexico and historic proofs of the armed resistance to the North American invasion

124

that began within twelve days of the beginning of the invasion. The New Mexican people were not conquered culturally or ideologically, and their conquest was only possible because of their abandonment by Mexican military authorities. The commander and governor of New Mexico evacuated the region and dispersed his small army, because he had been bribed by the North American government through their agent at the time. It appears these writers do not know about the letter sent to the Mexican central government by the citizens of the region, on the 31st of October, 1846.

Daniel Valdés, the only Chicano who until now has written a history of New Mexico affirms, "North American history has ignored the war of liberation against the North Americans" a lack of investigation, that can be found throughout the writings of traditional North American histories of the invasion of New Mexico. Therefore, from then until today, we have accepted North American authors' assertions that the frontier provinces were conquered without resort to arms and without opposition.

As to the invaders, they were convinced that belonging to the United States was a gift of providence supported by the belief in the racial superiority of the white American Anglo Saxons. In 1845, the newspaperman, John O. Sullivan justified the eagerness to expand into new lands, calling it Manifest Destiny, when it was in reality nothing more than a desire for conquest. The new Puritan belief was revived, according to which the cultivation of the land was ordained by God, that leaving it uncultivated was the fundamental basis for taking over indigenous and Mexican land.[244] According to the North Americans, the frontier inhabitants should be thankful that they were incorporated into their world. Mr. Benton of Missouri

[244] Ortega y Medina, Juan, *Destino Manifiesto*, Sepsetentas, México, 1973, p. 124.

125

insisted on the duty to save "inferior races", giving them all the benefits of Anglo-American institutions.[245]

The region of New Mexico had belonged to New Spain since its discovery and colonization at the end of the 17th century. Because of its distance from the center of the country it was a region on the edges of New Spains national life and this great distance and difficulty of access was the cause of a very precarious economic situation during the two centuries of colonial history. The prices paid for articles sent from Mexico were 300 percent higher than in Mexico City. Because of that, New Mexicans welcomed United States merchants, who in 1822, sold at much lower prices with independent Mexico deciding to keep the old economic road blocks against the North Americans. The United States on the other hand did not have export tariffs so that their prices were lower. From the beginning of their independence, the North Americans chose policies that favored the expansion of their country towards the west. As we have seen, North American history was always dominated by the desire for expansion, that of Mexico by the hope of conserving their frontiers. These two positions show that from the beginning the United States assumed an aggressive stance and Mexico had no other option than to be on the defensive.

North American merchants soon owned the basic industries of the province and took control of its economy. The Anglo Saxons, always Puritans, justified their greed by what had become a flourishing commerce through the myth of a cultural conquest before a military one. They believed that the New Mexicans wanted a democratic life under North American political institutions. Meanwhile the Mexican government established commercial restrictions to stop the North American economic

---

[245] Benton, Thomas Hart, *Thirty Years View*, D. Appleton, New York, 1958, vol. 1, p. 680.

advance, while the North Americans, on the other hand, publicized the benefits to be obtained if the region joined the United States. Many of the North Americans wrote diaries and memorials in which they told their people, in their own way, the history of the region exploited and then abandoned by the Mexican government with the purpose of making their compatriots see that a military intervention in the province was unnecessary since the territory had already been conquered culturally. For example, visitors of the period, Josiah Gregg and Susan Magoffin, referred to the cultural infiltration that took place with Gregg pointing out the belief of his merchant companions that the Mexicans were not opposed to annexation all the way to the province of Durango.[246] Susan Magoffin, wife of one of the merchants, stayed for several months in the invaded region and her diary confirms Gregg's ideas. The people of Santa Fe, she assured, "are until now very content with its governor, who is really a republican."[247] What she did not say was that the governor was assassinated by these so-called contented New Mexicans several months later.

These and other diaries of the period gave subsequent historians the certainty of the triumph of the North American cultural infiltration and began the myth of the peaceful surrender of a people who, it is supposed, had already been conquered culturally. Many Mexican historians have accepted this point of view, and without more investigation, incorporated it into our history. The archives of the Secretary of Exterior Relations of Mexico and of the North American Congress, however, provide a different version of the truth showing that in New Mexico, as in California, many of the merchants were spies from Washington

[246] Gregg, Josiah, *Commerce of the Prairies*, J.W. Moore, Philadelphia, 1849, p. 102.

[247] Magoffin, Susan Shelby, *Down the Santa Fe Trail and in to Mexico*. University of Yale Press, New Haven, 1926, p. 103.

in Santa Fe, among them James Magoffin, tried to convince the governor, General Manuel Armijo, of the futility of confronting the North American army of General Stephen Kearney. In the diary of Thomas Benton we read that Magoffin told James Polk, president of the United States, that he, Magoffin, was more than capable of impeding the armed resistance of General Armijo.[248]

When the Mexican-American War was declared between Mexico and the United States, Magoffin left for New Mexico with the army of General Kearney with Bancroft citing a letter from Senator Benton to Kearney in which Magoffin is presented as a man having the president's confidence.[249] However, upon reaching the frontier, Kearney sent him to Santa Fe escorted by Captain Cook. Undoubtedly, Magoffin did not want to risk a march across the desert without first having certain knowledge of how the city was defended. Upon reaching Santa Fe, he found it already had been infiltrated by the other secret agents, a fifth column that helped the peaceful conquest of the state.

In these events what exactly passed between James Magoffin and Manuel Armijo is unknown. It is supposed, however, that the governor of New Mexico was bribed, as there are documents in which it is noted that the North American merchant received $38,000 for Magoffin's services. In the archives of the United States' Department of War there is a letter from Magoffin to the secretary in which he states that he had been contracted by President Polk:

> I arrived at Santa Fe before General Kearney and prepared the way for the bloodless conquest of New

[248] Benton, op cit. p. 680.

[249] Bancroft, Hubert Howe, *History of Arizona and New Mexico*, The History Company., San Francisco, 1889. vol. XXVIII, pp. 414-416.

Mexico. Colonel Archuleti (sic) would have fought; I calmed him. It was he who later organized the revolt that cost General Price so much blood to put down. The fight was in him, in Archuleti (sic), and he would have sallied forth earlier taking Armijo with him, if it had not been for my efforts.[250]

Senator Thomas Hart Benton in his report before Congress, clarified the reason why Archuleta was opposed from the beginning to the invader by explaining what Magoffin had proposed to the colonel:

General Kearney had come to take the eastern region of New Mexico as part of Texas, leaving the western part untouched. Magoffin explained this to Archuleti (sic), showing him that that part would not be taken by the United States as it was too far to be protected by the central government, so he recommended that he (Archuleta) make a pronouncement and take that part for himself. This idea seemed fine with Archuleti (sic). He agreed not to fight, and General Kearney was informed that there would be no resistance to his entry. And there was none. Several thousand militia who were assembled there who could have held off a large army withdrew without a shot and without knowing why, Armijo ran away, and Kearney occupied the capital.[251]

What should be stressed is that Archuleta did fight in defense of his country, the North American war documents testify to it.

---

[250] "Letters to the President", in *Records of the War Department*, The National Archives, Wendell and Benthysen, Washington, 1872, vol. V, p. 49.

[251] Benton, op. cit. p. 683.

The New Mexican people were betrayed by the man who until then had kept them out of trouble. In my book, *El Comércio de Santa Fe y la Guerra del 47* can be read the brilliant trajectory of General Armijo until that moment. *El Republicano* of February 5, 1847, published a letter from Armijo in answer to the accusation by his compatriots of ineptitude, cowardliness, and of being the principal cause of the conquest of New Mexico. In it, Armijo defended himself against what he considered unjust charges. He alleged that in a territory of 5,700 leagues and with 56,000 men distributed all across it, it would have been impossible the recruit an army, and discipline and train it sufficiently to put it in a position to fight. He affirmed retreating to Chihuahua to reorganize and reconquer New Mexico.[252]

North American historians usually end their account of the conquest of New Mexico with the entry of Kearney into Santa Fe with the example of the unconditional surrender main proof that the people living in close contact with Anglo-American culture ended up, according to them, not only recognizing its superiority, but wanting to become part of it. According to this account, the history of the conquest of New Mexico ends with the bloodless taking of Santa Fe. However many documents exist showing how superficial this conclusion is which I will refer to below. Even in General Kearney's proclamation to the New Mexican people can be seen the beginnings of the resistance, "and I demand that those who have left their homes and have taken up arms against the troops of the United States return to them immediately if they do not want to be considered enemies and traitors who deserve to be punished and have their property

---

[252] "Carta de Manuel Armijo", in *El Republicano*, México, 5 de febrero d e1847, p. 79.

130

confiscated."[253] Certainly, the general committed an illegality by proclaiming, on his own authority, that New Mexican citizens would be stripped of their Mexican citizenship (and given United States citizenship), and that all rebellious acts would be punished as treason. Such charges were illegal and this act violating Mexican sovereignty was condemned some years later by the same North American Congress that had the power to bestow citizenship.[254]

Moreover, Colonel Doniphan reports that nearly everyday new rumors of rebellion reached General Kearney, and that the vicinity of Albuquerque was preparing a force to attack Santa Fe. The North American army entered the city on August 19, 1846, and then on September 2, the general left for Albuquerque with 750 men to destroy a detachment of patriots who had arisen against the invasion.[255] A few weeks later Dr. Lawrence Waldo, merchant of Santa Fe for many years, wrote to his brother, "It seems to me that we have committed an error in thinking that the people of this territory were disposed to accept the government of the United States. It could be said that not one likes it, and from what I can see not one in a hundred is happy about it.[256]

Two months into the invasion, a North American soldier reported that a group of Mexicans had been discovered training for a

---

[253] Hughes, John T., *Doniphan's Expedition*, Cincinnati, 1848, p. 99.

[254] Caushey, John Walton, *Early Federal Relations with Mexico*, doctoral dissertation, University of California, 1923, pp. 14-16.

[255] Hughes, op. cit.

[256] Twitchel, Ralph E., *Leading Facts of New Mexico History*, p. 245.

revolt.[257] Colonel Doniphan stated, "We have established a civil government and everything appears to be peaceful, the people satisfied, but to an astute observer this is all hypocrisy."[258]

The 31st of October, 1846, a group of New Mexicans sent a letter to the government of Mexico in which they related the details of the preparations to defend New Mexico from the invasion, the treason of Armijo, and his retreat to Chihuahua after having dispersed his small army. The New Mexican citizens who signed the letter asserted to the president of Mexico that if Armijo had wanted he could have prevented the invasion, as he had news of it beforehand, resources and powder, and moreover had the support of the people. They declared that they were not okay with the invaders and wanted the whole nation to know it.[259]

Upon General Kearney's departure for California, Colonel Price was named the military authority in the province and established a rigid vigilance over the region. In November of the same year, he arrested Ambrosio Armijo when he was found to have a letter for his brother, Manuel, in which he informed him that the New Mexicans were preparing a revolt and were only awaiting help from the Mexican government.[260] The Daily Missouri Republican newspaper commented that at the end of November a

---

[257] Hughes, op. cit. p. 112.

[258] Daily Missouri Republican, December 5, 1846, Liberty, Missouri.

[259] "Ciudadanos de Nuevo México al presidente de México", archivo de la Secretaria de Relaciones Exteriores (ASREM), exp. 2-13-2971.

[260] *Weekly Tribune*, Missouri, December 5, 1846, p. 3.

group of New Mexicans had bought large quantities of powder in Missouri.[261]

Meanwhile, the same group of New Mexicans that had sent the letter to the Mexican president continued preparing for their revolt. On December 12, they met at the house of the vicar, don Juan Felipe Ortiz. The meeting was called by don Tomás Ortiz, who had been the last president of the Assembly of the Department before the North American invasion. Tomás Ortiz made clear to the assembled group, all old Departmental authorities, that it was a duty for New Mexicans to rise up in arms against the invader. "It was criminal to be silent, he warned those present, without helping in some form the defense of the fatherland, especially when General Manuel Armijo had left the Department with the aim of blaming its inhabitants for turning it over, which he had really done himself." Ortiz asked those present to express their opinions, and all promised to spend their last drop of blood in defense of their Mexican fatherland. They then by acclamation elected Tomás Ortiz as governor of New Mexico, and don Archuleta commander of the Mexican Departmental forces. They also swore obedience to all orders of the leaders they had just elected. In addition, the meeting swore never to allow General Armijo to enter the territory and not to submit to any other government than that of Mexico, planning a coup d'etat for the 19th of December, 1846.[262]

They immediately sent patriotic publications to all of the Pueblo Indians and New Mexicans in the north of the Department., but on the 18th of December they met again and decided to postpone the insurrection until the 24th to get the cooperation of all of

---

[261] *Daily Missouri Republican*, December 5, 1846, Liberty, Missouri.

[262] "Ciudadanos de Nuevo México al gobierno de México", LE-1083, ff. 274-276.

New Mexico. Tomás Ortiz was assigned the Bado region, Diego Archuleta to Taos, and Domingo Baca went to look for the help of the inhabitants of Rio Abajo, while Pablo Domínguez and Miguel Pino travelled to Tesuca, since it was Christmas eve, and the North American soldiers were celebrating, it would be easier to take the garrison. There were orders to kill all of the North Americans and collaborators. However, on December 17 the conspirators were betrayed, and two days later taken prisoner. Don Tomás Ortiz and Diego Archuleta escaped to Chihuahua, but the rest were captured.[263]

One week later, the civil governor, Charles Bent, published a proclamation in which he accused the patriots of being "vicious men ... disillusioned, they could not hold any position in the society of men of standing and merit; desperate, they tried to lead a revolution against the actual government." The governor added that subversive doctrines were being spread among the settlements causing disquiet, "because the people who stay publish their plans." In the same proclamation the governor defended his government against the accusation that it wanted to impose major taxes and take over private land. Bent had established an office for registering land titles with the intent of protecting them. As to the news of the march of Mexican forces to retake New Mexico, Bent affirmed that they were false, since what resources could the Department of Chihuahua have when the political parties were dejected and reduced to nothing?"[264]

After the failed rebellion, the province seemed to calm down. Two weeks later, Governor Bent marched on Taos without suspecting that a new conspiracy had been planned for the 19th

---

[263] Twitchell, op. cit. p. 276.

[264] Carta de Charles Bent to the Department of State, December, 1846, Archives of the University of New Mexico, Albuquerque, Ritche Papers, Roll 2.

of January or less than a month after the failed one. John T. Hughes, who witnessed these events, accused the most prominent citizens of the province. According to his testimony, even those who had accepted positions with the North American government, and of course, Catholic priests, were in on the conspiracy. These latter exhorted their faithful to rise up against the heretics who had invaded their fatherland.[265]

On January 19, 1847, Bent, the first civil governor of North American New Mexico, was assassinated along with his retinue in the town of Taos. Pablo Montoya proclaimed himself chief of the revolt and asked the other settlements for help. This is the only revolt noted in the Anglo history of New Mexico, but it was mentioned only as an insurrection of the Indians of the Taos Pueblo without an explanation of its causes. In this way, the North Americans avoid discussing the discontent of the New Mexicans. After all, the North American people have the idea that the Indians were always savages and their rebellions happened without a justifiable cause. It is overlooked that its chief was not an "ignorant" Indian, but Pablo Montoya, a New Mexican ex-official. Colonel Price's report to the United States Congress clearly states that the Pueblo Indians and Mexicans killed the governor and the five people who accompanied him. "It shows that the object of the insurrection was to kill all North Americans and Mexicans who had accepted posts in the North American government."[266] Colonel Price reported to the Secretary of War that all North Americans in the region would suffer the fate of Governor Bent unless a strong military

---

[265] Hughes, op. cit. pp. 59-60.

[266] *Message from the president of the United States t the 2 houses of Congress at the commencement of the Session of the 30th congress*, December 7, Wendell and Van Benthuyen, Washington,1847, p. 520.

contingent could be sent, since "the opinion that New Mexicans are favorably disposed towards the United States government is totally false."[267]

The letters from Price to Congress to report on the situation of the insurrections in 1847, began on January 20, with the news that, "all of the cities and villages, with the exception of this one (he did not name it) and Querloti (sic) declared themselves in favor of the insurrection."[268] Two days later he wrote that from 300-500 had left Las Vegas, New Mexico, for Santa Fe to rebel. In all his letters he asked for reinforcements and heavy artillery.

The day following the assassination of Governor Bent, General Jesús Tafoya sent a circular to various New Mexican ex-officials. In it he presented them with a declaration against the North Americans and asked them to recruit all the men possible. At the same time he reminded them that their military appointments had been authorized by the Mexican government, and it was their duty to fight.[269]

According to Colonel Price's reports, the 20th of January, 1847, rebel letters had been intercepted asking the inhabitants of Rio Abajo for help. For this reason, on January 23, or four days after the assassination of Governor Bent, Colonel Price marched on Taos. He brought 353 men and four twelve-pound howitzers. The next day he found the enemy near the settlement of Cañada and prepared to attack. The New Mexicans had taken control of the elevated settlements in the mountains and of three ranchos.

---

[267] "Colonel Price to Secretary of War", February 26, 1847, National Archives Record, group 94, Adjutant General's Office (AGOO) exp. 23.

[268] Message from the President, op. cit. pp. 531-533.

[269] Twitchell, op. cit. p. 252

According to the subsequent report Price estimated the number of patriots to be 1,500, and even though they fought well, the superiority of the North American artillery, the four twelve-pound cannon, ended by defeating them. This was the first battle after the conquest and there died Jesús Tafoya, one of the leaders of the rebellion.[270]

The second battle was that of Paso de Embudo, where a force of 600-700 men attacked the North Americans, a force that ended in retreat by the Mexicans after losing 20 men. On the way to Rio Abajo the Mexicans arrived in Taos on the 3rd of February. The North Americans found it totally fortified for defense, and for two days they continually bombarded the settlement, and according to their estimates the two sides kept up a continual fusillade. The North Americans were able to penetrate into the church after a number of bombardments, and from there the houses where the patriots were supplied with food and ammunition. The patriots finally retreated to the west into the mountains. The fighting was so intense that one day later they asked for a cease fire and turned over their leader Pablo Montoya, who was hanged the next day by the North Americans. In total, nearly 200 New Mexicans died in the battles of Cañada, Embudo and Taos.[271]

In the meantime, on the other side of the province, Captain Hensley and his men found patriots under the command of Manuel Cortés, chief of operations in the valley of Mora. There they assassinated three North Americans of the region and a whole group of cattle rustlers. All the settlements of this valley, except Las Vegas and Queoloti, had declared in favor of the insurrection. "The whole population seemed ready to revolt", said the report sent by Colonel Price. The two groups of men

---

[270] Message from the President, op. cit. pp. 521-522.

[271] Ibidem, pp. 523-534.

encountered each other in San Miguel de Mora, from where they retreated after the death of Captain Hensley.[272] Holed up in Las Vegas, one of the two settlements favorable to the North Americans, the forces prepared to return to attack San Miguel de Mora. The following day another encounter took place in which the North Americans were victorious. The patriots and the inhabitants of the settlement retreated to the mountains and the North Americans destroyed the settlement.[273]

After these battles, in which the leaders Jésus Tafoya, Pablo Montoya, Pablo Chavez, and the Indian Tomás died, there were funerals for the fallen North American soldiers and the trials of the captives. Meanwhile, the North American forces through searches collected arms and munitions in Mexican hands.[274]

The trials of the prisoners took place on February 6, 1847, and were presided over by the brother of the assassinated governor. Louis Garrad, a Scots merchant recently arrived in the province, left a valuable testimony of the conduct of the invaders towards those who defended the integrity of their fatherland. Garrad wrote, "It seems to me presumptuous on the part of the North Americans to invade a country and afterwards accuse the citizens in revolution (defending their land) of being traitors." It is Garrad who serves as witness of the protest of the New Mexican general who, accused of treason, did not agree with the legality of the trial, swore his innocence and died valiantly while shouting, "to hell with the North Americans."[275]

---

[272] Ibidem, p. 532.

[273] Ibidem, p. 533.

[274] Cutts, James M. The Conquest of California and New Mexico. Horn and Wallace, Albuquerque, 1966, pp. 233-234.

[275] Garrad, Louis H. Wa-to-yah and the Taos Trail, edited by Ralph Bieber, Arthur H. Clark, Glendale, 1938, p.266.

That the charges of treason were illegal was proved one year later in a judicial review. In the trial it was shown that the defense attorney had argued that, not being North Americans, the accused could not be charged with treason. Also, he exposed that the judges did not accept his objection. One year later, the Secretary of War declared the charges of treason inadmissible, as only Congress has the right to give citizenship. This opinion was corroborated by President Polk on July 24, 1848.[276]

Despite the execution of the so-called conspirators, the revolt continued. In the official reports of Colonel Hughes to the Department of War we read:

> After the suppression of the rebellion in New Mexico, troops were stationed in nearly every place in the province. There was a higher level of vigilance and a stricter discipline was put into place. Guns and ammunition were not allowed in any house, not even Mexican gentlemen (which had been the case before) could travel in the province freely, spying on the movements of North American soldiers. They, angry about the brutal massacres and frequent assassinations carried out during the campaign, rarely respected the innocent and inoffensive. The soldiers slept with their arms, never left their garrisons, walked around town, visited other settlements or wandered into the countryside without their arms. They were prepared, day and night, for whatever emergency might occur. The North Americans and the New Mexicans treated

---

[276] Caught, op. cit. p. 16.

each other with suspicion and animosity. An atmosphere of suspicion reigned in the territory.[277]

After three months of repression, on May 20, a new attack was carried out in the area of the Santa Clara settlement. It could be seen that the Indians of Taos and other tribes had joined the Mexicans in their guerrillas and many of them fought under Manuel Cortés, called the "Santa Anna of the north", he was able to organize a group of guerrillas who worked as citizens during the day, but at night attacked the North American encampments. On the 20th of May, they stole 200 horses and killed a soldier under the command of Captain Robinson. For several days the group had for several days harassed the encampments and properties of the North Americans. A few days later, Major Edmondson's company arrived with 200 men to chase them down. On the 26th of May, 1847, the first battle of the second phase of the resistance took place. In the Red River Canyon, some 120 miles from Santa Fe, they found about 400 New Mexicans who exchanged fire for hours until Major Edmondson was obliged to withdraw. The patriots killed or captured all of the North American horses.[278] One month later, on June 27, Lieutenant Brown and two of his men were attacked and killed in Las Vallas settlement. Major Edmondson marched to the settlement, shot several of the attackers and sent 40 prisoners to Santa Fe.[279]

On July 6, the patriots under the command of Cortés attacked the camp of Captain Morris, took the horses and arms, killed five of

---

[277] Hughes, op. .cit. p. 519.

[278] Cutts. op. cit. pp. 236-237.

[279]St. Cooke, George P., *The Conquest of New Mexico and California*, Horn and Wallace, Albuquerque, 1964, pp. 123-124. *Message from the*, op. cit. pp.436-537.

his men, and escaped again. This is when Major Edmondson went to the Los Pias settlement, a place which, after an encounter unfavorable to the New Mexicans, he ordered destroyed. In the pockets of the prisoners were found letters written by General González giving the plan of the insurrection and asking the inhabitants of the settlement to be ready for action. Additionally, the documents confirmed that the North American forces had prepared to leave for the north with the greatest part of its troops, "that others would leave in a few more days, among them the artillery under the command of Captain Fisher, and that they would constantly have spies on the roads to keep informed of their departure, to give a military blow to the insurrection before the artillery left. On the 15 of July, 1847, Edmundson marched with his men and two cannon to the settlement of Loquesta, situated on the San Miguel River, and there surprised the New Mexicans sent by Generals Cortés and González. Being surprised, the New Mexicans scattered, and Edmondson was able to capture about 50 prisoners and recuperate a great number of horses. In his report, the major noted that the New Mexicans had fortified the settlement, barricaded its houses, and buried their possessions in the mountains.[280]

The 20th of July, Colonel Price reported that his force had been reduced by the departure of various regiments to the north of the country and as a result decided to concentrate his remaining men in Santa Fe. He reported that there were many rumors of insurrection and that he expected a large force from Chihuahua, "it is certain that the New Mexicans hate the North Americans."[281] The *St. Louis Republican* newspaper reported,

---

[280] Ibidem, pp. 239-240.

[281] Cooke, op. cit. p. 124.

141

"Almost the entire territory has been the scene of violence, fury and oppression by the soldiers against all the inhabitants.[282]

By the second half of August, 1847, one year after the conquest, an English traveler passing through New Mexico left this testimony:

> "I found in all of New Mexico a sentiment of bitterness and hostility against the North Americans, who had not tried in Santa Fe nor in other places to win the people over, but to the contrary, by their despotic and aggressive manner they were the cause of this hatred."[283]

Meanwhile, Colonel Price asked the Department of War for a thousand men to reinforce his position in Santa Fe. He wrote to the Secretary of War, "The opinion that the New Mexicans are favorably disposed towards the government of the United States is totally wrong. All the Americans in the region could be victims of the destiny of Governor Benton, unless we maintain a military force to frighten them."[284]

A year after the conquest, when according to the Congress in Washington that the situation in New Mexico was completely

---

[282] Duffus, R. L. The Santa Fe Trail, Longmans, Green, and Co., New York, 1930, p. 217.

[283] Ruxton, George F., Adventures in Mexico and the Rocky Mountains, ed. Leroy R. Haven, Norman Press, Oklahoma, 1950, p. 188.

[284] Cited by Frank MacNitt, "Navajo Campaigns and the Occupation of New Mexico 1847-1848, in the New Mexico Historical Review, University of New Mexico, vol. LIII, p. 173.

under control, Colonel Price kept asking for reinforcements.[285] A year and a half after the conquest, on December 29, 1847, Lieutenant Walker reported to the Department of War that he had sent Captain Armstrong with 40 men to Antón Chico, where Manuel Cortés was in rebellion. After the battle, Captain Armstrong captured some documents with detailed instructions from the Secretary of War in Mexico City for the organization of units of volunteers who could participate in military operations planned against the North Americans in New Mexico. Among the documents was one signed by Governor Frias of Chihuahua commissioning Manuel Cortés as a captain in service to Mexico. From this moment, Cortés, bandit and rebel, became head of the guerrillas in New Mexico.[286]

The treaty of Guadalupe-Hidalgo which, as we know, ended the war, was signed on February 2, 1848 and ratified on June 30, 1848. One month later, General Price fought the last battle of the campaign of New Mexico! This took place in Santa Cruz de Rosalía, near Chihuahua.[287] Rebel uprisings were constant from September 1846 to February 1848, including the month in which the Guadalupe-Hidalgo Treaty was signed.

Four years later, Larrainza, Mexican ambassador in Washington, wrote to the Secretary of Exterior Relations that the Daily National Intelligencer had just published a letter sent by one of their readers from New Mexico in which he expressed his disgust with the Mexican way of life, their resistance to North American authorities since they had been placed there, and the difficulties this produced. The newspaper attributed this to the hate and hostility that the Mexicans had against North

---

[285] MacNitt, op. cit. p. 175.

[286] Ibidem, pp. 190-194.

[287] Twitchell, op. cit. p. 262.

Americans.[288] K.D. Duffus' book, *The Santa Fe Trail*, includes the testimony of John Greiner, the government Indian agent in New Mexico, four year after occupation, "There are no North Americans in this region who dare to go out without being armed to the teeth and who keep a pistol and knife under their pillows. No one goes to sleep without taking these precautions."[289]

Even General Canby, chief of Union forces in New Mexico during the War of Secession in 1861, wrote, "The Mexicans have no affection for United States institutions (…) and have a strong, and until now repressed, hatred for North Americans."[290] The above would convince any impartial reader of the erroneous and incomplete thesis of a cultural conquest prior to the military one. We know that there were many New Mexicans who not only accepted the conquest, but who collaborated with the invaders from the beginning, but we also know that a good number of New Mexicans did not. Various documents in the archives at Santa Fe support the conclusion that prominent men declined to accept positions in the North American government of New Mexico during this period of conflict.[291] These documents will be cited in the chapter on repatriation, which presents irrefutable proof that a large number of New Mexicans did not want to become North Americans refuting the thesis of a cultural conquest before a military one is not historically correct.

---

[288] Archivo de la Secretaría de Relaciones Exteriores, expediente H/510 (73.0) 852, f. 11.

[289] Duffus, op. cit. p. 219.

[290] Heyman, Max L., Prudent Soldier, A Biography of Major General Canby. 1817-1873. The Arthur H. Clark Co., Glendale, California, 1959, p. 145.

[291] Benjamin M. Read Collection, State Records Center and Archives, Santa Fe, files numbers 35, 170, 295.

The Mexican government, conscious of this resistance, was reluctant to sell New Mexico and California. They knew that a large number of its nationals did not want to belong to the United States. Thus the emphasis in Article VIII of the Treaty of Guadalupe-Hidalgo, which gave the citizens the right to repatriation. As will be seen in the section on analysis of the United States' violations of the treaty, the North American government did not respect Article VIII. It must be repeated that the peaceful conquest of New Mexico was accepted by North American historians as a great cultural feat, and no one has tried in more pacific times to consult the documents. Even with the reports of United States overseas forces written in the decade of the 1960s about Southeast Asia, the myth of peaceful conquest persists.

FIGURE 5. LAS CALIFORNIAS

VI. RESISTANCE TO THE NORTH AMERICAN INVASION OF THE CALIFORNIAS

Since 1804, The California's had been divided into Alta and Baja California by the viceregal government. In the North American world of the era they were still called the same name, probably to ignore the viceregal decree (Figure 5).

The case of Alta California was analogous to that of New Mexico. North American groups, whalers, sea otter hunters, and merchants began to arrive from viceregal times. With the independence of Mexico the doors were opened to foreigners just as in New Mexico. In a short time, they bought or started businesses in the region. As in the neighboring province, during the rebellion against centralism of the 1830s, the North Americans were accused of "wanting to repeat the Texan feat."[292] The North Americans were marrying the daughters of the rich Mexican *hacendados* and by the end of the war had formed a clan. According to Thomas Oliver Larkin, a rich merchant and consul of the United States in the decade of the forties, the Anglo influence was so profound that they had convinced the Mexican authorities of California to declare independence and ask to be annexed by the United States.[293]

---

[292] Moyano Pahissa, Angela, *California y sus relaciones con Baja California*, Sep-ochentas, México, 1983, p. 24.

[293] Cleland, Robert Glass, *From Wilderness to Empire*, Alfred Knopf, New York, 1944, p. 203.

In the run-up to the war between Mexico and the United States (Chapter IV) the offers of the North American government to buy Alta California were mentioned, as well as the tangled mess of diplomatic negotiations to take over the province, including the frustrated invasion of Monterey by Commodore Jones in 1842.

With the ascension of James Polk as president of the United States the desire to acquire California intensified. He sent John Slidell with an offer of forty million dollars to purchase the province. When that did not work, Polk dedicated himself to plotting a program of annexation including having Thomas Larkin, his consul and confidential agent, work secretly to obtain the separation of the province. His plans failed for three reasons: a disagreement between the Californians and John Fremont, the insurrection of the North American colonists called the revolt of the Bear Flag, and the beginning of the war between Mexico and the United States.[294]

On the 13th of May, 1846, President James Polk declared war on Mexico; the 7th of July, Commodore John Sloat took possession of the port of Monterey, and on the 9th the news of the declaration of war arrived. We know that the occupation of California had been planned several years before from the explanations given by Commodore Thomas Catsby Jones at the taking of Monterey at the end of 1842. The North Americans were informed of the complete lack of protection of the California ports and also of the precarious state of the Mexican fleet. Their naval force and the pro-United States sentiment they thought they were sure to encounter, made the conquest of Alta California seem an easy task. Commodore Sloat, like General Kearney in New Mexico, published a proclamation offering the

[294] Ibidem, capítulo 13.

inhabitants of Alta California the protection of the United States government and all the rights of religion, property, and citizenship to which they had become accustomed.

Two days after the occupation of Monterey, Captain Mervine took possession of the Port of Yerba Buena, afterwards known as San Francisco. On July 15, Commodore Stockton arrived to replace Sloat in command of the Pacific fleet. He immediately proceeded to occupy the remaining California ports without opposition. As in New Mexico and later in Baja California, the North Americans attributed the lack of resistance to the strong pro-United States sentiment in the region. What had happened in New Mexico happened again in California and Baja California: their authorities, Armijo and Pico, abandoned the region after disbanding their forces that could have defended it. Also in Baja California the political leader, Palacios Miranda, decided to join the North Americans. In New Mexico, General Armijo took refuge in Chihuahua, in California, Generals Pio Pico and Jose Castro, left for Sonora leaving their citizens leaderless. The invasion, the abandonment by its authorities, and the absence of a military force left them stunned and thus, it took several months to get organized before the Californians, like the New Mexicans and later the Baja Californians, decided to resist.

In the port of Los Angeles, Commodore Stockton put Captain Archibald Gillespie in charge of 50 men. Then, he sent Kit Carson with the news that the province had been totally overtaken. It never seems to have occurred to them that the Californians would defend their country. The revolt against the invaders began in Los Angeles on September 23, 1846, three months after the invasion. The majority of historians attribute the revolt to the anger against the character of Gillespie, commander of the garrison. Under the command of Capitan José María Flores, around 600 Californians proceeded to capture the North Americans in Los Angeles and organize the defense of the city.

Their arms consisted of old shotguns, lances, and clubs. One of the soldiers managed to escape, and within a few days Stockton was aware of the situation. On September 24, the combatants of the Los Angeles resistance published the following proclamation to the public:

> Citizens: for one and a half months, due to the disgraceful cowardliness and incompetence of the principal authorities, we have seen ourselves subjugated and oppressed by an insignificant band of adventurers of the United States of America, who, putting us in a state worse than slavery, are dictating despotic and arbitrary laws, by means of which weighing us down with onerous taxes, wanting to destroy our industries and our agriculture, and forcing us to abandon our property to be taken and divided up among them. Will we permit ourselves to be subjugated and accept in silence the heavy chain of slavery? Will we lose the hereditary land of our fathers which cost them so much blood? Will we leave our families victims of the most barbarous servitude? Will we wait until seeing our wives raped, our innocent children whipped by the American lash, our land sacked, our temples profaned, painfully dragging out a life full of shame and disgrace? No! A thousand times No! Compatriots, death before this! Who does not feel his heart beating and his blood boiling contemplating our situation? Who will be the Mexican who will not lower himself and who will rise up in arms to expel our aggressors? We believe that no one is so vile and cowardly. Therefore, the majority of the inhabitants of this district, justly indignant before the presence of our tyrants, give the cry for battle, and with weapons in hand, swear to support the following articles of this plan:

1) We, the inhabitants of the department of California, as members of the great Mexican nation, declare that it has been our desire to belong only to her, free and independent.

2) Therefore, the intruding authorities named by the invading forces of the United States are considered to be invalid and illegitimate.

3) We swear not to lay down our arms until the North Americans, enemies of Mexico, are expelled from Mexican land.

4) Every Mexican citizen from 15 to 60 years of age who does not take up arms to support this plan will be declared a traitor, under pain of death.

5) Every Mexican or foreigner who directly or indirectly helps the enemies of Mexico will be punished in the same manner.

6) All property of North American residents that have directly or indirectly taken part or helped the enemies of Mexico will be confiscated and used for the expenses of the war, and their persons sent to the interior of the (Mexican) Republic.

7) Everyone who opposes the present plan will shot down.

8) All residents of Santa Barbara and the northern district will be immediately invited to participate in this plan.

Field near Los Angeles, September 24, 1846[295]

After the taking of Los Angeles, the patriots controlled the Chino Rancho, refuge for a number of North Americans residing in the region. They returned to Los Angeles with the prisoners, forcing Gillespie to surrender and leave the city. In the settlement of San Pedro the North Americans fortified themselves in hopes of aid sent by Stockton. Stockton sent Captain Marvin in the ship Savannah with 300 men who, along with those of Gillespie, proceeded to try and retake Los Angeles. On the way, there was an encounter with 150 Californians who had been able to take a four-pound cannon with which to harass the North Americans. These latter returned to San Pedro waiting for a better day. The city of Los Angeles remained in Mexican hands for four more months.[296]

On December 6, 1846, the battle of San Pascual took place in which the patriots attacked the forces of General Kearney who had arrived from New Mexico to complete the conquest of California. According to military reports and the diary of Captain Emory, the battle of San Pascual was a victory for the Californians, who had excellent cavalry armed with enormous lances.[297] For some unknown reason the winners did not make prisoners of General Kearney's people.

Meanwhile, because the Californians attacked constantly, Commodore Stockton arrived in San Diego on December 12,

---

[295] Bancroft, Jubert Howe, *History of California*, vol. 1, The History Co., San Francisco, 1866, p. 310.

[296] Cughey, John, *A Remarkable State's History*, McGraw Hill Book Co., New York, 1970, p. 108.

[297] Emory, William H. *Notes of a Military Reconnaissance*, Wendell and Van Behthuysen, Washington, D.C. 1848, p. 109.

1846 and sent 180 men to help General Kearney on the route from San Pascual to San Diego. The Californians by then had reorganized the Mexican government in California, electing Captain José Flores as interim governor. They conducted their military operations using guerrilla tactics, with which they were able to harass Stockton's men. These, lacking horses, sent a group of marines to Ensenada from where they brought back 500 head of cattle and 140 horses and mules, that they had taken from ranches by force.[298]

Despite the victories, by the end of 1846, after three months of battle, the Californians' munitions were used up and their attempts to obtain reinforcements had failed. Moreover, Alta California did not have land communications with the rest of Mexico and North American naval forces were too strong for Mexican ships to pass their blockade.[299] At the beginning of January, 1847, the combined forces of Kearney and Stockton marched from San Diego to Los Angeles. The Californians waited on the banks of the San Gabriel River, where another military encounter took place. Even though they had the advantage of position, the lack of munitions forced them to retreat. The next day they were defeated in what became known as the battle of La Mesa. The 10th of January, Stockton and Kearney took Los Angeles and raised the North American flag that had been replaced four months earlier.

As for the north of California, the patriots had been able to keep Captain Fremont and his men in Monterey. When news arrived of the Stockton and Kearney's march on Los Angeles, Fremont also left for Los Angeles. A North American of the region warned the patriots who waited for him near Gaviota, causing

[298] Purade, Richard, *The Silver Dons, the History of San Diego*, Union-Tribune Publishing Co., San Diego, 1963, p. 82.

[299] Cleland, op. cit. p. 231.

Fremont to cross the San Marcos pass towards Santa Barbara. After innumerable vicissitudes he was able to reach Santa Clara, where Californians under José Antonio Carrillo awaited him. The Californians tried to surprise him at Rancho Sespe, but failed to bottle him up in a battle they ended up losing. At Rancho Cahuenga they surrendered.

All that was asked of the Californians was the handing over of their artillery, which consisted of two cannon and perhaps a half dozen muskets, a promise that they would obey the laws of the United States and to give their word that they would not rise up in arms against the United States again.[300] In the chapter studying the violations of the Treaty of Guadalupe-Hidalgo, we will see the situation in California after the end of the war.

Even though Baja California did not become one of the lost provinces I would like to include it in this discussion of the resistance to the North American invasion since it is a little known period in our national history. It shows that the idea of nationality was very present in the second half of the last century in the faraway province of Baja California. To the contrary of many states in the center of the Republic that had declined to send men to repel the North American invasion, the farthest provinces, New Mexico, California, and Baja California, fought the invader and left documents of indisputable patriotism and national identity. The ease of consulting the archives makes the following section much more complete than other sections of this book.

On August 17, 1846, although not one North American had gotten to Baja California Commodore Stockton declared the end of the conquest of the Californias, announcing the conquest even

---

[300] Cleland, Robert Glass, *History of California, the American Period,* the MacMillan Co., New York, 1922, p.224.

before it began. The cause of the confusion was ignorance of the geography. Commodore Stockton did not realize that Baja California was a separate political entity. Since 1804, the viceregal government had divided California into two different provinces, but from the way he acted it is clear he did not realize this. Five days after his proclamation, Stockton ordered the blockade of the coast of Mazatlán and for this totally indirect motive caused the arrival of the first North American ship of war to the coast of Baja California.

On September 14, 1846, the U.S. Cyane entered the bay of La Paz looking for Mexican ships with the objective to interrupt commerce between La Paz and other Mexican ports. Believing himself to be in conquered territory, he asked the local political chief, Colonel Francisco Palacios Miranda that he stop trading with Mexico, and declared the area neutral in the war between Mexico and the United States. Commander Du Pont never mentioned conquering or taking La Paz. He simply limited himself to praising the cooperation of Governor Palacios and of the inhabitants of the port, and informed Stockton, commander of the forces in California, of the following:

> Baja California has been totally neglected for the past two years, its inhabitants, who have fought against this neglect and lack of government, are very poor— it is difficult to understand how they can allow the flag of such a useless government to fly over their territory—even though I believe that they are ready and anxious to raise ours as soon as they are assured of its protection.[301]

---

[301] Nunis, Doyce B. Jr., ed., *The Mexican War in Baja California: the Memorandum of Captain Henry Halleck*, Dawson's Bookshop, Los Angeles, 1877, p. 20. citing a letter from Commander Du Post to Commodore Stockton.

At the time of these events there was a firm confidence in Manifest Destiny, and Du Pont was a man of his times. He was convinced of the Mexican admiration for North American institutions and sure of the desire that the inhabitants of occupied Mexico wanted to raise the North American flag. Some groups in Baja California supported the North American invasion, but there were more who defended national integrity in the fight against the intruders. The La Paz archives have the report of the Mexican ships in the port on September 14, 1846, when they were taken by the corvette U.S. Cyane of the United States fleet: there were two brigantines, two sloops, four schooners, and a pilot boat, all the property of Mexican citizens, three of whom were from La Paz, one from the Mining District of San Antonio, another from Cabo San Lucas and two from Mazatlán.[302]

Governor Palacios Miranda appealed to Commander Du Pont for the return of the ships since, "this peninsula lacks everything necessary for life and except for roasted meat, there is no flour, no corn, nor seeds of any kind". He thought that return of the ships was only fair, given the friendly welcome they had received.[303] By the submission of governor Palacios, Du Pont did not think it was necessary to leave part of his forces in La Paz, and hence Baja California was not conquered in 1846. The only war measures the U.S. Cyane carried out was the taking of the ships and the declaration of a blockade of the port.

In November, 1846, Commodore Stockton sent a North American whaler to collect provisions in Baja California. A small force under Captain Gibson collected 60 horses, 220 head of cattle, and 500 sheep that he brought to San Diego. Three months later another group of Stockton's men went to San José

---

[302] *Archivo Histórico de La Paz*, "Pablo L. Martinez", Legajo 44, "Expedicion Norteamericana", s.f.

[303] Ibidem.

del Cabo to investigate the report that a French ship had brought munitions. The news said that Anastasio Bustamente would invade Alta California with an army of 1,500 men provoking Commodore Stockton to insist to the Secretary of War the necessity of occupying Baja California.[304] Finally, they were aware that they had not conquered Baja California.

Meanwhile, the last governor of California, General Pio Pico, escaped from the invaders, and with his Secretary of Government, José Matias Moreno, arrived in Baja California the 22nd of November, 1846, to cross over to Guaymas and ask for help from the central government. Santa Anna finally answered his letters in December, 1846, via the Secretary of Exterior Relations, by admitting his desire to help but also that he could not do so given the current conditions in the capital.[305]

In January, 1847, the United States' Secretary of War, William L. Marcy, formally ordered the invasion of Baja California, to raise the flag in the region, and to take the key points of the peninsula; however, his orders only reached Kearney in April of that year.

The Territorial Deputation of Baja California met in February, 1847, in Santa Anita on the outskirts of San José del Cabo, to name a political chief to replace Palacios Miranda who was considered a traitor. Everyone was surprised when, in September of 1846, he declared himself to be neutral in the conflict between the United States and Mexico. In the following four months no more American ships appeared. The men of the Territorial

---

[304] Colección de documents de la Casa de Representantes, *Executive Documents Num. I*, serial 537, 30th Congress, second session, pp.1047-1052, Washington D.C., 1848.

[305] Long, Robert W., *Life and Times of José Matias Moreno*, doctoral thesis, Western University, San Diego, California, 1972, pp. 175, 177.

Deputation decided to organize in defense when the North Americans would arrive, and designated Mauricio Castro as political chief. A native of San José and a man of great energy and patriotism, he decided to make war against the invader and started to organize the resistance[306]

On March 29, 1847, Captain John P. Montgomery arrived in San José del Cabo with orders to take the settlement, proceeding to ask for the surrender of the local authorities and the hand over of all public property to the United States. In addition, he obliged the inhabitants to swear strict neutrality. Like Kearney in New Mexico, Captain Montgomery published a proclamation that offered the rights and privileges of North American citizens to the locals. The 3rd of April, 1847, he repeated the same ceremony in Cabo San Lucas, and reported that he had found the inhabitants friendly and fairly passive toward the change in flags.[307]

In April, 1847, another ship arrived in La Paz, the Portsmouth, and Colonel Francisco Palacios Miranda, who had continued in office despite accusations of treason, received Montgomery asking that members of both nations meet to discuss the terms of the occupation. Thus, they signed a treaty that public properties would pass into North American hands in exchange for the respect of the local authorities and the neutrality of the municipal employees. They also offered to respect the Mexican soldiers if they agreed not to resist.

In the documents directed to the North American Congress there is a list of the authorities of La Paz who signed the surrender document. Lieutenant Colonel Francisco Lope Uriza, Francisco

---

[306] Martinez, Pablo L. *Historia de Baja California*, 1972, pp. 175-177.

[307] Long, op. cit., pp. 186-187.

Villegas, Teófilo Echeverría and Francisco Palacios Miranda. Don Ángel Lebrija was named customs inspector for the United States and Juan de la Fuente captain of the port.[308] Colonel Palacios Miranda limited himself to asking for the return of the ships confiscated in September 1846, and to directing a letter to Commodore Stockton to relate the suffering of the inhabitants of the peninsula because of the lack of food. In addition, he complained that his petitions of the last six months had not been addressed, despite the fact they had not resisted the occupation.

There were volunteers from San Diego who, because they believed Baja California would become North American, helped facilitate the occupation by informing the authorities of nearby towns about the changes in the terms of the treaty and explaining the rights and privileges that North American citizens enjoyed. Mauricio Castro, Secretary of Exterior Relations, wrote about this, saying that when the North Americans arrived in April, 1847, they had announced that no one would lose their Mexican citizenship, which turned out to be wrong, because when the armed forces arrived in the territory they obliged the local governments and authorities to swear allegiance to the laws and constitution of the United States. "Surprised, these small settlements, tricked and threatened by force, had to comply despite their wishes."[309]

Until this moment, the army had not been used in the conquest of Baja California. Since the beginning, the war ships patrolling the coast had been enough to control the situation. But when the North American authorities entered Santa Anita the Mexican government organized and immediately made gestures to send an army. A letter from Mauricio Castro to the Mexican government

---

[308] *Executive Documents, num. 1*, pp. 1059-1065.

[309] Archivo de la *Secretaría de Relaciones Exteriores de México* (ASREM), Expediente 538-1848.

159

listed the names of the chief patriots: Dominican Father Gabriel González, Franciscan Father Vicente Sotomayor, Don José Matías Moreno, Don Vicente Mejía and the town councils of the Comondú and Mulegé settlements. Castro lauded these settlements for being examples of patriotism, since it was they who asked for arms and munitions from the commanders of Sinaloa and Sonora to organize guerrillas.[310]

Companies A and B of the First Battalion of New York Volunteers left Santa Barbara, California on the 3rd of July 1847 under the command of Colonel Henry Burton, named governor and military commander of Baja California. In his trip south, he passed by Ensenada, where he left a detachment. He arrived at La Paz the 20th of July, in the ship Lexington and informed Congress that they were well received by the inhabitants, and the 29th of July, Burton published the following proclamation:

The Military and Naval Commanders of Baja California to its inhabitants.

> Californians: Having taken possession of this territory, the United States, and having raised the pennant of J.B. Montgomery, captain of the frigate Portsmouth, in the month of last March and April, today proceeds to occupy it with the forces at his command in the name of the government of the North American Union. However, the laws that governed before the war will remain in full force, as long as they do not contravene the constitution of the United States, or are modified or revoked by the competent authorities. The undersigned swear to having done everything within their power to protect and sustain the peaceful citizens in the full

---

[310] Ibidem, no date.

enjoyment of their rights and civil and religious privileges and invited the actual authorities to continue in the exercise of administering justice, punishing criminals, and upholding the laws. The political and military government will remain under the charge of the military commander, and the arrangement of the mails and exterior commerce to the oldest naval officer, under the instructions of their respective heads. [signed:] La Paz, July 29, 1847. Henry J. Burton, Lieutenant Colonel commanding the forces of the United States and political chief of Baja California. - Theodor Bagley, captain of the United States frigate, Lexington, and the oldest officer of Baja California.[311]

Armed opposition took place in the settlement of San Antonio, but the leaders were jailed. In August, 1847, the resistance began. The city council of Mulegé informed the government of Sonora that they did not recognize the foreign authorities, "(. . .) this patriotic neighborhood is in agreement with this city council concerning being governed by foreign authorities, and joining the Sonora government"[312] The note elated the Mexican authorities of Sonora and they sent it to the comandante general" of the state as the following letter testifies:

With the note from your excellency of the 20th instance, in which you transmitted that of the president of the city council of Mulegé, I received a copy of the record that contains the rejection by that organization and neighborhood of the authorities of

---

[311] *Bancroft Library Archives*, University of California Berkeley, Cowen Collection, Microfilm no. 13-3-799-1847, August 16, 1847.

[312] Ibidem, agosto 20, 1847.

the United States occupying that territory, as well as their obedience to the Mexican government and the recognition of obedience to that of Sonora.

I possess the greatest sympathy for all the adversity in which those Mexicans find themselves and satisfaction for the steadfastness with which they have maintained their love of country. This government is ready to obtain help and to save them. I tell your honor that if we receive, as is hoped at any moment, arms, they will be taken care of immediately, to which effect we should maintain in more frequent contact because of the nearness of that port to here. I hope you will inform me of the forces and arms you consider necessary for a good result in Baja California. This government will not spare any effort in defense of the country when it becomes necessary.[313]

God and Liberty, August 27, 1847

Meanwhile the Mexican government named Captain Manuel Pineda to replace the traitor Palacio Miranda as military commander of Baja California. Along with several men and supplies, he traveled in the brigantine Magdalena, disembarking in Mulegé at the end of September and immediately began to organize the people against the invader. He was helped by Vicente Mejía of Mulegé, and Fathers Vicente Sotomayor of San Ignacio, and Gabriel Gonzalez of Todos Santos. They counted on the support of the common people who had wanted to attack the intruders. Pineda wrote to the Comandante General of Baja California informing him of his arrival:

---

[313] Ibidem, agosto 27, 1847.

The sixteenth of the present instance, I disembarked in the port of Guaymas and presented myself to the comandante general of Sonora. The dignified leader with much effort helped me with six thousand rounds of rifle shot, fifty lances, a cannon with its corresponding ammunition, a bugle, three soldiers and another bugle. I continued my march on the twenty-third, and on the twenty-fourth I disembarked at this place. At the same time, Don Vicente Mejía put himself at my orders with the force he had armed for the defense of the country and his arms, two casks of powder, forty lances and six casks of lead, and the arms of each person that had been gathered by this illustrious city council who had asked for them. He also ordered the rest of the forces in his jurisdiction to meet, so that I am busy organizing and disciplining the group with which I must march on the third of next October to confront the enemy in La Paz. The ex-political chief, Don Francisco Palacios Miranda, as soon as he knew that Mr. Mejía had raised forces from the population, embarked, along with the American Davis to the port of La Paz where the enemy are.

It fills me with glory to inform you of the enthusiasm and disposition that I have found in these true sons of our beloved country, recommending to your honor Mr. Vicente Mejía who has not ceased for a moment to organize the forces and has contributed with his own resources to the defense of our independence.[314]

----

[314] Ibidem, septiembre 27, 1847.

The following was directed to the inhabitants of Mulegé proclaiming:

> Fellow citizens and friends, my heart has never experienced the great joy of walking on lands that I have always considered to be the first step in the glorious military career in which I have ascended to my present rank.
>
> Towns of Baja California, here you have me as your chief, with superior forces, with arms and munitions, to guide you to the glorious époque in which these adventurers a thousand and one times shamed by their unjust cause will have to surrender to defenders of the fatherland who want nothing more than to avenge the shame with which they have taken this territory, its flag, and the sacred rights of our nationality.
>
> Yes, Mexicans, the time has come to make ourselves into an impregnable wall upon which these unnatural immigrants will crash. As I exposed myself to the risks of the sea and enemies in my travel here, I call upon you to unite as true Mexicans and together win the laurels that await us.
>
> The sad situation that you have experienced has not been because of our supreme government, since it has always tried to elevate you to the rank of civilized men as one of many that form part of our nation.

What can I do at such a great distance? Without the faintest idea of your situation, when at the same time your ex-political leader has not had any more ideas than to revile you with his nasty, vile, and shameful cowardice, perhaps hoping that these mercenaries will reward him and his terrible treason.

No, companions and friends! Deafen the scene of your disgrace. You have known me for the past fifteen years and you are satisfied with my energy and my military comportment; I swear to you on the furrows of my beloved fatherland that I will never, ever, deviate from the path of honor until my death . . .

Manuel Pineda[315]

In effect, the invasion had taken the Baja Californians by surprise, who after the first moments, became aware of the situation and reacted by opposing it. The North Americans ignored the danger since there had been no opposition in the beginning. Also, Burton, the commander of the forces of Baja California, believed that "they lack arms, munitions and patriotism." He stayed in La Paz with barely one hundred and eleven men to watch over a population of around ten thousand, disseminated in an enormous area. According to a census by the ex-governor Palacio Miranda, three thousand inhabitants lived in San José, a thousand five hundred in Santiago, a thousand in San Antonio, a thousand five hundred in Todos Santos, two thousand in La Paz, and a thousand more among San Ignacio, Mulegé and Comondú.[316]

---

[315] Nunis, op. cit. p. 93.

[316] *Bancroft Archives*, Microfilm no. 12-3-799-1847, November 8, 1847.

Meanwhile, the patriots in Comondú, some seventy men, were organized under the command of José Matías Moreno and with the name Guerrillas Guadalupanas de Comondú, Defenders of the National Independence. On November 8, 1847 Moreno published the following proclamation:

Citizen José Matías Moreno, commander in chief of the Guerrilla Guadalupana de Comondú, defender of the fatherland, to the inhabitants of the settlement of Todos Santos.

Fellow citizens: with great satisfaction and glory, I take the liberty of speaking to you, not as a guerrilla, but as a citizen animated by the best sentiments and intentions in defense of the country. Following the consequences of this beginning and confiding in your well known patriotism, I invite you to take up arms against the unjust invader that has until now not said why he has come or what he wants.

The North Americans have become political bandits. They will flatter you while they can with the object of making you fall under the weight of their destructive claws to later dispose, at their whim, of your docility.

Fellow citizens: the nation has been invaded by an immoral enemy who, taking advantage of our political disruptions has had the temerity to reach the gates of Mexico. The republicans, as the rest of Spanish America, will teach them what country and liberty are. In such circumstances it is necessary to write with the point of a sword some warlike pages of our political history.

Speaking like this, I am not doing anything more than expounding a well known truth, which is the following: North America has no other motto, political or private, than robbery and trickery. Fellow citizens, two paths are open to us, the North American offers slavery and disgrace, Mexico, honor and liberty. Look to the past, contemplate the present, and do not forget the future that Mexico has made to live free of the influence of a foreign power. Also be aware that a handful of adventurers do not have enough physical or moral power to defeat the great nation of Mexico. In the field of battle I will be your companion, in your homes, your friend. If fortune smiles on me you will gain the laurels, but if it goes against me I will accept with dignity the blows it wishes to give me.[317]

Also in San Ignacio and Mulegé, volunteers were organizing for battle. By September, 1847, only La Paz and San Antonio had been taken by the North Americans.

When Colonel Burton learned of the guerrilla activities he decided to send Commander Selfridge in the corvette U.S. Dale to Mulegé. This gave place to the first encounter that attempted to stop the movement of arms and munitions through the port. The ship made a stop at Loreto, where it was learned that two hundred Mexicans had arrived who were organizing to march on La Paz. In passing, Selfridge became aware that the principal instigator of the rebellion was Father Gabriel González, superior of the Dominicans of Baja California.

---

[317] Ibidem, octubre 2, 1847.

According to Mexican documents, the U.S. Dale arrived at the port of Mulegé flying the British flag. Once anchored, they lowered it and raised the North American flag. Captain Pineda, who had been sent as military commander, protested this infraction of international law and drily replied to the request to surrender:

> Informed by the instructions that you passed on to the judge of this settlement, I must tell you this place is held by Mexican forces that I have the honor of commanding, and that I will never ignore nor be indifferent to the unjust war of the United States to the Republic of Mexico to which I belong. I protest your actions before the nations of Europe, that you should not have anchored your ship in these waters flying the British flag, and then raise the flag of the United States, the country you belong to, and for this reason I could not have my forces teach you a lesson and not end with a cease fire. The ex-political chief, Don Francisco Palacio Miranda, who because of his cowardice appeared neutral to your government, today joined the forces in La Paz. This main headquarters will be just the opposite, and will maintain all communications with the Mexican government, even though the entire United States fleet wants to prevent it. This headquarters, with the valiant soldiers it has at its command, will defend itself and will take up arms until the last drop of blood is shed.[318]

---

[318] Nunis, op. cit. p. 154, cited from the diary of lieutenant William L. Crashaw, microfilmed by the Bancroft Library.

Confronting the threat of a strong resistance, Commander Selfridge ordered Lieutenant Craven with fifty men to take the schooner Magdalena which had to be burned as unusable, since the Mexicans had taken everything usable. According to North American documents, Selfridge ordered Lieutenant Craven again on October 1, 1847, to ask for the surrender of Mulegé a second time, and while he awaited the response, the U.S. Dale prepared for battle. The encounter that took place in Mulegé is controversial as there is no agreement between the North American and Mexican versions, which will be compared later. According to the report sent by Lieutenant Craven to Commander Thomas Selfridge, the encounter was of little importance. On October 2, 1847, and in response to the Mexicans refusing the entry into the port, Lieutenant Craven disembarked sixty men ready to fight. He was able to take the left bank of the arroyo and advanced towards the settlement.

According to his report, the enemy hid and only shot three times from a house which he immediately ordered burned. He climbed a hill where his men rested and for the second time he was attacked at a distance by the Mexicans. Leaving a detachment of his men to watch the area, Lieutenant Craven and a group of his men went down into the settlement which was deserted with their gun boat following them to the arroyo. The third attack at a distance then took place in which, according to Craven, he followed the enemy for half a mile, but when they fled into the mountains he decided to return to the Dale as night was falling.[319]

In summary, he was afraid to open a battle in unfamiliar terrain. His intention was to take the settlement and get the guerrillas to

---

[319] *Bancroft Archives*, microfilm no. 12-3-799-847, October 3, 1847.

surrender, but he failed at both objectives and thus his short version.

The Mexican version was sent by Captain Pineda to his superiors, explaining how he organized the defense of Mulegé in which he sent sub-lieutenant Vicente A. Avila to cover the right flank while Vicente Mejía covered the left. Pineda personally took charge of the center. The North Americans disembarked approximately sixty men, with the corvette and boats opening fire on the Mexicans as soon as they saw them.

> The said corvette shot 135 shots of shrapnel, bullets and grenades, and the boats thirty something, but the valiant Mexicans who defended the ambush, viewed with the greatest contempt the artillery and infantry fire of the enemy. And you could only hear them heartedly cheer "Viva la República Mexicana". Finally, Comandante General, since the beginning of the battle at nine in the morning, the officers and men of the National Guard of the heroic settlement of Mulegé discussed attacking the enemy. Between four and five in the afternoon, the enemy shamefully ran away leaving all their artillery and arms that they had thrown on the ground, despite being a force superior to that which I have under my command.[320]

His troops were left "with the glorious satisfaction of having given them a lesson." The so-called battle of Mulegé was a great psychological victory for the Mexicans in which the surprise of the retreat of the North Americans in Mulegé received satisfactory praise from Mexican authorities. Anastasio Bustamente, at the time General in Chief of the Western

---

[320] Flores, Jorge, *Documentos para la historia de la Baja California*, v.2, Ed. Intercontinental, México, 1946, p. 110.

Division, wrote to Mulegé congratulating them for the defense, "Such a valiant example given by a little settlement which has barely forty houses, promises happy results in both Californias, and it is not beyond presuming that the enemy's attention will now be directed to this area to at least slow down the invasion they are planning for Sonora."[321]

Antonio Campusano, Commander in Guaymas, wrote,

> This headquarters has had the greatest pleasure in the heroic comportment of you and these intrepid Muleginos, worthy of taking a brilliant page in Mexican history, to whom in the name of the Supreme Government of the Nation to whose knowledge I must recommend them, such a happy acknowledgement and from this headquarters I give you my most express thanks.
>
> History of all time has taught us that a people do not allow the oppressive yoke of slavery when they want to be free. And as union is what makes force, this headquarters promises to keep you in harmony with the political authorities. We unite in your exciting sentiments with your subordinates to form a compact group prepared to gather new laurels in the field of battle, supported by the God of justice, in the belief that this headquarters is ready to help you in everything we can.[322]

In addition, according to a report from Guaymas dated October 8, 1847, Colonel Campusano had sent 100 rifles 100 carbines, 50

---

[321] Ibidem, October 8, 1847.

[322] Nunis, op. cit. p. 34, cited in the diary of Lieutenant Craven, microfilmed by the Bancroft Archive.

lances, a four pound cannon, munitions, several sets of pistols and food.[323]

The US Dale withdrew from La Paz, where the North Americans were preparing the defense against a Mexican attack. For the rest of the invasion the settlement of Mulegé remained free. The port, however, was blocked to prevent the entering or leaving of warships.[324] What happened in Mulegé excited the patriots and Pineda wrote to the commander of Sonora:

> The 7th of the present month I started my march with the guerrilla of Don Vicente Mejía from Mulegé and a squad of the Compañia Presidial de Loreto under the command of Second Lieutenant Manuel Calderón hoping that these valiant Mulegeños and the few dragoons of the Compañia Presidial de Loreto will result in another glorious day for the Fatherland as had been the case the first of October of the present year (....) On the 9th I arrived at this settlement and it filled me with glory to see the great enthusiasm of these inhabitants to march against the enemies of our fatherland.[325]

The 18th of October, 1847, a demonstration in San Jose del Cabo erupted against the invaders. The same happened in Comondú, where a North American died with the patriots destroying the ranches that they suspected the owners of having sympathy for the North Americans.

---

[323] *Bancroft Archives*, Microfilm, no. 13-3-799-947, 7 October, 1847.

[324] Long, op. cit. p. 195. Nunis, op. cit., citing the DuPont diary.

[325] Ibidem, p. 200. Nunis, p. 36.

Colonel Burton informed his superiors that there were many clandestine meetings taking place to raise forces against the North Americans, including a religious festival to that end at Todos Santos, as the parish was openly hostile to the invaders.[326] On October 23, 1847, the people of San José del Cabo also rebelled taking down the North American flag and expelling the private North American inhabitants and declaring that the invasion was over. But the victory only lasted a week, since on October 30, the Pacific Naval Squadron under the command of commodore Shubrick arrived to put down the rebellion of the Mexicans when the commodore found that the pro-Americans had suffered continuous hostilities from the guerillas. The commodore published a proclamation directed at the citizens of San José and declared that the United States was not planning on returning Baja California to Mexico, and consequently, invited the inhabitants to be loyal to the new government. "The flag of the United States is destined to fly forever in the Californias," said his declaration. Even President Polk said that his country would not return the Californias.[327]

At the same time, Shubrick, fearing a revolution, sent an expedition to Todos los Santos to look for the guerrillas, and when he withdrew from San José del Cabo on November 8, 1847, left a detachment of 24 men under Lieutenant Heywood, with provisions for one month, a nine pound cannon, and seventy-five carbines. In addition, he wrote to the United States governor of California asking for reinforcements. He said that a land force was necessary so that the invaders could maintain the ports of La Paz and San José when the hurricane months would

---

[326] Nunis, op. cit., p. 37.

[327] Martinez, op. cit., 377-378. Long, op. cit., 200-205.

require the retirement of his fleet. Without this help Shubrick was afraid the patriots would reclaim their land.[328]

At that time, a proclamation appeared from the Territorial Council:

> From the Honorable Territorial Council of Baja California to its inhabitants:
>
> Fellow citizens, on a day which we breathe free of the yoke that has oppressed us, this assembly, full of the greatest enthusiasm has returned to the exercise of its functions and although it is difficult for it to carry out its task with the tact demanded by the critical circumstances in which we find ourselves, but animated by a patriotism without limits, we will dictate several measures that are necessary for the defense of the fatherland:
>
> Mexicans! The voice of the fatherland requires from you the defense of our nationality, and this assembly full of the greatest confidence hopes that you will now and forever reject the seductions of those who without honor and for private gain try to mislead you to a shameful slavery. People of the south of Baja California, you have borne witness to the sentiments that animate the settlements in the north of this territory dragged down by the elements and naked scarcity, [*with patriots*] abandoning their homes, families, and interests, bravely volunteering themselves to the fight in support of our independence; and why should you not feel those same sentiments of honor and liberty? and what

[328] Executive Document, number I. pp. 1112-1115.

keeps you from forming guerrillas to fill out the ranks of our brothers? Californians: join us like in the year 21 [*Mexican Independence*] and we will be invincible to teach the perfidious invaders that have had the boldness to profane our soil; and if luck abandons us we will die with glory and the civilized world will know the value of a people who love liberty. Yes, citizens, was it not bravery the defense of the pass at Thermopylae that those valiant Spartans wanted to show that when a people wants to be free no human power can stop them. Long live the Fatherland! Long live Independence! Long live the Mexican Republic! Long live the Supreme Government.[329]

When the forces led by Moreno, Mijares and Mejía approached San José del Cabo and found that the settlement was controlled by Lieutenant Heywood and his men on November 19, 1847, they advanced to the outskirts of the settlement and demanded its surrender. Heywood, holed up in the parsonage, refused. The Mexican forces, which did not have cannons and their arms were only old muskets, rifles, sticks, knives and lances, withdrew to a little hill called La Lomita to organize an attack. Before sunset the battle began.

The next day, the group of 150 men renewed the attack with Antonio Mijares and his 40 men attacking the front, while the rest went with Mejía, Angulo and Moreno to scale the North American fort. The hostilities ended with the death of Mijares and a retreat from the attack on the fort. While the guerrillas reorganized, on November 21, two United States shark fishing boats arrived in the port, the Magnolia and the Edward. Their crews disembarked to support their compatriots and the

---

[329] Long, op. cit., p. 198, cited from the diary of Colonel Burton.

175

Mexicans withdrew. A few days later two North American warships with 50 men and provisions for Lieutenant Heywood arrived, at which time the guerrillas withdrew to the settlement of San Antonio leaving a group in Median Flores, 25 miles from San José del Cabo. In San Antonio 300 fighters were ready to engage the occupiers, but the ship Portsmouth in San José del Cabo impeded any assault by the Mexican forces.[330]

Meanwhile, as the unfortunate encounter took place in San José del Cabo, Colonel Pineda with his men prepared an assault on La Paz. This town had been under martial law since the rebellion in San José, and its commander, Colonel Burton, counted on an organized municipal guard consisting of 28 Mexican traitors led by the old Mexican governor, Francisco Palacios Miranda to protect the town. Burton went to the extreme of demanding that whoever did not accept the United States government leave the region within twelve hours.[331]

The Mexican guerrillas opened their attack on the morning of November 16, 1847. The North Americans were taken by surprise as they did not know that there were patriots in La Paz. When Pineda could not immediate take the plaza, he repeated his attack and then withdrew in face of the superior fire of the North American artillery. The following day they returned to the attack, only to retreat again after setting the house of ex-president Palacios Miranda on fire. On November 18, the North Americans attacked the guerrillas, but they also failed. The siege of La Paz lasted 10 days. Colonel Burton asked for help and munitions from the Pacific Squadron and when the Mexicans returned to the attack on November 27, the invaders had received reinforcements. During the attack of the 28th the Mexicans were

[330] Archivo de la Secretaría de Relaciones Exteriores de México (ASREM), Expediente 538-1848.

[331] Nunis, op. cit. ,pp. 35-40, cited in the diary of Du Pont.

forced to retreat in the face of a six-pound gun, and on December 5, because of the failure of their attacks on the North American fort, they decided to abandon La Paz. Eight miles from La Paz, in Zacatal, they left a small group of men, and the rest withdrew to San Antonio from which they continued to harass the North Americans with sporadic attacks.

The political leader, Mauricio Castro, commented in his report to the central government about the attack on La Paz:

> Without walls, without cannon, nor other approaches of war beyond their heroic chests, 80 patriots under their principal commander in the port of La Paz sustained a well concerted attack against an enemy of 130 North American soldiers, and other ingrate Mexicans, who had to run to their trenches where only with their cannon and grenades could they defend themselves against our intrepid soldiers.[332]

At the same time on the other side, Commander Du Pont wrote in his diary:

> Things were very bad; the country is in a state of complete resistance with the Mexican forces terrorizing those who had been friendly to us. Mounted groups of the enemy ran around the town and it was abandoned by its inhabitants. Colonel Bruton asked for a force of 500 men, because the population of Baja California was much more warlike than the Alta Californians.[333]

---

[332] *Bancroft Archives*, Microfilm. No. 13-2-799-847, Feb. 10, 1848.

[333] Martinez, op. cit. , pp.376-380.

On January 1, 1848, the last of the ships of the Pacific Squadron left San José del Cabo under the command of Commodore Shubrick. This was the signal for the patriots to rejoin the fight. For the rest of the month they devastated the area around San José with the goal of collecting what was necessary to support the settlement. They took horses and cattle from the surrounding area, burnt crops, cut communications, and on January 21, captured a ship that was bringing supplies to the North Americans in San José. The next day, the Mexicans were able to capture eight of Heywood's men and on the 10th of February, 1848, the town had fallen to the guerrillas such that the North Americans could not leave their fortifications.[334] No one knew that on February 2, the Treaty of Guadalupe-Hidalgo had been signed, ending the war!

The siege of San José continued for 21 days and when it appeared that Lieutenant Heywood had no other option but to surrender, when a North American warship sent by Commodore Shubrick arrived.

On February 15, 1848, the battle of San Vicente took place. The men from the recently arrived ship attacked with 32 pound cannon, and Pineda's forces left the settlement. They were chased across a sugar cane field, a banana plantation, and a flat plain of 400 yards while the ship Cyane shot their potent cannon and sowed terror among the guerrilla forces. Thus, ended the siege of San José del Cabo, where the North American artillery proved its superiority.[335]

---

[334] Cazadero, Manuel, "¿Pudo México ganar la guerra contra los Estados Unidos?", en *Anuario de Estados Angloamericanos*, 8 p. V. 5, Facultad de Filosofía y Letras, UNAM, México, 1973, pp. 120-121.

[335] Connor, Seymour, and Odie Faulk, *La guerra de intervención*, Ed. Diana, México, 1975, pp. 55-56.

Since 1826, North American generals had been preoccupied with investigating the technological advances Napoleon had given to artillery. The United States had sent Lieutenant Tyler to Europe to familiarize himself with these advances, and in 1838, Joel Poinsett, who had been ambassador to Mexico, was named Secretary of War. This functionary organized the field artillery of the North American army following European innovations. In the 15 years prior to the war, three journals were published dedicated to spreading this new knowledge within the army.

From the beginning of the war, it was obvious that there would be an artillery duel, and that the North American superiority was much greater. The Mexicans fired 650 shots to the enemies 3000.[336] In addition, the federal cannon were small and old, no one bothered to replace them because they thought the most important part of the army was a capable officer corps. In the first battle, that of Palo Alto in Tamaulipas, the North Americans used two siege cannon of 18 pounds and a total of 16 batteries, plus 932 artillerymen of the regular army. The Mexican army counted 14 cannon of 4 pounds. According to military histories of the war, Mexico only used up to 18 pound cannon while the North Americans used up to 32 pounders. Thus was the encounter of a world with updated technological advances against the other that gave more importance to traditional cavalry and the bravery and competence of military officers. The reach of the North American cannon was greater than that of the copper balls of the old Mexican cannon that could only reach the front lines of the North Americans by skipping on the ground to extend their range.[337] The Mexican army thus suffered five times

[336] Archivo de la Secretaria de Relaciones Exteriores de México (ASREM), Expediente 538-1848, f. 2.

[337] Bancroft Archives, Microfilm, no. 13-3-799-847, Feb., 5, 1848.

the casualties in battle with the North Americans as Mauricio Castro, political chief of Baja California, reported to his government:

> Those settlements, dear sir, took on a battle superior to their strength because they fought against an enemy that defended itself with cannon that were military state of the art. It is true that we fought for our independence, but "what did we do to protect it?"[338]

To continue our account, we should note that the Mexican forces abandoned San José del Cabo and retired to Todos Santos and San Antonio. Lieutenant Wise informs us that, "the spirit of the people sustained them and they sent Don Juan Nepomuceno Ayala, Don Mateo Magafía and Father Sotomayor who gave them 100 rifles, 16 powder kegs, 10 casks of lead, 1,800 bolts of cotton cloth, and 50 loads of flour to get help from Sonora." At this point the peace treaty had been signed, but in the peninsula the news did not arrive until the end of April, 1848, and the battle continued. In San José del Cabo, another warship anchored in the bay to watch over the port. Lieutenant Heywood, wrote to his commander informing him of what was happening and asked for permission and men to chase down the guerrillas.[339]

In La Paz, Colonel Burton obtained enough horses to send a group of men to San Antonio in March,1848. On the 14th of March, there was an encounter in this town in which the North American triumphed. However, the patriots won a good battle when they attacked the North Americans as they were returning to La Paz. A week later, a New York Company of volunteers arrived, led by Captain Naglee to reinforce Colonel Burton. On

---

[338] Nunis, op. cit., p. 52 op. cit. , p.219.

[339] Long, op. cit. ,p. 219.

March 26, 1848, Burton marched with 217 men to San Antonio and the following day captured Pineda and his secretary. Being wounded Pineda stayed in San Antonio while the rest of his men left for Todos Santos. This was the reason Burton left for that place, while Captain Naglee's volunteers arrived there first, attacking from one side while Burton attacked from the front. The combination of their forces gave them the victory, winning Todos Santos, where they took Father Gabriel Gonzalez prisoner. The North American newspapers criticized the cruelty of Naglee and his volunteers who assassinated, in cold blood, many Mexicans and Yaqui Indians.[340]

On March 31, 1848, Colonel Burton sent the same Captain Naglee with his men to look for guerrillas in the area of Bahia Magdalena. To the same end he also sent Lieutenant Halleck to La Paz via San José. He stayed in Todos Santos with his men constructing military works that would put an end to Mexican guerrilla activities in the valley, forcing them to retreat to Santiago, a little village 16 leagues from San José.

By April of that year, many of the guerrilla chiefs had been captured, and among them the political chief of Baja California, Mauricio Casto, who after the capture of Pineda shared the military command with Father Gabriel González. With this, the last campaign, the North American forces returned to La Paz on April 12, 1848. The conquest of Baja California ended thus: it took six months to vanquish the patriots of Baja California, despite a powerful fleet that had the most advanced military technology. It was in reality a heroic resistance. The peace treaty was signed two months before the last battles. The time from the battle of Mulegé on Oct. 1, 1847, to the final battle in Todos Santos on April 12, 1848, was six months during which Baja California, an impoverished land with a thin population, was

---

[340] Martínez, op. cit., pp. 386-387.

conquered but whose inhabitants became guerrillas who were determined to continue being Mexican. Even after the arrests of their leaders, Burton reported how a group of patriots reunited in Mulegé, and he asked that the naval blockade continue to avoid the importing of arms and men from Mexico.

This month of April, was when they received news of the peace treaty, and that Baja California would remain Mexican. All those who had betrayed their country by collaborating with the North American forces trembled in fear, desperate to save themselves along with their property, and met in La Paz on July, 5, 1848. They considered themselves the Assembly of Representatives of Baja California, and planned their separation from the Mexican Republic and solicited annexation by the United States, threatening that if they were refused they would turn to England.[341]

Meanwhile, Captain Pineda and Father González returned to the peninsula where they had been exiled by the North Americans who feared their influence. Upon their return they organized their revenge on the traitors.

On July 15, 1848, Commodore Jones, Commodore Shubrick and Colonel Burton responded to the appeal of the Assembly by declaring that Baja California would be returned immediately to the government of the Republic of Mexico, and recognizing the danger to some who had helped, offered them free transport to Alta California. They also offered economic compensation for losses suffered at the hands of the guerrillas. But they warned they would not help organize a rebellion against Mexico and that those who did not leave the peninsula with the United States forces would not be protected, and that they had to sign up to leave no later than August 20, 1848. Two ships, the

---

[341] Nunis, op. cit., pp.69-70.

Southhampton and the Lexington would transport the dissidents while another three would carry the North American troops. Colonel Burton announced to the Mexican government his withdrawal from the peninsula on August 31, 1848, and to be turned it over to the official Mexican representative, Mauricio Castro, who had filled the office of political chief during the war.[342]

The refugees embarked on the North American ships the 30th of August. Even though some stayed because of lack of resources, between 300 and 350 people left. Among them was Patricio Miranda, the ex-governor, Father Ignacio Ramirez, head of the diocese and various civilian ex-authorities.

On September 1, 1848, Commodore Jones gave the order to lower the United States flag and with it North American occupation of the peninsula of Baja California was formally ended. Upon the exit of the North Americans, Nicolás Lastra was left in charge of the civil government and Captain Manuel Pineda of the military. The situation in the peninsula was disastrous. To the poverty and isolation was added the ruin and desolation left by the war. The countryside had been devastated by the guerrillas. The cattle and horses had practically disappeared. However, traditions, religion, culture and race remained intact.

The effort needed to continue being Mexican cost dearly. Jorge Flores, in his *Documentos para la historia de Baja California*, gives an idea of what was required of those who had participated in the heroic defense of the peninsula. "Upon a census of eight thousand people, 900 men enlisted, or more than ten percent of the total population. The rest of the country, with a population of

---

[342] Flores, op. cit., p. 90.

seven million was only able to enlist seventy thousand men, or one percent of the total."[343]

[343] Ibidem.

VII. VIOLATIONS OF GUADALUPE-HIDALGO:CHANGE OF THE FRONTIER

The Treaty of Guadalupe-Hidalgo was not simply an agreement to end the war, as is noted in the previous text. With its twenty-three articles it was an attempt to modify the subsequent relations between the two countries. However, despite the good will of the delegates, it was full of problems. For the lack of an assessment of the geographic limits, the quarrels over the fixation of the limits did not stop until a century later, when the dispute over El Chamizal was settled, a territory located between Ciudad Juarez and El Paso (Figure 6).The lack of precision in many of the articles also provoked innumerable diplomatic disputes that were at the point of starting a new war in the following decade (1850-1860). In the following chapters I will try to point out these faults, as well as the violations of the treaty on the part of the government of the United States. The Treaty of Guadalupe-Hidalgo continues in force: and that is its importance. It is a document that is alive for a large number of inhabitants on the frontier who still invoke its articles demanding the United States government respect it. In this chapter, a certain number of the treaty's articles have been chosen for discussion, those, that according to the documents consulted, were the most violated, to show the lack of foresight, failings, and misunderstanding that it has caused. I also want to demonstrate the ill will on the part of the people on the North American border towards everything Mexican. It is so difficult to solve the problems of the undocumented, of the braceros and still today of the chicanos, because the roots extend back to the treaty in Articles VIII, IX, and XI. I will try to demonstrate this in the following.

The curious thing about the treaty of Guadalupe-Hidalgo is that it satisfied no one; on the Mexican side it is considered the harshest treaty in our history for the enormous territory we lost, and the North Americans, who wanted to expand to the South

185

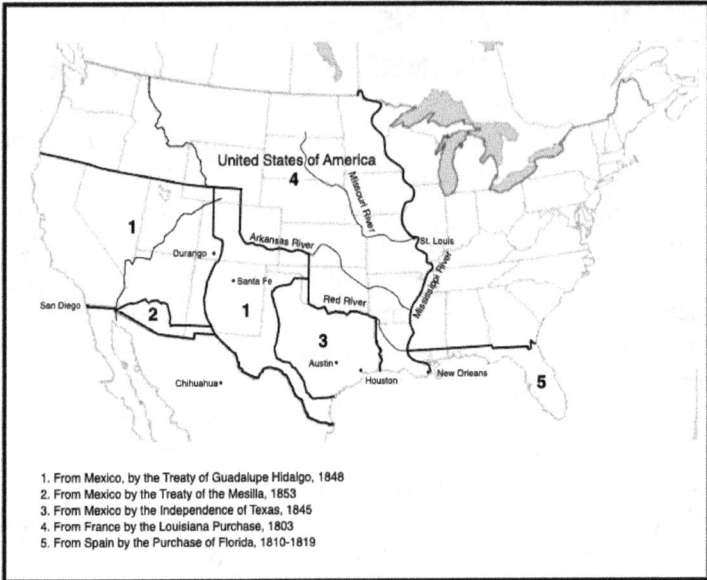

1. From Mexico, by the Treaty of Guadalupe Hidalgo, 1848
2. From Mexico by the Treaty of the Mesilla, 1853
3. From Mexico by the Independence of Texas, 1845
4. From France by the Louisiana Purchase, 1803
5. From Spain by the Purchase of Florida, 1810-1819

FIGURE 6. TERRITORIAL EXPANSION OF THE UNITED STATES FROM 1783 TO 1853 (BASED ON CARL N. DEGLER ET AL. HISTÓRIA DE LOS ESTADOS UNIDOS (LA EXPERIENCIA DEMOCRATA), ED. LIMUSA, 1984, P. 212.

Pole, find it of little advantage for them. Those who signed the treaty, on both sides, were vilified in their respective countries.

Looking back, one can come to the conclusion that the treaty was a minor issue, as Mexico was on the verge of disappearing as an independent nation, at least for a time. Instead of remembering what we lost we should point out what we defended and were able to conserve until today.

The treaty put an end to the war but did not achieve peace. In the chapters that follow, we will see how its own provisions were cause of a continuation of the diplomatic battle and the innumerable armed encounters on the frontier. The North American attempts to appropriate more Mexican territory continued after the Gadsden Purchase. Baja California and Tehuantepec were on their agenda, but they never obtained them. In the following pages we will see the attempts at invasion and the answers from the Mexican government and people. This effort to maintain the integrity of the territory is one of the most honest and dynamic chapters of our history, but because it lacked much excitement it is not well known, even though it should be. It is witness to the fact that once more the defense of the country was made by the diplomats and not the politicians or the military.

According to the Treaty of Guadalupe-Hidalgo the line of the frontier would be delineated by a group of commissioners of the governments of both countries. According to Article V of the treaty, the measurements were to be made following the map published in New York in 1847 by J. Disturneli. The commissioners were to meet within a year of the exchange of ratifications of the treaty.[344] What the authors agreed to, that the limits of the frontier would run down the middle of the Rio Bravo (Rio Grande), caused a myriad of problems for both countries.

In effect, the Rio Bravo or Grande, collects the ice melt and rain from an enormous drainage. Move its channel, and land and towns would be moved from one country to the other. As incredible as it may seem the treaty authors did not know this had happened. They were politicians and diplomats, not geographers. Also, the problem was not easy. This was shown by

---

[344] Zorrilla, Luis G., Historia de las relaciones entre México y los Estados Unidos, Editorial Porrúa, México 1965, p. 241.

subsequent conventions to delimit the frontier. It was not until 1938 that construction of a canal was finished where the dividing line was to be.

Sepúlveda, in his book *La frontera norte de México*, summarized the manner in which they arrived at a solution to the problem of a moveable dividing line.[345] The well known case of El Chamizal had it origins in the change of the channel of the Rio Bravo and its tendency to move southward to the disadvantage of Mexico. We know that after the signing of the treaty the first litigation due to the channel concerned three settlements, Isleta, Socorro and San Eleazario. These three settlements had belonged to Chihuahua since their founding and thus it was thought they would always be. Then, in January 1849, the governor of Chihuahua received a letter from the political leader of Paso del Norte, who was informed that soldiers of New Mexico had taken possession of the three settlements and expelled the Mexican authorities. He explained that he assumed that the pretext for the invasion was that the channel of the Rio Bravo had changed. It had formed a new arm leaving the mentioned settlements to the left (north) of it. It was a geographic question that needed to be settled by clerks and not soldiers. He asked that the governor protest to the government of the United States.[346]

The said letter is, it seems to us, very interesting. First, because when violations of territory are discussed, the Gadsden Purchase is always mentioned as the first invasion. It is said with reason that the motive to possess that territory was for the construction of a railroad. What, then, was the reason for the invasion of

---

[345] Sepúlveda, César, La frontera norte de México, Editorial Porrúa, México, 1970, p. X.

[346] Archives of the Secretaría de Relaciones Exteriores de México (ASREM), file LE 1095, ff. 9-13.

Isleta, Socorro, and San Eleazario? There were six thousand poor Mexican inhabitants so that the economic advantage of their appropriation was minimal. However, the invasion happened. It can only be explained by the desire for land that dominated the Anglo Saxons. They had been profoundly dissatisfied with the dividing line and coveted the land all the way to the Sierra Madre, as demonstrated by the filibuster expeditions, unauthorized military expeditions into Mexican territory to incite or promote a revolution. In this situation comes the importance of the case of these settlements. It demonstrates, once more, the Anglo manner of obtaining more territory. As a result, it is strange that the case is not included in historic accounts of the era.

When the prefect of Mexican El Paso complained before the magistrate of Frontera, New Mexico, the magistrate answered by asking for the land titles of the three settlements, adding that no one in these settlements had complained about the change in jurisdiction. Not only did the North Americans ignore the reclamations of the prefect of El Paso, they threatened him to be

prepared in case of disturbances.[347] It was the Secretary of Exterior Relations himself, Luis Cuevas, who wrote to the United States ambassador. He pointed out the gravity of the situation, given that by Article V of the treaty these territories continued to be Mexican. He asked for respect of the treaty until

the Commission on Limits had decided the question.[348] It is curious that the Mexican government continued asking for respect of the treaty as they had done for years over the Texas issue. It served them nothing, but it appears to have continued to be the policy of the Secretary of Exterior Relations. He was afraid that the taking of the three settlements by North American

---

[347] Ibidem, f. 47.

[348] Ibidem, f. 47.

soldiers would provoke new friction "and that would be the beginning of grave, very grave incidents that later might be impossible to resolve." He believed that this invasion was not an isolated incident, but rather was related to others reported in the press.[349] This fear, complicated by indigenous incursions and filibuster invasions, would be the prelude to the sale of the Gadsden Purchase.

By April, 1849, news arrived that the United States Secretary of State had given orders that their troops leave the territory until the Commission on Limits determined otherwise.

They received no further information from the Secretary of State. Mexico continued complaining and the North Americans kept ignoring the problem. As they had supplanted the authorities of the three settlements at the end of 1849, they considered the problem solved. Because of bigger problems the incident was forgotten and six thousand Mexicans became North American citizens. The Anglo procedure was the following: invasion of the coveted land, change of the authorities, pretense of a referendum, threats, protestations of innocence on the part of federal authorities, annexation of the territory. The same procedure used in Texas.

This was repeated one more time, in the Gadsden Purchase, and from then on Mexico took care that it did not happen again. The case of the three islands in the Pacific, occupied by the United States, was not a violation of the Treaty of Guadalupe-Hidalgo. The Mexican government simply forgot to include them in the article of the limits as these only talked about islands in the Gulf of Mexico. Conversely, the case of Isleta, Socorro, and San Eleazario was indeed a violation of the same article of the treaty.

---

[349] Ibidem, f. 7.

VIII. VIOLATIONS OF GUADALUPE-HIDALGO: THE REPATRIATION

The discussion of the treaty lasted exactly 25 days, for which it can be called a treaty made in haste. Many points were barely reviewed in which Mexico came out the loser for not having clarified their signiflcance. A large number of geographic mistakes, omissions, and vagueness later became serious diplomatic problems. So it was with Article V, by omitting to note that Mexican jurisdiction stretched three leagues into the Pacific, the Santa Catalina islands ended up in the possession of the United States. The course of the Rio Bravo (Grande) also was not specified so that the following year, as we have seen, the United States occupied the little settlements that according to the United States had been placed on their side of the river. The same happened to the article dealing with repatriation. In it the general rights of Mexicans in California and New Mexico to leave or stay were ceded. Since the manner in which people should repatriate and to whom they should address themselves for permission or help was not specified nor regulated, each nation interpreted for themselves how it should be done. This lack of precision was the origin of the second diplomatic dispute of the peace treaty.

The Treaty of Guadalupe-Hidalgo, ratified the 30th of May, 1848, consisted of 23 articles, among which were two that referred to Mexicans in territory obtained by the United States:

ARTICLE VIII
Mexicans now established in territories previously belonging to Mexico, and which remain for the future within the limits of the United States, as defined by the present treaty, shall be free to continue where they now reside, or to remove at any time to the Mexican Republic, retaining the property which they possess in

191

the said territories, or disposing thereof, and removing the proceeds wherever they please, without their being subjected, on this account, to any contribution, tax, or charge whatever.

Those who shall prefer to remain in the said territories may either retain the title and rights of Mexican citizens, or acquire those of citizens of the United States. But they shall be under the obligation to make their election within one year from the date of the exchange of ratifications of this treaty; and those who shall remain in the said territories after the expiration of that year, without having declared their intention to retain the character of Mexicans, shall be considered to have elected to become citizens of the United States.

In the said territories, property of every kind, now belonging to Mexicans not established there, shall be inviolably respected. The present owners, the heirs of these, and all Mexicans who may hereafter acquire said property by contract, shall enjoy with respect to it guarantees equally ample as if the same belonged to citizens of the United States.[350]

According to this article, the Mexican government interpreted it as giving them the implicit right to send representatives to repatriate those who did not want to be converted to North American citizens. Thus, as the rest of the annexed territory had not been organized, they sent three delegates or commissioners: one to California, another to New Mexico, and another to Texas.

The commissioner named to New Mexico was don Ramón Ortiz, who arrived in April, 1849, as emissary of the Mexican government and offered the New Mexicans land and equipment

---

[350] Álvaro Matute, *Antología en el siglo XIX*, UNAM, 1973, p. 450.

necessary for agriculture and transport of their families. Ortiz, also governor of Chihuahua, informed the Mexican government of his mission. He communicated that the North American governor for the territory of New Mexico had received him well and offered to cooperate in his task. The day after his arrival in New Mexico, Ortiz went to the county of Bado, ". . . which was where it was thought that fewer people wanted to be repatriated to the Mexican Republic." However, said Ortiz in his report that out of one thousand families in the county, nine hundred wanted to return to Mexico. The reason given is significant, "even though they knew that despite the guarantees in the peace treaty they would lose all their properties, to lose everything would be better than to belong to a government where they would have fewer guarantees and would be treated worse than the African race."[351] From there he went to La Cañada county, but the first day he enlisted over 100 people, and the governor of New Mexico sent a message in which he accused Ortiz of worrying the people and thereby prohibiting a continuation of the register. Thus, he went to Santa Fe, where he met with the governor and made him see that his accusations were groundless. Ortiz was able to convince the North American governor of the necessity of sending agents to the settlements so that all New Mexicans would learn of the possibility of returning to Mexico and continue being Mexican citizens.

Three hours after the agent in Santa Fe posted his notices, continued Mr. Ortiz, more than 200 people wanted to sign up to return to Mexico. The governor of New Mexico called him back and prohibited him from using his agents under the pretext that the anxiety would extend to the capital. He also reported that he had received communications from all of the prefects of the districts, complaining that since the arrival of the Mexican

---

[351] *Archivo de la Secretaría de Relations de México* (ASREM), H/524 5, 849, 2-21-13 2971, ff. 4-8.

commissioner, all the people refused to obey them almost openly. In response, Ortiz asked the governor to put this in writing so he could pass it on to the Mexican government, a request that the governor did not receive, so Ortiz also could not obtain an interview. When the date stipulated in the treaty to finalize the repatriation neared, the commissioner received letters from two of the most well-known men in the area. They told him that the governor of New Mexico was doing everything in his power to impede the exodus that accompanied repatriation. The newspaper, El Republicano de Santa Fe, refused to print the lists of citizens who wanted to be repatriated. Every citizen who wanted to return to Mexico had to sign up in their prefecture of origin with the purpose of avoiding concentrations of people. Even this they were unable to accomplish since the prefects, by a strange coincidence, were not present. Despite all the obstacles, the Mexican commissioner to New Mexico reported that "80,000 people wanted to be repatriated." This calculation was exaggerated, as it is believed there were only 60,000 inhabitants.

Don Ramón Ortiz sent to the Ministry of Exterior Relations the document he had received from the New Mexican government in which he was prohibited from returning to the settlements in the territory under the pretext that "he had gone beyond his official duties giving the people too much information about the treaty's provisions that led to the discontent.[352]

The 24th of July, 1849, the Secretary of Exterior Relations sent a message to the Mexican ambassador in Washington, to make claims against the conduct of the governor of New Mexico towards the commission of the Mexican government, asking to

---

[352] Ibidem

continue the Repatriation Commission, as stipulated in the Treaty of Guadalupe-Hidalgo.[353]

On September 18, 1849, Luis de la Rosa, Mexican ambassador in Washington, sent a diplomatic note to John Clayton, Secretary of State of the United States. In it he presented the complaint of the Mexican government over the obstacles placed before their commission for the repatriation stipulated in the treaty. Among other things he complained that, ". . . he could not even inform the Mexican citizens about emigration through the press because the editors of the few existing newspapers refused to publish his postings". De la Rosa repeated the right of his government to promote emigration, as implicitly stipulated in the treaty, at the same time asking that orders be given that the commissioners could carry out their tasks. He also explained the necessity of sending commissioners to the territories that had belonged to Mexico since it was their duty to settle expenditures and destination points.[354]

The answer was not long in coming. Eight days later, the 25 of September, 1849, De la Rosa received a copy of the messages sent between the Secretary of State and the Secretary of War of the United States. In them, it was clear that the United States had never considered that Article VIII of the Treaty of Guadalupe-Hidalgo would include the right of sending commissioners. According to them, "The treaty cleared up a principal recognized by this government: the right of every citizen or subject to transfer his obedience to whatever government", but the

[353] Nota del secretario de Relaciones Exteriores al ministro de México en Washington, 24 de Julio de 1849, ASREM 2-13-2971, f. 19.

[354] Carta de Luis de la Rosa, ministro de México en Washington al secretario de Estado de los Estados Unidos, ASREM H/524 5849/2, ff. 17-19, 18 de septiembre de 1849.

repatriation would depend only on the desires of each citizen. As a result, according to them, the right to send commissioners was not implicit in Article VIII of the Treaty of Guadalupe-Hidalgo.[355]

The last diplomatic note about repatriation was on November 20, 1849. De la Rosa communicated the news that the United States affirmed that Mexico asked for something not expressly given in the treaty. De la Rosa expressed his amazement at the pretense that repatriation could be accomplished without commissioners to direct it. He noted that the United States Secretary of War included in his note his complaint against the supposed disturbances caused by the commissioner to New Mexico.[356]

The repatriation of Mexicans from New Mexico ended without having found a diplomatic solution. We know that Commissioner Ortiz could not return to New Mexico, but he was able to bring a number of Mexicans to the La Mesilla region, which was later sold to the United States so they could build a railroad.

As to the change of nationality, this continued to be discussed since many had not decided in this regard in the time allowed by the treaty. Additionally, Article VIII stipulated that, "those who stay in the indicated territories a year after the passage, without declaring their intention to retain their Mexican allegiance will be considered as having decided to take United States citizenship." Consequently, all those who were not aware of this stipulation, without knowing it, became United States citizens.

---

[355] Carta del secretario de Guerra de los Estados Unidos al secretario de Estado, ASREM 2-13-2971, ff. 20-22, 25 de septiembre de 1849.

[356] Carta del ministerio de México en Washington al secretario de Relaciones Exteriores, ASREM 2-13-2971, ff. 20-22, 25 de septiembre de 1849.

Some who did not know how to write, also tried to repatriate themselves, however, they were impeded from doing so only because they did not know how to sign their names.[357]

In the archives at Santa Fe three testaments of New Mexicans are found who not only did not want to change nationality but who rejected posts in the new government in order to maintain their Mexican citizenship. The first was José Francisco Leyva, to whom was offered the post of senator in the territorial legislature of New Mexico. Among other things he said:

> Add two things to that already stated: the first is that I must be considered a foreigner in this region because neither my origins nor my sentiments are anything other than Mexican; and as for the second, I have never stopped desiring to be a citizen of my country whose laws and customs will be the only ones I will ever recognize.[358]

On November 6, 1851, José Baca rejected the post of general of the First Brigade of the Central Division for the following reasons: "That I find myself enrolled in the register of the National Guard of the Republic of Mexico which prevents me from conducting the requirements of Article 63 of the (Mexican) Organic Law of July 15, 1848, and I cannot do less for my nation than spill my last drop of blood.[359]

---

[357] Carta del ministro de México en Washington al secretario de Relaciones Exteriores, ASREM 2-13-2971, f. 20, 20 octubre de1849.

[358] Benjamin Reed Coll, State Records Center, Santa Fe, New Mexico, folio 87501, num. 170.

[359] Ibidem, num. 35.

The third testament that we possess, although there may have been more that we did not find, was that of Vicente Valdés, who on November 8, 1851 rejected the post of commissioner to organize the registration of the territorial militia.

> I consider myself incapable of accepting it for the sole reason that I have declared myself a Mexican citizen, which I will remain my entire life. It appears the peace treaty assures me of this imperceptible right, and while no law requires me to renounce it, I am resolved to take no action nor any order from any other government than that to which I belong. I hope that you will entrust the commission to another person, since I cannot carry out, nor do I want, nor should I, accept it.[360]

Article VIII of the Treaty of Guadalupe-Hidalgo says the following:

> Mexicans now established in territories previously belonging to Mexico, and which remain for the future within the limits of the United States, shall be free to continue where they now reside, or to remove at any time to the Mexican Republic, retaining the property which they possess in the said territories, or disposing thereof, and removing the proceeds wherever they please, without their being subjected, on this account, to any contribution, tax, or charge whatever.[361]

The Treaty of Guadalupe-Hidalgo was very precise about repatriation. Article VIII was the only article to talk about it, and as we have observed, it stated that the inhabitants of the lost territories could stay where they resided or move to the Mexican

---

[360] Ibidem, num. 295.

[361] Matute, op. cit., p. 456.

Republic. There was no mention of the possible dispatch of commissioners to organize the repatriation. Mexico sent commissioners, which means that they added significantly to Article VIII. That was the error. They should have asked that a diplomatic commission specify the form of repatriation. The treaty did not give Mexico the explicit permission to send commissioners to the lost provinces. However, six months after the signing, August 19, 1848, the Mexican government sent a decree in which they allocated 200,000 pesos of the first three million paid by the United States to cover the costs of moving all those Mexicans who wanted to live in Mexico. Not only the commissioners, but even the consuls were required to help in the move.[362]

This decree was not based on the Treaty of Guadalupe-Hidalgo, even though Mexico was free to make such a decree within its own territory. That which it had no right to make, according to the Secretary of War of the United States, was to send commissioners to United States territory to repatriate people who lived there. It is evident that the Mexican government considered it implicit that North American permission would be granted to the commissioners as is shown by the note from the Mexican ambassador in Washington to the Secretary State. In it he harshly criticized the governor of New Mexico, saying, "that he had obstructed the work of the commissioner, thereby violating the rights of his government to promote emigration following the stipulations of the treaty.[363] Not only did the Mexican government of the time, but also later historians have thought that Mexico did have the right to send commissioners. Luis Zorrilla in his *Historia de las relations entre México y los Estados Unidos de América*, thought that the North American

---

[362] Zorrilla, Luis G., Historia de las relaciones entre Mexico y los Estado Unidos de America, Editorial Porrúa, 1965, p. 259.

[363] ASREM, 2-13-2971.

authorities of New Mexico obstructed the work of the commission and thus violated the first paragraph of Article VIII.[364]

For Zorrilla the transfer of a group of illiterate families could only be done if a government agent informed them of the conditions, bought them equipment and food, and conducted them to the new place of residence, as occurred with the little group transferred to La Mesilla. The Mexican government should have requested a treaty in which the diplomatic right to send commissioners was contemplated. As they did not do this, they assumed a right that did not exist, having been rejected by the United States. According to United States, "the treaty clarified a principal recognized by this government; the right of every citizen or subject to change his allegiance to whatever government he wishes." but considering repatriation or transfer of nationality to be up to the individual.[365]

Against this response was total silence on the part of Mexico. There are no documents, but we suppose that the Secretary of Exterior Relations was aware of the absurdity of the situation and that in reality there was no diplomatic solution to insist that the United States government recognize this implicit right. The document alluded to, that of the answer by the Secretary of War of September 25, 1849, does not seem to have been known to the two historians who have studied this topic. Neither Luis Zorrilla, nor Benjamin Read, in *Illustrated History of New Mexico*, mentions the document. This is probably the reason for which both authors defended Mexico's right to send commissioners.

The only inexplicable point in all these problems was the attitude of the governor of New Mexico. At first he allowed the entry of

---

[364] Zorrilla, op. cit., p. 260.

[365] ASREM, 2-13-2971, f.22.

the commission and offered to cooperate with him in regard to repatriation. When the number of persons who wanted to emigrate alarmed him, as all the labor in the territory was Mexican, he invented or pretended that the commission was sowing confusion and rebellion. He never mentioned that they were violating the treaty or that they had no right to send a commission. The same happened with the Secretary of State of the United States. It was the Secretary of War who found that Article VIII, invoked by Mexico, did not grant implicitly or explicitly the right to send a commissions.

In conclusion, we can say that the Secretary of War of the United States and the governor of New Mexico did not deny the right of repatriation of Mexican citizens to Mexico (seeing as it was obviously implied by Article VIII), and thus, the Mexican government was not so wrong in supposing it.

The Treaty of Guadalupe-Hidalgo in its second paragraph says:

> Those who shall prefer to remain in the said territories, may either retain the title and rights of Mexican citizens, or acquire those of the citizens of the United States. But they shall be under the obligation to make their election within one year from the date of the exchange of ratifications of this treaty; and those who remain in the said territories after the expiration of that year, without having declared their intention to retain the character of Mexicans, shall be considered to have elected to become citizens of the United States.

The warning about the change of nationality appears to us to be counter to international law. To change nationality at that time required that a person renounces his original citizenship to be able to acquire a second. The logic is that whoever desires a new nationality must explicitly ask for it. The United States, however, wanted to obtain new citizens, who after a year had not elected to remain Mexican. The manner in which the United States viewed citizenship is curious. In their hurry to avoid international problems and promote their interests, they granted citizenship too easily, remember that when General Kearney invaded New Mexico in May 1846, he immediately granted citizenship, and then declared as traitors those who defended their country.

IX. VIOLATIONS OF GUADALUPE-HIDALGO: CALIFORNIA

As we have seen, the war (the only official war between Mexico and the United States) ended with the peace treaty signed on February 2, 1848. The cession, according to the North Americans, or the forced sale, according to the Mexicans, of California was formally recognized as part of the Treaty of Guadalupe-Hidalgo. This region had been under the control of the North American army since July 1846, when Commodore Sloat declared it a territory of the United States. From that moment until 1850, when the United States Congress accepted it as a state, California was governed by a series of military officers and civilians who tried to impose order on a chaotic situation.

Even when the authorities were North American the legislation in force continued to be Mexican. In this way, California could have continued for a long time as the agricultural and cattle territory it had always been, but the discovery of gold transformed its importance.

Several months after the signing of the Treaty of Guadalupe-Hidalgo gold was discovered in California. It is said that it was found before 1848, but it was not generally known. This event began the frenzied emigration from the United States to the West, and especially California. In a few months, there was an incredible exodus from other parts of the world; thousands of people defied all kinds of dangers attracted by the dream of overnight riches. Also in a few months, unlike in New Mexico, the population of California doubled, such that the Mexican commission sent to repatriate their compatriots did not find great centers of population who wanted to repatriate. As a result, North American violations of Article VII of the Treaty of Guadalupe-Hidalgo did not consist, as in New Mexico, in negating

203

repatriation but in expelling locals from the land. It is important to make known that few North American historians include these facts in their narration of the period. For example, Hubert Bancroft, author of a series of books on the states of the American union, a collection considered to be a classic of his country, only mentions in passing that there was hostility towards the Mexicans.

Between 1849 and 1856, California produced $500,000,000 of gold. Gold fever unhinged the Anglo population to such an extent that assaults and murders were the order of the day. The owners of the greater part of the territory were local natives, the Mexicans or Californians, who were the first to suffer the North American abuse. On November 19, 1849, the Mexican ambassador in Washington wrote in a note to the Mexican consul in San Francisco asking that the consul in San Francisco provide protection for the Mexicans in California as it was known that they were suffering all kinds of humiliations.[366]

By that time, according to the treaty, the Mexicans of California should have been considered North American citizens, and for that reason the outrages were doubly illegal, since in addition to violating the treaty they were violating the Constitution of the United States. The abuses against Mexicans were also against the provisions of Article IX of the Treaty of Friendship and Commerce.

As the persecution of the Mexicans developed along with the gold fever the Anglos took all of the estates belonging to Mexicans in the mines in the center and north of California by force. The Commander General of Sinaloa wrote to the Secretary of Exterior Relations informing him about the disconcerting

---

[366] Archivo de la Secretaria de Relaciones Exteriores de México (ASREM), Expediente LE 1095 ff. 198-200.

204

news in California, and above all of the pleasures that the gold and the port of San Francisco produced, "where robberies and murders grow daily leading to such hate of the Mexicans, Spanish and Chilenos that the increase in violence makes it impossible to live there, they rob them, they humiliate them, they make them leave by force."[367]

The answer was not long in coming, showing the preoccupation the government of Mexico had for the lot of the inhabitants in the lost territories and that they wanted to do something for them. Since it was evident that the actions against them constituted a violation of the treaty the Secretary of Exterior Relations asked for provable facts on their plight and that they inform the Mexicans that they could present protests to the Mexican consul. He also asked the commander in Sinaloa that he communicate the affair to the Ambassador of Mexico in Washington who should in turn protest to the North American government, and let them know that Mexico considered them responsible for damages to the Mexicans. In addition, he appealed to the governments of Sonora and Sinaloa that they receive those who returned to Mexico and give them vacant land on credit. In case the governments of those states could not do so, the central government would indemnify them.[368]

In response to the Mexican protest, the North American Secretary of State answered that the charges were vague and that the Mexicans in California should present themselves to the local authorities. Only in unresolved cases should they turn to the federal government in Washington. He emphasized his desire to

---

[367] Ibidem, ff. 185-187.

[368] Ibidem, ff. 189-191.

fulfill the obligations of the treaty and attributed what was happening in California to the reigning chaos and confusion.[369]

In April, 1850, a law was passed in California by which foreigners needed a license to work in the mines. In view of the fact that the North American authorities said they could not prove who was a native Mexican in California and who were recent arrivals, everyone suffered under the law. The government of Mexico complained once more for this violation of the treaty and the bias of the authorities. Additionally, the Anglos had armed themselves against the foreigners forcing them to turn in their arms. The old owners of California saw themselves reduced to the level of strangers persecuted without the right to defend themselves.[370]

There were many violent encounters. The settlement of Sonora in the south of California, was converted into a refuge for thousands of Californians and recently arrived Mexicans. Shortly after the passage of the law of 1850 requiring the payment of a tax on foreigners, which was as we said an illegal act, 2,000 Anglo miners arrived in the settlement of Sonora shooting the Californians and Mexicans, burning the mining camp and lynching dozens of Mexicans. The majority of the Mexicans and Californians abandoned their rights and fled to Spanish speaking counties. It would be difficult to calculate the number of Mexicans and Californians lynched in the decade of 1850-1860.

---

[369] Toribio Esquivel Obregón, Apuntes para la historia del derecho en México, t. IV. Antigua Librería de Roberdo, Mexico. 1948, p. 426.

[370] Hubert Howe Bancroft, The Works of Hubert Howe Bancroft, v. XXIII, ARNO Press, New York, 1866, pp. 405-407.

Some historians affirm that there were 3,000-4,000 from a population of 10,000.[371]

In May, 1852, miners from the Rough and Ready company prohibited foreigners in its mines. The Californians found so little protection in their new citizenship and so many abuses, that they emigrated to the south of the state, to cattle lands, as they had lost their mining tools or were not allowed to use them. Only the internal situation in Mexico prevented a complete exodus.[372]

One grave consequence of the violation of the rights of Californians and Mexicans was that many of the displaced persons were converted into guerrillas or highwaymen. Almost all of the histories written by Anglos used the appellation "bandits", without taking into account that they were fighting for their own land and possessions. A contemporary of these events described the situation thus:

> After 1846, a strange metamorphosis took place among the humble classes of the Californian natives [since] before the North American conquest they were a peaceful and satisfied population. There were no organized bands of criminals. The North Americans not only took possession of their country and government, but also in many cases they expelled them from their ancestral lands and their personal property. The injustice caused resentment and frequently they were treated by the lowest North Americans as strangers and intruders who had no rights in their native land.[373]

---

[371] Carey McWilliams, Al norte de México, Siglo XXI, México, 1972, p. 150.

[372] Bancroft, op. cit., pp. 403-408.

[373] Carey McWilliams, op. cit., p. 151.

The majority of these "bandits" had fought for their country in the 1847 war with the United States and in the decade of 1850-1860 patriots and thieves united to constantly strike the gringo. They assaulted the herds headed north, laid siege to the mines, and sacked mining towns. Among the most well-known were Joaquín Murrieta, Procopio Soto, Juan Flores, Pancho Daniel Vásquez, Luis Bulvia and Antonio Moreno.

The most famous among them appears to have been Joaquin Murrieta, whom the Californians called "El Patrio". Murrieta terrorized the North American population from 1851-1853. He had so many exploits that his name became legendary. Stories of his innumerable exploits converted him into a generous bandit in the style of Robin Hood such that his uprising was a benefit to his race. Some say he came from a rich California family, others that his real name was Carrillo. It is certain that he caused terror on the highways and mentioning him caused goosebumps among all the travelers. He had, according to legend, the fastest horse in the whole state and a charm that captivated thousands of his men. All suspects identified themselves as members of his gang, and various towns fought over the honor of being his hometown. The innumerable stories about him obscured his true identity. Many believed that he never existed and was a collective image of a cross between the anti-gringo Californian bandit and the Mexicans who sacked the south of the state. Even his death at the hands of Captain Love has been put into doubt.

The state legislature subsidized the formation of a company of soldiers whose mission was to capture Joaquín. They offered $5,000, a great fortune, for his head. After three months pursuing him, Love presented Joaquín's head preserved in a jar of alcohol. The authorities accepted that it was Murrieta and his head displayed across the state. Since no one had ever seen him they accepted the testimony of a Sonorense who had known him as a child! The *Star of Los Angeles* newspaper made fun of the news and reported that Joaquín had been seen in the south of the state at the same time his death was announced. Whatever the truth, in Southern California they never believed that Love had killed Murrieta.

One can doubt his existence, but the myth is real. The life of Joaquín Murrieta became the most important folklore legend in California. Several years later his first biography was published that affirmed his aristocratic birth and vengeance as the motive for his actions. He was presented as a peaceful miner expelled from his land by the North Americans who, in addition to beating him, raped his wife and hanged his brothers. From this moment he began his career as a bandit. After his death, or his disappearance, his name became a symbol of hate against the gringos.[374] He had many imitators, among them Tiburcio Vázquez who declared, "A spirit of hate and vengeance took possession of me. I had many battles for the defense of what I consider my rights and those of my fellow citizens. I believed that we were unjustly deprived of the social rights that belonged to us."[375]

The acts of violence by Mexicans and Californians in turn served to justify the North American violence. Companies of armed men were formed to chase down the bandits and troops were requested from the United States army. If that had been all, the agitation would probably have lasted longer. The worst were the Anglo miners, ranchers and artisans who took up the custom of lynching Mexicans and Californians. "In the decade of the sixties

---

[374] Leonard Pitt, The Decline of the Californias, University of California Press, Los Angeles , 1969, pp. 77-82.

[375] Carey McWilliams, op. cit., p. 152.

209

lynching of Mexicans was so common in Los Angeles that the newspapers did not bother writing about the details."[376]

Although Article VIII of the peace treaty the United States had promised to respect the property of the inhabitants of California during this time the Californians were gradually dispossessed of their possessions. They had assured that "their actual owners, the heirs of these and the Mexicans who in the future might acquire by contract the indicated properties, could enjoy them as much as if they belonged to citizens of the United States."[377] But they did not do as promised.

The same United States Congress violated the provisions of the treaty by approving the law of March 3, 1851, in which Mexican landholders had to present their property titles to a judge who would determine their legality. The interminable litigation that this established was the cause of many Mexicans losing their properties. In 1856, a California law required that the owners of the land pay for the improvements that the invaders had inflicted under pain of losing the land!

All of this was known to Washington, who, following its custom, never admitted to violating the Treaty of Guadalupe-Hidalgo. On the other hand, they did accept the laws that invalidated it, another example of the well-known North American characteristic of self-justification. The history of the looting of the land of the Californians is representative of the manner in which the government of the United States changed their own law whenever it was in their interest to do so.[378]

---

[376] Ibidem, p. 153.

[377] Alvaro Matute, ed. Antologia, México en el siglo XIX, UNAM México, 1973, p.456.

[378] Esquivel Obregón, op. cit., pp. 534-535.

At the entry of a great number of Anglos into California on the occasion of the discovery of gold, they discovered ranches and haciendas of enormous dimensions. History shows that the recent arrivals began to plot a legal way to take control of these lands. It is known that western North Americans believed that a "higher law" gave them the right to these lands in the hands of the hated Mexicans. "For them", the historian Bancroft informs us, "everything that was Mexican was suspect and mysterious, not to say diabolical,"[379] and as free United States citizens they believed they had the right to take these lands, notwithstanding their obligations under the Treaty of Guadalupe-Hidalgo. They spent years hearing from their ambassadors and leaders that only Anglos could fully develop these lands and that the grants of Spanish and Mexican lands were totally anti-American, followed by their characteristic self-justification of proclaiming the need to establish more democratic institutions.

Two years after the conquest, the first riot against the owners of extensive land holdings took place which failed because the military commander of California did not want to have problems with Washington. However, in March 1849, Captain Halleck presented the first report on land holdings by which the government could use the legal process to dispossess the land from its owners in California. In it, it appeared, that many of the documents of the land grants had problems or were incomplete. The second report was by William Carey Jones of March, 1850, who as confidential agent of the Secretary of the Interior had investigated the situation in depth. He arrived at the conclusion that the majority of the documents were legal and that the best course of action was to respect them and take legal action against the suspicious ones.[380]

---

[379] Bancroft, op. cit., pp. 534-535.

[380] Ibidem, pp. 536-537.

Indian Territory

Missouri River

New Mexico

Sioux

Platte River

Omaha

Pawnee

Arapaho

Missouri

Oto
Delaware

Iowa
Kikapoo

Mississippi River

Cheyenne

Shawnee
Kaskaskia, Peoria
Otawa
De New York
Cherokee
Quapaw
Semaca

Osage
Cherokee

Canadian River

Creek

Shawnee

Chickasaw

Choctaw

Arkansas River

Coahuila-Texas

Red River

Sabine River

Gulf of Mexico

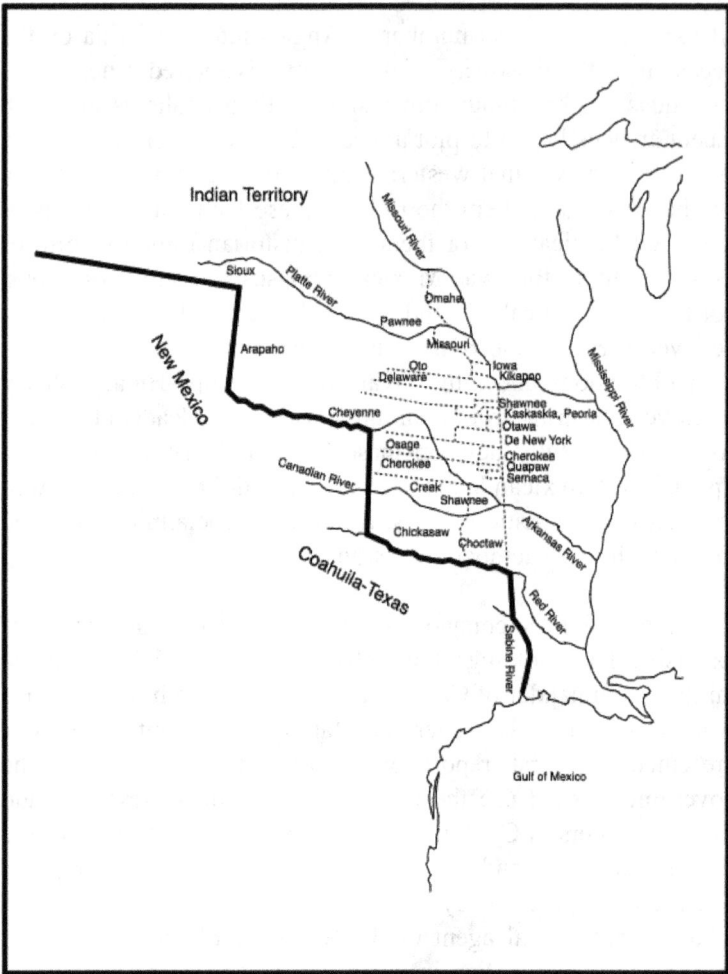

FIGURE 7. TRANSFER OF NORTH AMERICAN INDIAN
TRIBES TO THE FRONTIER WITH MEXICO, 1825-1842.
(BASED ON LUIS ZORRILLA, HISTÓRIA DE LAS
RELACIONES ENTRE MÉXICO Y LOS ESTADOS
UNIDOS DE AMÉRICA, ED. PORRÚA, VOL. 1, 1965, P.
288.)

This report should have closed the case, but that is not what happened because of the very strong desire for land among the Anglos. Senator Gwin took charge of trying to resort to fraud, and old Senator Benton was opposed to having the Californians appear before the courts, saying that that would be directly against the Treaty of Guadalupe-Hidalgo. However, Senator Gwin's fraudulent plan was adopted, which constituted an incredible example of Anglo denial. Gwin argued that not only did his plan not violate the Treaty of Guadalupe-Hidalgo, it protected it, since it assured that the land grants would remain in the hands of its legal owners. The only thing, he said, that North Americans were asking for was the protection of the courts. He concluded that it was better to oblige the owners of the grants to appear before the courts, even if they ran the risk of losing their property resulting from the high cost of litigation. In other words, the legislators approved the dispossession since, as they said, if the North Americans in California did not have properties the conquest would be effectively annulled. The grants covered an area of 12,000,000 acres.[381]

Even the most chauvinistic North American historians recognize that the act of 1851 gave rise to abuses and dispossessed many people of their property.[382] Many owners who had returned to Mexico also lost their properties, since according to this law, they only had two years to present the documents. The majority of the absentees, given the distance and bad communications, did not even know of the law's existence. When they returned, they and their descendants, found themselves without land. Thus, it was that the old Mexicans were dispossessed of their land and marginalized and from owners and gentlemen they became supplicants.

---

[381] ibidem, pp. 538-540.

[382] ASREM, Exp LE 1095, ff. 200-203.

X. VIOLATIONS OF GUADALUPE-HIDALGO: INDIGENOUS TRIBES

From the establishment of diplomatic relations between Mexico and the United States the latter country insisted on the convenience to Mexico of making a cession or sale of territory in return for taking charge of the repression of the numerous bellicose Indian groups that lived in the frontier zone. Poinsett said as much in his first attempt to buy territory[383] with all of the subsequent envoys sent by the United States emphasized the same point. Mexico was accused over and over again of not being capable of confronting the Apache and Comanches who besieged the frontier settlements. The heart of the problem, as indicated by Poinsett, was that Mexico, following the old Spanish tradition, recognized the citizenship of the Indians. The United States on the other hand considered these groups to be foreign nationals and did not accept any responsibility in their depredations. No one considered that it had been their own people who, through the years, who had caused the collision with the tribes by constantly pushing them to the southwest. There were tribes originally from the Great Lakes who came to occupy territories neighboring Mexico. Following Darwin's law of the survival of the fittest, they expelled the weakest, pushing them to the south. "Between the years of 1825 and 1840, the government of the United States transferred thousands of dispossessed Indians in the east to the territory west of the Mississippi River (Figure 7).[384]

---

[383] Bosch Garcia, Carlos, Material pata la historia diplomática de México, Escuela Nacional de Ciencias Politicas, UNAM, México, 1957, p. 28.

[384] Canales, Isidro, Invasíon de los indios bárbaros, Universidad de Nuevo León, Monterrey, 1958,p 44.

The region of the Great Plains encompassed the present day states of Montana, a third of Wyoming, and half of the territories of Colorado, New Mexico, Texas, Oklahoma, Kansas, Nebraska, South Dakota, and North Dakota. Thirty-one Indian tribes lived in this area of which 11 were native to this region including the Arapahoes, Assiniboin, Blackfoot, Cheyenne, Comanche, Crow, Gros Ventre, Kiowa, Kiowa-Apache, Sarcee and Teton Dakota. Prescott Webb, in his study of these Indians tells us that they were nomads depending for their survival on big game and the buffalo and could communicate with each other by means of a sign language.[385] Spain was never able to force their submission, given that they were nomads without permanent settlements that could be destroyed or surrounded. It is interesting to note that Spain was able to establish dominion over more civilized Indian populations, but with nomadic populations they nearly always failed. Their system of conquest could not be applied to nomads.

By 1848, the Indians of the Southwest had been divided into two categories: the inhabitants of settlements and those of the deserts and plains. These latter, the nomads of the Southwest, had over the centuries overwhelmed the inhabitants of the settlements, later, terrorizing the Spanish colonies for many years. The Apaches dominated the desert that extended between the colonies of California and Arizona. In the same way the Spanish had separated the colonies in southern Arizona from the settlements in California and New Mexico.[386] In 1847, the Apaches took advantage of the war between Mexico and the United States to attack again and again the settlements of New Mexico taking advantage, as it seemed to them, of a magnificent

---

[385] Prescott Webb, Walter, The Great Plains, Appelton Co., New York, 1931, p. 80.

[386] McWilliams, Carey, Al norte de Mexico; Siglo XXI, México, 1972, p.52.

opportunity to get a little plunder.[387] The inhabitants of the frontier Mexican states lived in constant terror of the indigenous incursions. The Anglos took maximum advantage of these circumstances to prepare for their invasion of Mexican and Spanish territories by promising the inhabitants a thousand and one times that the United States would give them protection against the Indian attacks. As we have already seen, this was also one of the most used reasons in the petitions for buying territory; that Mexico could not defend its frontier regions from the Indian attacks. When General Kearney invaded New Mexico, the first promise he made was to safeguard the territory from Apaches and Navajos. Naturally, from 1825, the year in which diplomatic relations were established between the two countries, and the war of 1847, the Indian attacks were one of the topics most frequently discussed. In the very complete compilation of documents conducted by Dr. Bosch, the reference to Indians in diplomatic notes were continuous. From the beginning, the United States offered "that in return for this cession of territory, they promised to liberate Mexico of all aggression by these tribes."[388] One of the greatest ironies of this history, as we have seen, was the United States' inability to accomplish this repeated promise.

Poinsett arrived in Mexico in June, 1825. Exactly one year later, the Mexican government sent its first report on the Indians. The ambassador claimed that, according to reports of two Comanche captives, all their tribe was preparing, with help from the United States, to invade the Mexican frontier. The president of Mexico asked that the United States government stop the sale of arms to

---

[387] Lavender, David, Bent's Fort, University of Nebraska Press, Lincoln, 1954, p. 321.

[388] Bosch, op cit., p. 29.

the Indians.[389] This same request was repeated dozens of times in the following twenty years, and naturally the United States ignored them, since they knew they could not control the ambition of their men on the frontier. Proof of this was that in the Treaty of Guadalupe-Hidalgo of 1848, a subsection of Article XI that prohibited the sale of arms to the Indians, was rejected by the North American Congress.[390] The problem of the Indian tribes was complicated very quickly by commerce on the frontier. North American merchants traveling from Missouri to Santa Fe, New Mexico, were constantly besieged by Indians to whom their colleagues had been selling guns. If the tribes had been in Mexico their acts would have been considered the responsibility of the Mexican government, since as we have said they were considered Mexican citizens. On the other hand, if the tribes were not Mexican the government of the United States, considering them foreign nations, did not accept any responsibility. They also did not want to prohibit the sale of arms, a measure that directly affected their own merchants. As a result, Poinsett counseled his government not to present reclamations for Indian incursions against Mexico because that country would close the zone to North American merchants.[391] They filed away the reclamations to be able to throw them up against Mexico at the appropriate moment, as was their custom.

The North American ambassadors following Poinsett continued to emphasize more and more the depredations of the Indians and to accuse Mexico of fomenting aggressions against North American citizens. To Mexican reclamations, the ambassadors

[389] Ibidem, p. 61.

[390] Matute, Alvaro, ed. Antologia, México en el Siglo XIX, UNAM, 1973, México, p. 459.

[391] Bosch op. cit., p. 75.

217

were evasive or rejected the claims of depredations for supposedly not having any foundation.[392]

The situation worsened in the decade of 1830s. The law of expulsion of the Indians was approved by the North American Congress in May, 1830. In the 10 years that followed the Indian tribes that lived in the states of the Gulf of Mexico and the Atlantic were expelled to the west. The same happened to the tribes from the region of the Ohio River to the Great Lakes.[393] The displacement produced a new shock between the tribes being pushed to the south or in other words, to Mexico. At this time, the Mexican government complained of attacks by Cherokee, Creeks, and Kickapoos in November 1830.[394] This reclamation is a perfect example of the tribal collision. The Kickapoo were from the Great Lakes; the Creeks and Cherokee from the state of Georgia! Displaced by the government of the United States they harassed the Mexican frontier settlements in the 1830s.

At the insistence of Ambassador Anthony Butler, Mexico agreed to sign the Treaty of Friendship, Commerce, and Navigation in the year 1831. What interests us in this treaty is Article XXXIII, in which is stipulated the obligation that each country had to maintain the peace among the Indians who lived in their territory, preventing them from further incursions.[395] We know that the United States did not bother to fulfill its obligations, as the

---

392 Ibidem, p. 131.

393 McNickle, D'Arcy, Las tribes indias de los Estados Unidos, Eudeba, Buenos Aires, 1976, p. 50.

394 Bosch, op. cit., pp. 130-131.

395 Zorrilla, Luis G., Historia de las relaciones entre México y los Estados Unidos de América, 2 vols. Porrúa, 1965 México, p. 112.

Mexican frontier was constantly invaded by bellicose Indian tribes that came and went over the border.

The provinces of New Mexico and Chihuahua continued to be devastated by the Indians until the eve of war. President Polk took advantage of these events to brandish them as one of the reasons that Mexico should cede the province of New Mexico. In his message to Congress, Polk said, referring to the Indians:

> Mexico has been and continues being too weak to suppress them [...] it would be a blessing for all those states in the north that their citizens be protected against the savage Indians by the force of the United States. If New Mexico were retained and governed by the United States, we could effectively stop these tribes from committing similar attacks.[396]

Meanwhile, discussing the provisions of the treaty, the Chihuahua legislature let the central government know that they would not accept the treaty without the inclusion of an article that would force the United States to control the warlike activities of their Indians.[397] They knew that the United States would keep pushing the tribes to the southwest and wanted to protect themselves from more incursions. Nicolas Trist, as a result, asked his government to accept the inclusion of an article, that according to him, only repeated Article XXXIII of the Treaty of Friendship and Commerce of 1831.

Thus it was that Article XI was included in the Treaty of Guadalupe-Hidalgo from 1848-1853, the year in which it was repealed by the Treaty of the Gadsden Purchase. For twenty

---

[396] Polk, James ed., Luis Cabrera, Diario del Presidente Polk, Antigua Librería Robredo, vol. II, Mexico, 1948, p. 461.

[397] Zorrilla, op. cit., p. 276.

years the United States government insisted on having jurisdiction over Mexican frontier lands on the pretext that this would enable them to control the tribes. While they had such control they were unable to meet their obligation. Five years after the Treaty of Guadalupe-Hidalgo they were willing to pay whatever was necessary to achieve the suspension of Article XI. Let us see what was in the article with the following:

> Considering that a great part of the territories, which, by the present treaty, are to be comprehended for the future within the limits of the United States, is now occupied by savage tribes, who will hereafter be under the exclusive control of the Government of the United States, and whose incursions within the territory of Mexico would be prejudicial in the extreme, it is solemnly agreed that all such incursions shall be forcibly restrained by the Government of the United States whensoever this may be necessary; and that when they cannot be prevented, they shall be punished by the said Government, and satisfaction for the same shall be exacted all in the same way, and with equal diligence and energy, as if the same incursions were meditated or committed within its own territory, against its own citizens.

The following paragraph regulates the prohibition of its (the United States') citizens to buy captives from the Indians, as well as horses, mules, and other objects stolen from Mexico. It continues to talk about its promise to rescue and restitute persons captured by the Indians. The final paragraph of Article XI reiterates their obligation:

> For the purpose of giving to these stipulations the fullest efficacy, thereby affording the security and redress demanded by their true spirit and intent, the Government

of the United States will now and hereafter pass, without unnecessary delay, and always vigilantly enforce, such laws as the nature of the subject may require. And, finally, the sacredness of this obligation shall never be lost sight of by the said Government, when providing for the removal of the Indians from any portion of the said territories, or for its being settled by citizens of the United States; but, on the contrary, special care shall then be taken not to place its Indian occupants under the necessity of seeking new homes, by committing those invasions which the United States have solemnly obliged themselves to restrain.[398]

After reading this article we see that the North American government did not fulfill, in the final analysis, either the first or the final paragraphs. It is credible that the North Americans had accepted the first paragraph, since as we have seen, they spent twenty years saying that Mexico was incapable of stopping the indigenous incursions. What is not understandable is how they could accept the last paragraph since they had spent years pushing the Indians into waste lands. The Congressmen who discussed the treaty to ratify it knew that the last paragraph would be impossible to accomplish as the decade of the fifties was of expansion towards the conquered territories, and thus, towards lands occupied by the Indians.

Six months later after the ratification of the treaty, the first incursions by the tribes were being felt with the ranches located between the Rio Grande and the Nueces being the first to feel them. Later they turned to Reynosa and Camargo, but it was Ciudad Mier that was the most impacted, as it was attacked twenty times over the following fifteen years. None of the three towns had heard of North American forces pursuing the Indians.

---

[398] Matute, op. cit., pp. 459-460.

The settlements in Tamaulipas suffered damages of more than thirty-five million pesos.[399] Despite the North American promises — all of the invading generals had promised to end the Indian incursions — the inhabitants along the frontier continued to live under the terror of the nomads. In Nuevo Leon things were not much better. The tribes got almost to Monterrey after harassing all the frontier settlements. Zorrilla gives us the number of attacks: "n 1848, there were 34 attacks on more than a half dozen settlements and towns. The incursions of the tribes in Mexican territory were so frequent that the frontier states, after a period of hope, began to reorganize their militias to fight against the Indians. The North American government had proven to be just as ineffective as the central government of Mexico. The Chihuahua legislature approved warrants which permitted the government to pay one hundred and fifty pesos for each dead Indian over the age of 14 and for Indians taken prisoner. As for Sonora, they were so devastated by the Apaches that they asked the government to apportion soldiers to all the settlements so that they could defend themselves. All able bodied men had to serve in the militias, and be on a permanent war footing."[400]

From Coahuila there was similar news. In November, 1851, the government of the state wrote to the Secretary of Exterior Relations describing the serious misfortunes that they suffered due to the Indian attacks. They were worried that the barbarians might reach the states of San Luis Potosí and Zacatecas, "who perhaps ran the same risk as those located along the dividing line with the United States, if they did not adopt defense and security measures." They noted that the frontier states were considering

---

[399] Zorrilla, op. cit., pp. 278-279.

[400] Ibidem, pp. 279-280.

an alliance to defend themselves.[401] A little later a communication from the residents and land owners of Coahuila state arrived: "since the time of the peace treaty with the United States, the incursions of the barbarians who live within the United States territory and particularly of the Comanches have been continuous and repeated." After complaining in detail, they accused the United States of not having contained these incursions by force and, as a consequence, of not having fulfilled Article XI of the treaty.[402]

The central government was always preoccupied by the frontier situation. The attacks by the tribes were not new. As we have seen the government had made innumerable attempts to colonize the frontier and thus defend it. In July, 1848, a decree of the Mexican government asked that the people of the frontier to be aware of the frontier recently established to conserve the integrity of the territory and "to defend the frontier states from the frequent incursions and cruelties of the savages." A law was passed that reestablished the presidios and military colonies. They divided the territory in three, the Eastern Frontier, the Chihuahua Frontier and the Western Frontier; 18 colonies were distributed within them: 7 in the east, 5 in Chihuahua, 5 in Sonora and one in Baja California. The land around each colony was divided into lots, and subsidized by the government, and given to the soldiers for them to cultivate. After a service of six years a bonus of ten pesos and a piece of land that had been cultivated was given to each soldier. Rippy in his book about the relations between Mexico and the United States emphasized that

---

[401] ASREM, 1-3-685, f. 9.

[402] ASREM, C/R-1-1, Ff. 364-370.

the number of cavalry troops Mexico planned to station on the frontier was superior to the number of North American troops.[403]

Over three years colonies were established in the designated points or places that could be attacked by Indians. In May and June of 1850, the colonies of Norte y Paso del Norte were established and in May and July of 1850, those of San Carlos and Pilares. In the eastern frontier, Rio Grande, Guerrero, Monclova Viejo and Monterrey were established. By 1851 the military colonies included: 1) Camargo; 2) El Pan en Lampazos; 3) Monterrey en Paso de Piedra; 4) Rio Grande en Misión Nueva; 5) Guerrero en Piedras Negras; 6) Monclova Viejo en Moral; 7) San Vicente en el viejo presidio de Agua Verde; 8) San Carlos en el viejo presidio de San Carlos; 9) Del Norte en el Presidio del Norte; 10) Pilares en Vado de Piedra; 11) Paso, 14 leagues from El Paso; 12) Jano, near the villa of Janos; 13) to 17) the five colonies of Sonora in the presidios of Bavispe, Fronteras, Santa Cruz, Tucson and Altar; and 18) Rosario in the mission of Santo Tomás, Baja California.[404]

By the end of 1850, Mexico recruited 434 soldiers and 972 horses for the eastern colonies, 296 soldiers and 220 horses for Chihuahua, 240 soldiers and 306 horses for the west. By December, 1851, there were 1,093 soldiers and 689 mules or horses. This represents a true effort on the part of the governments of the frontier states to meet the indigenous threat, as the continuous upheavals in the interior of the country kept soldiers near the capital. Diplomatic attempts were made to contain the tribes and in October, 1850, and in July, 1852,

---

[403] Rippy, Fred, The United States and Mexico, AMS Press, New York, p. 77.

[404] Cited by Rippy, the U.S. and Mexico, op. cit., in Vicente L. Manero, Documentos on colonist on, p. 78.

224

treaties were signed to permit the Seminoles and the Muskogee to establish colonies in the east and in Chihuahua.

In 1851 the North American filibuster invasions began with the doubtful proposition of helping Mexico in its battle against the Indians. In the same year, the diplomatic complaints against the United States worsened. In August, 1851, the Secretary of War and Navy sent a report to Exterior Relations:

> The copies that I have the honor of accompanying with this letter […] bring to your attention the transgressions the United States citizens committed, especially calling to the attention of his excellency the President, the conduct which has been observed encouraging the barbarians to pass into the Republic to rob cattle that on their return they sell or trade.[405]

Eight days later, the Secretary of Exterior Relations answered this news by announcing that he had already given orders to the ambassador in Washington to present reclamations to the North American government. A little later, the ambassador had to complain about the lack of fulfillment of the Treaty of Guadalupe-Hidalgo.[406]

In November of the same year of 1851, the ambassador of Mexico in Washington reported that he had learned that the North American government was looking for a way to offer Mexico a large sum of money to change Article XI of the Treaty: "Lately, I have learned in a nearly undeniable manner that Mr. Letcher has brought instructions on this issue and that he probably will try to mix them in with the negotiations relative to

---

[405] ASREM, LE 12-1-32 f. 7.

[406] ASREM, Ibidem, f. 5.

the Treaty of Tehuantepec."[407] By this note we know that already in mid-1851 the United States government had become aware that it could not comply with Article XI of the Treaty of Guadalupe-Hidalgo.

In January, 1852, the Secretary of Exterior Relations communicated to the United States ambassador in Mexico that, given the inability of his government to protect the frontier, Article XI had to be modified. President Arista had decided that both armies should make war on the Indians. The costs would, according to the treaty, be defrayed by the United States government, and he asked that the Mexican army would have the right to determine the number of soldiers that each country should contribute and regulate their service and allocation. He asked for compensation for the damages caused to that time. In addition, the Secretary of Exterior Relations presented a formal reclamation "for the support given to the Indians to buy stolen goods and for selling them all sorts of arms, including prohibited ones, that helped their activities."[408] Already on the eve of the signing of the Treaty of the Gadsden Purchase, the Mexican government continued complaining of the violations of Article XI, accusing the United States of not having defended the frontier with enough soldiers.[409]

All that we have seen shows us the seriousness with which the Mexican government tried to protect the frontiers as much from the Indian incursions as from the filibuster expeditions. The same Fred Rippy in his book *The United States and Mexico* said that from the documents of the period he had tried to determine if Mexico had wanted to protect itself, concluding that it had.

---

[407] Ibidem, ff. 14-15.

[408] Ibidem, ff. 277-284.

[409] ASREM, C-R 1-1 ff. 469-470.

The Mexican government presented 366 reclamations that added up to thirty-two million dollars to the commission created in 1868. He added that despite the chaotic conditions on the Mexican frontier, the North American diplomats could not refute these reclamations.[410]

As we have seen, the government of the United States did not meet its obligation under Article XI of the Treaty of Guadalupe-Hidalgo. Confronting such a failure one should ask why. According to the terms of the treaty, the United States had an obligation to watch over 180,000 Indians who lived in the territories obtained from Mexico. The Indians took advantage of the chaotic situation that developed at the end of the war and attacked both sides of the frontier. In addition, they very cleverly exploited the hatred between the two countries with the result that both thought that the other had instigated the Indians against them.

In the following, we will see the attempts, though weak, of the North American government to meet Article XI of the treaty. From time to time they informed Mexico of their activities to show their good will.

After the war with Mexico and confronting the enormous deficit it had left, the United States government decided to promote savings. The new territories became to be considered a white elephant, and the Whigs proposed that they be returned to Mexico until they could be paid for. The great problem consisted in knowing how to reduce the military costs, protect the inhabitants of the new territory and make sure the Indians did not invade Mexico. Military establishments were needed to maintain the peace with and between the tribes, but since Congress wanted to economize, no more actions were taken in this regard

---

[410] Rippy, op. cit., p. 80.

from 1848 to 1852. The debates on this issue generally changed into discussions of the responsibility for the war with Mexico or on the continually growing problem of slavery.[411]

When the North American executive reminded Congress that Mexico demanded recompense, it named four more agents to the Department of Indian Affairs. As they had not developed a concrete policy to resolve the problem of the Indians, 18 months after the ratification of the treaty, they still had not commissioned agents to take charge of the Indians of California and New Mexico. In September, 1850, those charged with obtaining peace treaties with the Indians of the frontier were commissioned, but this commission had no financing, and in addition, made no efforts to extend the laws that regulated commerce and peace among the Indians of the north and of Texas. The same Secretary of the Interior presented a complaint declaring that until the laws were observed in Texas they could not control the incursions on the Mexican border.[412]

The problem was complicated in 1851, with the beginning of the filibuster incursions. The North American government could not control the sale of arms to the filibusterers and the Indians. The spirit of the inhabitants of the frontier was hatred and rancor towards Mexico for not having been able to obtain mining lands. Thus, their own colonists worsened the situation. By gradually taking the land of the Indians, these latter were pushed to assault the frontier populations to be able to live, with the North American government shutting its eyes. In 1851, the finances of the Department of War were reduced from nine million to seven and a half million dollars. Instead of sending troops to the

[411] Rippy, Fred. "The Indians of the Southwest in the Diplomacy of the United States and Mexico", in Hispanic American Historical Review, II, August 1919, pp. 370-373.

[412] Ibidem, pp. 366-368.

frontier, discussions in Congress were centered around proposing measures to shrink the army.[413] In the period 1848-1852 there were never more than 150 cavalry troops on the frontier nor more than 600 soldiers.[414] Even though the Departments of Interior and Indian Affairs complained, Congress could not have cared less about complying with Article XI.

As we have mentioned, the Secretary of State did not do more than receive Mexican complaints and reclamations. In October, 1851, the North American ambassador in Mexico, Joseph P. Letcher, proposed to the Secretary of Exterior Relations a discussion of various points, among them the request for a modification of Article XI. The United States confirmed that its stipulations were impossible to fulfill and had to be changed to become effective.[415]

Mexico in turn became aware of the impossibility of maintaining peace on the frontier if the United States did not meet its obligations nor permit the passage of Mexican troops chasing the tribes. For the time being, in January 1852, Mexico showed its desire to discuss Article XI as long as it was reimbursed for the United States' failure to fulfill reclamations up to the date of the modification.[416]

During the rest of the year the problem of the Isthmus of Tehuantepec was discussed, giving the impression that Article XI was put to one side. In August, 1852, the Secretary of Exterior Relations asked the governor of Sonora to prepare a detailed list

---

[413] Ibidem, pp. 369-371.

[414] Ibidem, p. 378.

[415] Zorrilla, op. cit., pp. 287-288.

[416] Ibidem, p. 288.

of the indigenous incursions and the damages caused. Since Mexico estimated the damages to be between 39 and 40 million dollars and the United States only offered five and no opportunity to bargain diplomatic discussions did not progress. Unfortunately, the problem of Article XI became complicated with the Treaty of Tehuantepec and later with that of the Gadsden Purchase.

As we know, at the beginning of 1854 the Treaty of The Gadsden Purchase was ratified. With one of its points annulling forever Article XI of the Treaty of Guadalupe-Hidalgo, as well as XXII of the Treaty of Friendship and Commerce.

The Mexican reclamations resulting from the invasions carried out before 1853 were discussed 15 years later in the Convention of Arbitration of 1868.

The expansion of the North American colonies towards Indian lands continued and the attacks on the Mexican frontier did not cease until the decade of the 1880s.

XI. VIOLATIONS OF ARTICLE XI OF GUADALUPE-HIDALGO

Filibuster Invasions

The ink had not dried on the signatures of the Treaty of Guadalupe-Hidalgo when rumors began about the organization of new expeditions whose object was to fence off more parts of the national territory. Everyone not satisfied with the treaty and anxious to extend their power over more lands, financed and armed groups of adventurers ready to obtain land. The North American government had the obligation, per Article XI of the treaty, to stop attacks on the Mexican frontier, an obligation which remained pure theory and in practice they did little to enforce.

The Southern inhabitants of the United States thought that their country had the responsibility to annex more Mexican territory, not only to expand slavery, but to affirm their duty to propagate their superior institutions on inferior peoples. Providence, they said, connected them to Mexico, a country which was confounded by constant revolutions, and further, the average (*US*) citizen blamed the unfortunate national life (of Mexico) to the heritage of the Spanish Conquest, and justified United States' aggression with the assurance that they had to bring their liberationist institutions to the other side of the border. As Professor Weimberg said: "The decade of 1840 was possessed by a spiritual exaltation suggested by the superiority of North American institutions."[417]

---

[417] Weimberg, Albert, Destino Manifesto, ed. Paidós, Buenos Aires, p. 105.

Fortunately, the North American government did not share this sentiment. After the war and the violent discussions in Congress about the annexation of all of Mexico, only Southerners held the idea of obtaining more land from the neighboring country. In California, the newspapers proclaimed the right of the United States to occupy North Eastern Mexico with the purpose of "elevating the standard of living and redeeming its inhabitants from the corruption of the government and its dictators."[418] In addition, they thought that the North American government was obligated to annex Baja California and Sonora after the Mexican War. The *Daily Alta California* reported to its readers that common sense should have shown to the government the necessity of keeping at least one of the coasts of Baja California. The less belligerent thought that with patience, and keeping other powers from becoming involved, Baja California and Sonora would be theirs sooner or later. The editors of the most important newspaper of San Francisco showed their desire to wait philosophically for the development of Manifest Destiny.[419]

To these reasons, it is necessary to add that the climate of adventurism, obtaining easy money, and cheap romanticism that reigned in the Californian atmosphere since the discovery of gold, only encouraged the recent arrivals. Sonora appeared to them as a place where gold fever would extend as they thought that the California deposits should extend into the neighboring state. In Sonora, the central government tried to establish five military colonies, but given the political chaos, only one was established. The soldiers defending the state never exceeded 500. It is necessary to add the tremendous depopulation of the frontier, where Comanche and Yaqui attacks were still devastating. There were several Anglo adventurers who thought

[418] Allen, Joseph Stout, The Last Years of Manifest Destiny, Filibustering in Northern Mexico. p. 15.

[419] Ibidem. pp. 45-47.

they were the only ones who could defeat the Indians and bring peace and stability to the State of Sonora, but they arrived too late to the Californian gold rush and thus were left in search of other sources of easy money.

The majority of the so-called filibusterers began their relationship with Sonora by offering their services to the authorities to hunt Indians.[420] Disillusioned and unemployed they were ready to do anything but work. The majority belonged to the Southern middle class, sure of their racial and institutional superiority. When the Sonoran authorities branded them as meddlesome and persecuted them, furious, they tried to "help" the state by force. The territory of Baja California played a secondary role in these expeditions carried out between the end of the war and the signing of the Gadsden Treaty. They were only interested in La Mesilla as a base to get to Sonora.

Notwithstanding the importance of the filibuster expeditions to Sonora the Texans were making other plans to invade at the same time.

At the end of 1846, the old idea was reborn in Texas, that geographically, the area from the Rio Grande to the Sierra Madre Oriental belonged to them. Thus began a series of fraudulent maneuvers of a group called "buffalo hunters" who wanted to take control of the aforementioned territory under the pretext of establishing a so-called Republic of the Sierra Madre, which would, of course, allow slavery and the immigration of Anglos.[421] As before the war, the newspapers gave ample publicity to the adventure, including the names of the Mexicans who would help to establish it. This time, however, the project

---

[420] Ibidem, pp. 20-52.

[421] Zorrilla, Luis G., Historia de las relations entre Mexico y los Estados Unidos de America, ed. Porrua, vol. I, Mexico, p. 199.

did not obtain official approval. President Polk's diary shows that as soon as he heard of the project he considered it a violation of the Treaty of Guadalupe-Hidalgo and prohibited it.[422]

Although there are documents on the particulars in the Secretary of Exterior Relations archives the facts presented are incomplete. As a result little is known about the failed attempt to organize the Republic of the Sierra Madre. There is not even agreement on the date of the declaration of independence of the seven northern states of the Sierra Madre. Gastón García Cantú gives the date as June, 1848, while Zorrilla puts it one year later, with the documents dated January, 1849.

According to the information collected, the idea of the creation of such a republic dates to 1839, when a group of dissident Mexican federalists united with the North Americans with the object of founding it in the region. Here again there is confusion, given that North American historians called it the Republic of the Rio Grande. A third name is found in Nance's relation, that cites a letter from the Texan deputy, José Antonio Navarro, directed to the president of the Free Frontier States of the Mexican Republic (*Estados Libres Fronterizos de la Republica Mexicana*).[423] Perhaps this was the reason that there has not been a complete history written about the strange plan to separate the frontier states from the rest of the Mexican Republic. Nance states that the authorities of the Rio Grande were almost all old ex-functionaries of the bordering states with Vice President Francisco Vidaurri, ex-Governor of Coahuila and Texas; Manuel María del Llano, of Nuevo Leon, y Juan Nepomuceno Moyano, ex-Mayor of Matamoros, representing Tamaulipas. The new

---

[422] Polk, James, Diario de presidente polk, Antigua Librería Robredo, vol. I, México, p. 464.

[423] Nance, Joseph Milton, After San Jacinto, University of Texas Press, Austin, pp. 252-258.

government declared that their territory included the states of Tamaulipas, Nuevo León, Coahuila, and the portion of Texas west of the Rio Nueces. To the south it extended to the Sierra Madre Occidental including Zacatecas, Durango, Chihuahua, and New México.

On January 23, 1840, the government of the new country posted a decree, entitled the Organic Law of the Republic, in which it was stated that they had no ties to the Mexican government, and that they planned to fight against the current administration until it was destroyed. Remember that the government of the Republic of the Rio Grande was made up of fanatical federalists.

The Republic did not last long. After various battles against the centralist armies of General Arista, its leaders were obliged to ask for asylum in Texas. There, President Lamar was courteous, but resolved not to involve himself in their problems, since he was interested in obtaining Mexican recognition of his country through English influence. After a time, during which the Mexican government again rejected recognition of the independence of Texas, Lamar began negotiations with President Cardenas, President of the new Republic. According to the very controversial treaty between the Republic and Texas, the government of the Republic of the Rio Grande, recognized the independence of Texas, in exchange for the latter's recognition of its own.[424]

Meanwhile, President Cardenas obtained the support of the North American businessmen of the region who resented the re-establishment of centralist control on their businesses. In the district of Victoria y Béjar Cardenas was also able to awaken the enthusiasm of the inhabitants of Texas while the newspapers in

---

[424] Ibidem, pp. 290-293.

the area continued to ponder the richness of the Mexican cities and the lucrative sacking that could be done there.

After innumerable vicissitudes, in September 1840, nine months after the declaration of independence, the federalists of the Republic of the Rio Grande were able, with the help of Texas, to take control of Victoria, Tamaulipas.[425] There they organized the provisional government of the free and sovereign state of Tamaulipas that only lasted until October 6, when they had to abandon Victoria before the attack of General Arista. The reality of their failure caused the generals of the Republic of the Rio Grande to decide to come over to the centralist cause, thus finishing the short life of the Tamaulipas Republic. By December, 1840, they had disbanded their troops and sent the Texan volunteers home, not without first having woven an immense tangle of intrigue and betrayals.

The idea of an independent country, what the press of New Orleans called "a sister nation anxious for the assistance and sympathy of North Americans" remained dormant in the spirit of the southern United States.[426] President Polk, however, rushed to send orders to the attorneys of Saint Louis, Missouri, Arkansas, Louisiana, and Texas in an effort to stop all adventurer actions. The war had just ended and the United States government did not want to get involved in new invasion projects.

The history during these times is a true puzzle. In January, 1849, the Mexican consul in Havana notified the Secretary of Exterior Relations that its secret agents had discovered that two North American citizens, John Wist and Frances Meker, said to have a party in Tampico to achieve their ends, had travelled to Tampico with the intention of fomenting a pronouncement of annexation

---

[425] Ibidem, pp. 300-339.

[426]

by the United States. The consul communicated this to the Secretary of Exterior Relations, Luis Cuevas, who sent orders to Tampico not to let these men disembark.[427] From this we can deduce that Wist and Meker were part of the "buffalo hunters" group that Polk had ordered be arrested. The official letter is found in the folio entitled "República de la Sierra Madre" en the archives of the Secretary of Exterior Relations.

In an official letter that dates from February 3, 1840, the Senate asked Luis Cuevas to report on the actions taken to determine who the agents were who wanted to go to Tampico "with the object of promoting the independence of that state and the formation of the Republic of the Sierra Madre".[428] Thus it became clear that the two filibusterers were associated with the intent of invading Mexican territory.

The investigations began while Cuevas ordered the governor of Tamaulipas to arrest the individuals and judge them according to the law.[429] Fifteen days later news arrived from the consul in Havana, who communicated that the two filibusterers were agents of the cabinet in Washington who had solicited visas to go to Tampico from his consulate. Upon being refused they appeared to have gone to Mobile from where they must have left for Tampico.[430]

We know that on June 16, 1849, there was published in Brownsville, Texas, in English, the declaration of independence

---

[427] Archivo de la Secretaria de Relaciones Exteriores de México (ASREM), LE 1095, f, 74.

[428] Ibidem, f 76.

[429] Ibidem, f 75.

[430] Ibidem, f. 85.

of the Seven Northern States of the Sierra Madre, a copy of which is in the Exterior Relations archives.

It is known from these documents that on the same day the conspirators planned to publish the same declaration in Matamoros. An official letter from the governor of Chihuahua was directed to Cuevas 12 days later, in which he stated that due to the vigilance of General Ávalos, the announcement of independence was prevented on June 16, in Matamoros. What we do not know is how General Ávalos became aware of it, and how he frustrated the proclamation. In this same official letter the governor of Chihuahua asked for more military forces for the frontier "to frustrate the planned attempts by the few who wanted the independence of those states."[431]

The printed version of the declaration of independence reached the Secretary of Exterior Relations by General Arista, who sent to Cuevas asking in the name of the president that the foreigners and Mexican dissidents be discovered and punished.[432]

At the same time, Arista wrote to the governor of Tamaulipas informing him of the independence attempts and asking that he send 40 infantry to Matamoros to establish a strict watch over the town.[433] The information I was able to collect ended with an official letter from the Secretary of War to the governor of Tamaulipas in which he announced the arrival of new military forces in the region.[434] According to Zorrilla, the so-called invasion had degenerated into "an attempted attack on the

---

[431] Ibidem, f. 93.

[432] Ibidem. f. 88.

[433] ASREM H 250, 72-73, 6-2-27, ff, 3-4.

[434] ASREM LE 1095, f. 98.

238

customs house at Matamoros and in recovering in Mier, 15 wagons of confiscated merchandise."[435]

The historian Rippy, in his article on frontier problems, notes that the first big phase of the conflict between Mexico and the United States after the war relates to import laws. According to the federal law of October 4, 1845, the importation of all kinds of sugar, flour, butter, bacon, beets, rice, coffee, tobacco, baled cotton, cotton thread and cheap textiles had been forbidden. Additionally, the import duties of the permitted products were high causing what Rippy called the merchants' war that began in 1850 with the guerrillas of José María Carvajal.[436] Texan by birth and educated in Kentucky and Virginia, he was incited to rebellion by the desire to lead the Texan merchants' movement against the Mexican government, and to make a last attempt to create the Republic of the Sierra Madre. The North American merchants and the rich Texan merchants provided the money to arm filibuster expeditions and the name of the Republic of the Sierra Madre was no more than a subterfuge to attract Mexicans not ready to be annexed by the United States but who liked the idea of forming a new Republic free of the central government.

Thus it was that the third attempt to create such a republic was begun. In September 1849, Luis de la Rosa, ambassador in Washington, reported to have received a warning from the vice-consul in New Orleans about an expedition that was being organized in Round Island, "protected until now by various North American warships." The vice-consul assured him that the said expedition was directed towards Yucatan or Tampico to

---

[435] Zorrilla, op cit., p. 298.

[436] Rippy, Fred, The United States and Mexico, AMS Press, New York, p. 98.

promote the proclamation of the Republic of the Sierra Madre.[437] The response of the Secretary of Exterior Relations, dated October 11, 1849, baldly said that, "the necessary measures had been taken."[438] Zorrilla affirmed that "the United States acted with energy for the first and only time" and sent seven warships to impede the passage of the filibusterers. He added that five of them were caught but not brought to trial because public opinion in New Orleans prevented it.[439]

As we have said, the importation laws put into force after the war infuriated the Texan merchants. On April 4, 1849, Mexico permitted the introduction by Tamaulipas of critical supplies, free from all duties, against the interests of the Texans, who ran large scale contraband operations in the region.

On September 3, 1851, Carvajal published the Plan de la Loba, wherein were stipulated all of the requirements of the merchants, among them the permanent reduction of import duties, a soft touch in the punishment of the smugglers, and the withdrawal of federal troops from Tamaulipas. According to Zorrilla, the Plan included the virtual separation of this state from the rest of the country.[440]

Talk of establishing the Republic of the Sierra Madre returned, which would be accomplished, according to Carvajal, with the complicity of the governor of Tamaulipas and the military commander of the region.[441] Several hundred Texans and

---

[437] ASREM, LE 1096, f.96.

[438] Ibidem, f. 97.

[439] Zorrilla, op. cit., p. 299.

[440] Ibidem, p. 300.

[441] ASREM, 6-2-28, ff4-7.

enlisted ex-Mexicans were able to take Matamoros in October, 1851, and hold it for eleven days. They then returned to Texas, where the North American soldiers deserted to the last man to join the cause, which was nothing other than to take over Mexican territory. It was in this month that President Fillmore made his proclamation against the filibuster operations. In the archives of the Secretary of Exterior Relations there is an extended history by Carvajal about the Republic of the Sierra Madre, since North Americans were included in its ranks and the diplomatic claims were many.

José Fernando Ramirez, Secretary of Exterior Relations, accused the United States of violating the Treaty of Guadalupe-Hidalgo for allowing the continuous passage of Carvajal and his men from one side of the border to the other.[442] He specifically blamed not only the merchants and the landowners of Brownsville as instigators of the rebellion to annex frontier lands, but also the businessmen of Tehuantepec who did everything possible to distract the attention of the Mexican government.[443]

In the opinion of the consul in Brownsville who accused the residents of Brownsville of lending aid to Carvajal, Carvajal's rebellion "threatened to dismember a large part of Mexican territory."[444] For his part, the ambassador in Washington, Luis de la Rosa, presented claims "for tolerating and dissimulating so that the Texan authorities allowed the passage of 500 armed men towards Mexico." This was a clear violation of the treaty, and the

---

[442] ASREM, 1-1-61, ff. 3-4.

[443] ASREM, H 250, 73-72, 4 ff. 7-8.

[444] ASREM, 1-1-69.

ambassador declared that the United States government was responsible for these actions.[445]

In response to this note, Daniel Webster, Secretary of State, answered that his government did not have laws prohibiting aggressions considered as part of a national uprising and had no news about hostilities on the part of North Americans against Mexican citizens.[446]

The case of Carvajal was typical of the relations between the two countries: each time a grave problem came up on the frontier, the government of the neighboring country (the United States) pretended not to know anything but promised to investigate.

To Webster's answer, on the point that the movement was internal, the consul in Brownsville disagreed. He noted that it was a rebellion supported by foreigners, as the Texans had not agreed to the dividing line established by the Treaty of Guadalupe-Hidalgo, wanting to extend it to the Sierra Madre.

At the beginning of 1852, the consul became aware of the presence of Carvajal in Brownsville and pushed for his arrest. He was told that it could only be done if there were charges against Carvajal.[447] It is clear that the local authorities were not interested in making Mexican government charges against Carvajal. It was said that his guerrillas were backed by King and

---

[445] ASREM, H 250 72-73, 4, ff. 7-8.

[446] Ibidem, ff. 37-39.

[447] ASREM, 1-1-69.

Kennedy, two of the largest cattle producers in the south of Texas.[448] The situation became more tense.

In March 1852, when the *Picayune* of New Orleans reported that General Harney was doing everything possible to prevent the passage of armed men toward Mexico. The reporter added that given the small number of soldiers at Harney's command, Carvajal would not find it difficult to cross by one of the innumerable passes.[449]

In the middle of the attempts to buy La Mesilla (Gadsden Purchase), and certainly to pacify the Mexican authorities, the North American government organized a jury on the Carvajal question. In March, 1852, they announced that Carvajal and eleven United States citizens were arrested. They would not be tried until the new session of the court, in June, and were thus allowed to go free on bail. Immediately, Carvajal began preparing his fourth intervention into Mexican territory, which took place in December, 1852, taking Reynosa and reaching Nuevo León.

To gain public support, Carvajal's people announced the Republic of the Sierra Madre, from which to prepare expeditions to Cuba and Tehuantepec.[450] Before such news, Luis de la Rosa, again addressed Webster, reminding him of his protests from October, 1851. He asked that Webster show his support of the

---

[448] McWilliams, Carey, Al norte de México, Siglo XXI, Mexico, p. 119.

[449] ASREM, 6-2-28.

[450] ASREM, 1-1-69.

treaty by ordering that the necessary measures be taken to protect the border.[451]

In April, 1853, he was still speaking of Carvajal, who had recently invaded Mexican territory. One month later, Lucas Alamán, then Secretary of Exterior Relations, wrote to Luis de la Rosa, telling him that Carvajal was again free. Conkling, the North American ambassador in Mexico, declared that according to the laws of the United States, based in English common law, "a person arrested by a Liberal accusation had the right to be promptly tried and confronted witnesses. If these did not appear at trial, he should be given his liberty."[452] Of course there were no witnesses against Carvajal as the Texans did not consider it a crime to invade the hated Mexico. His actions were not only applauded by the public, but were backed and encouraged by them, as well. Like in California, the filibusterers were popular heroes.

The Carvajal case was one of the most prickly to keep our government occupied until 1862 (the French Intervention). The curious thing is that Carvajal, after being checked along the entire border, ended up becoming governor of Tamaulipas, named by Juárez himself, who in 1865 sent him to Washington in search of a loan to prosecute the war against the French. Carvajal negotiated in his own style, a transaction for thirty million pesos guaranteed by half a million hectares (1.2 million acres) of mining land in Tamaulipas and San Luis Potosi, plus 80% of all federal and state income, calculated to be three million pesos annually; and in addition in exchange for the loan, 500 square leagues (1500 sq. miles) of agricultural land in those two states, with the right to colonize them and privileges to build a railroad from Matamoros to San Luis Potosi. These famous guarantees

---

[451] Ibidem,.

[452] ASREM, H 110, 73-0, "853"/1, ff. 128-129.

were so many and so extensive that Matias Romero, then ambassador of Mexico in Washington, did not accept them.[453] Proof, it seems to us, that governor Carvajal never rejected his fanatic admiration for the United States of America. It was with reason, that at the beginning of his career, "he was publicly called a traitor, bought by 'gringo gold'."[454]

A final note on Carvajal exists in the archives of the Secretary of Exterior Relations. In December 1872, the investigative Commission of the Northern Frontier took the testimony of José de la Mora, a citizen of Matamoros, who declared that in the siege of that city in the year 1855, General Carvajal brought a large number of North Americans and that during the siege all of the help and provisions came from Brownsville.[455]

As in California, the average Texan was in agreement with the intent of the invasion and believed that his country had the duty to take more Mexican territory. The filibusters of their era were like film artists in ours. They were always absolved by juries of their region. However, the government of the United States at that time had other interests. President Taylor decided at the end of 1849 to support Article XI of the Treaty of Guadalupe-Hidalgo and remembered that the invasions were violations of it and as a result the invaders were not protected by their government.[456]

Nance (see Chapter 4) explains that the Whigs, to whose party Taylor belonged, were not expansionists. His successor,

[453] Zorrilla, op. it. pp. 451-453.

[454] ASREM, 4-2-5646, ff. 1-3.

[455] Ibidem, ff. 3-5.

[456] Zorrilla, op. cit., p. 299.

President Fillmore, pronounced a proclamation in October 1851, in which he threatened the filibusterers with denying them all protection. In the archives of the Secretary of Exterior Relations there is a letter from President Fillmore directed to the general commander of the Department of the West, in which he asked to use all necessary means to obstruct the filibuster expeditions.[457]

Mexican Attempts to Protect the Frontier

In July, 1848, President Joaquin Herrera passed the first of the colonization laws given after the war. Following this decree, various military colonies were established on the frontier with the aim of defending the region, and the colonial civil government could proceed to form a municipal government under civilian control. The law also established the division of the frontier in three parts, the east with the states of Tamaulipas and Coahuila, the center with Chihuahua, and the west formed by Sonora and Baja California. He also directed that ten thousand pesos be paid annually to the Indians to keep the peace.

The colonization plan was very similar to the Spanish presidio system in which each area would have a military organization.. Volunteer soldiers would receive cultivatable land when his enlistment was over. To promote the establishment of these colonies, the government was ready to advance six months' salary and provide the land necessary to build living quarters. In addition, taxes were forgiven to married colonists and to those who got married in the first four months of the colonization. The law of 1848 expressly excluded foreigners from the frontier colonies. Certainly, the Texan experience had motivated such a clause.[458] At first, the problems were so severe that by 1850 it

---

[457] ASREM, 1-1-65, f. 12.

[458] Stout, op. cit., pp. 28-30.

had only been possible to found nine of the 18 colonies planned and more only partially so. With time, the colonies were abandoned because of Indian attacks, lack of protection and governmental inefficiency. However, some politicians and military from the frontier states continued to show interest in the said colonies. One of them, Mariano Paredes, explained to the Chamber of Deputies on August 16, 1850, his plans for the frontier.[459]

The colonies were supposed to be organized by civilians whom the central government would help by suppressing taxes for 25 years. It was necessary that Guaymas be tax free for 25 years to stimulate commercial development in Sonora. As for the colonists, these were to be only Europeans and Mexicans, as North Americans were prohibited from colonizing. The concession of 177 irrigable acres was given to each head of family and the assurance that their property and liberty would be respected. To those who wanted to have cattle, they gave 4.425 acres of land. They wanted to continue with the impresario system which had begun in Texas whereby a single person was given a contract to import a certain number of colonists, in this case European colonists, in a certain area that would, in time, be incorporated into the nation. The only obligation was that they could not sell their properties for 80 years. As a means of assurance, Paredes asked for the creation of a naval guard to patrol the area between Cabo San Lucas and the mouth of the Colorado River. Its mission would be to defend and inspect all the ships that crossed the zone and to make a list of their cargos

---

[459] Mariano Paredes, Proyectos de leyes sobre colonización y comercio en el estado de Sonora, presentados a la Cámara de Diputados por el representante de aquel estado en la sesión extraordinaria de dia ... 1850, Ignacio Cumplido, México, pp. 3-5.

to control contraband and the filibusterers.[460] Paredes's plan was not accepted by the Chamber of Deputies most certainly because the plan included foreigners in the colonization.

In January, 1852, Juan M. Almonte presented a new plan for the frontier. Unlike his predecessors, Almonte did not propose colonization but rather to put an end to the Indian attacks. Only when the region was secure could one speak about populating it. His plan required a study of the zone, the division of the land into lots and its later sale. In the plan he established that the state governments would have the ability to give out the land and create new towns. The central government would supply 500 pesos to transport each family to the interior, paid in installments, and with low interest. Above all, Almonte asked for intensive publicity in favor of colonization from the principal European countries, especially Germany and Belgium. Foreigners would be free of taxes, military service, and municipal obligations for five years. He even went so far as to ask for illegal European immigrants.[461] The proposals of Paredes and Almonte were never approved by Congress. Meanwhile the situation on the frontier got worse every day.

The Secretary of Exterior Relations was aware of the problem. It is evident that what Mexico lost was the work of its politicians, and that which was saved, the work of its diplomats. In 1850, a circular was sent to the state authorities in which they were prohibited from extending permits to foreigners to travel to Baja California.[462] From that year until the beginning of the troubles of the Reforma, the protests of the Secretary of Exterior

---

[460] Stout, op. cit., pp. 30-31.

[461] Juan M. Almonte, Proyecto de leyes sobre colonización, citado pro Stout Allen, op. cit., pp. 34-36.

[462] Zorrilla, op. cit., p. 304.

Relations multiplied. There are many documents attesting to this fact in the midst of the political confusion, and of the sure and consistent defense of the territory by the diplomats. These were to such a degree, the commander of the United States forces on the frontier sent a note to the Secretary of War of the United States, in which he comments that over the years they had received complaints in regard to defending the said territories from the Mexican ambassador in Washington, many of them, according to the commander who sent the note, without foundation or very exaggerated.[463]

The existence of this note resulted in an unfortunate discovery. It seems that there was a national consensus that no one was protecting the frontier. Although the claims for violations of the territory or attempts to do so make up a large file which contradicts this. The North American consuls were well aware of everything concerning invasions of Mexican territory and faithfully reported the main part of articles about Mexico published in the most influential newspapers, through which we know that high federal and state authorities were discussing the Mexican situation. The Mexican ambassador in France, for example, sent a report about an article published in the *New York Herald* where it was reported that the Attorney General had declared that his country had an obligation not only to annex California and New Mexico, but also Chihuahua and Sonora. The Attorney General added that on another occasion the United States would put its frontier to the south of Mexico so that no more disputes would ever arise.[464] Expansion euphoria was such that the governor of Chihuahua asked the Mexican Congress "to

---

[463] ASREM, LE, 1096, f. 15.

[464] Ibidem, f. 128.

affirm and ratify in the most solemn manner possible that the state of Chihuahua belonged to the Mexican Republic."[465]

President Fillmore in two messages to Congress (1850-1851), declared that the army of the frontier was insufficient to fulfill the Treaty of Guadalupe-Hidalgo. And in October, 1851, he announced a proclamation prohibiting all United States citizens from joining filibuster operations, warning them that the government would not protect them.

Notwithstanding, the Mexican reaction was minimal as they no longer believed in the good intentions of the neighboring government. A letter of the then ambassador of Mexico in Washington in which he tries to explain Fillmore's proclamation was due to having just frustrated an invasion of Cuba from Corpus Christi. Spain demanded satisfaction and was supported by England and France. Even the most radical newspapers were making moderate statements, and underlining the difficulties of having a war with Spain. They also asked for moderation in Mexican relations and reported on the rapacity of the filibusterers.

The Mexican ambassador in Washington also mentioned, as another reason behind the proclamation that prohibited United States citizens from joining the filibusterers, that is the treaty on Tehuantepec, as he said that the government of the United States would take advantage of all means to accomplish the ratification of this treaty. In sum, he guessed that Fillmore's proclamation would remain unenforced and was sure Fillmore would not energetically try to prevent the filibusterers.

More than six months after the proclamation, the Secretary of Exterior Relations, José Fernando Ramirez, continued sending

---

[465] ASREM, 2-1-1875, f. 5.

his claims to the neighboring country for the invasion of Mexican territory. It is curious, but in his letter to the North American envoy, Ramirez complained "of the harmony between the two countries being continually broken, and especially since October, 1851, by continuous thefts, violence, assassinations, and violations of the territory". October, 1851, was the month of President Fillmore's proclamation, and Ramirez asked for the reason why the North American government had reduced its forces on the frontier.

The First Filibuster in California

In January, 1851, the newspaper, *Daily Alta California*, reported to its readers that the quartermaster general of the army, Joseph Morehead of California, had stolen 400 rifles and 90 boxes of ammunition from an expedition. Two months later the governor offered 1500 dollars for his arrest, accusing him of organizing an expedition of conquest against Mexican territory.

Morehead, seeking easy riches in the mines of Sonora, decided to organize a group of adventurers to invade the state. The San Francisco newspapers compared his action to that of pirates on the high seas. [466]

After innumerable difficulties, Morehead, along with some of his men, were able to escape towards Sonora embarking for Mazatlán.

In Mexico and California, the news of the expedition caused great concern. The newspapers revived the old hate against the "Yankees", while in California they asked citizens not to cooperate with the adventurers, as Mexico was a friend and the

----

[466] Stout, op. cit., p. 42.

251

United States had the obligation of impeding filibuster expeditions.[467]

Arriving in Mazatlán, the Mexican authorities inspected the ship and found no arms or ammunition and permitted the entry of the group who said that they were miners in search of work. This is all the documents say, and it is not totally certain that this was actually them. Stout says that following some historians, they stayed in Sonora as miners until the arrival of the William Walker expedition. Others are sure they returned to the United States. Whatever may be, the Morehead expedition is the first that wanted to invade Sonora.

In May of that year, the Secretary of War wrote to the commander of the Pacific region, reminding him that one of his duties, according to the Treaty of Guadalupe-Hidalgo, was to defend Mexican territory from attacks by Indians "or of others who originate in the United States".[468] On December 2, 1851, President Millard Fillmore, in his message to Congress, denounced the filibuster expeditions and asked the local representatives to stop them. Stout assures us that, in practice, the United States government and the authorities of California did very little to impede them."[469] The Californians, for their part, thought that the United States should annex Baja California and Sonora.

Economic and political disorder reigned in California. Great numbers of immigrants kept coming in search of easy money and fame. France, too, was having difficult moments being in an economic crisis after the revolution of 1848. As a result, a great

---

[467] Ibidem, p. 43.

[468] Ibidem, p. 46.

[469] Ibidem, p. 47.

252

number of gallic adventurers decided to try their luck in California spurred by the news about the ease of finding gold nearly 20,000 French immigrated to California between 1849 and 1851.[470]

However, when they got to California gold fever had devastated the area and earning money was as difficult as anywhere else. Despite this, the newspapers reported that in 1848, Guaymas had exported five million pesos of gold and silver. It was believed that the gold veins in California extended into Sonora, along with the rumor that the Mexican government wanted to establish colonies to protect the frontier as much from the attacks of the Apaches as from the North American invasions, and that the French were capable of doing both things.

In 1850, the French in California heard that the Mexican vice consul in San Francisco was looking for colonists who were not North American to found a town on the frontier. The Mexican government, it was said, promised financial help when they arrived in Guaymas. It was for these reasons that the French appeared enthusiastic about the attempt at colonization in the northwest frontier of Mexico. But in reality, the French immigrants in California were adventurers, not colonists, and only took advantage of the situation to enter Mexico looking for mines and easy money. The French attempts were the same as the North Americans'. It is for this and other reasons that the history of the filibuster expeditions in northwest Mexico is so confused.[471]

First French Attempts at Colonization

---

[470] Ibidem, p. 50.

[471] ASREM, 2-C-R-1, ff. 41-42.

The first attempt at legal French colonization was that of Charles Pindray, who passed through Guaymas with 88 Frenchmen in November 1851.[472] Pindray had organized the expedition at the insistence of William Schleiden, vice consul of Mexico in San Francisco. The government of Sonora, thinking that the expeditions would help them against the Apache, allowed the French three leagues of land near Cocóspera, in the valley of the San Miguel river, 30 horses, 30 mules, 30 burros, and 1800 pesos in silver. The expedition was in Cocóspera for several months. The French had received land to cultivate but what they were looking for were gold and silver mines. It was at this time that the authorities became aware of the revolutionary past of Pindray and realized his only interest were the mines and decided to expel him from the country. He finally died and his men returned to California. Thus ended the first legal attempt to colonize Sonora. At the same time, Sainte-Marie and Pierre Charles de Saint Amant, consuls of France in California, planned new expeditions in search of abandoned gold mines in Sonora. They were able to find one, but the lack of nearby water ruined the project. Meanwhile, they continued making efforts to recruit another group of compatriots willing to join the adventure.

Gastón Raousset de Boulbon. The Second Expedition to Sonora

Raousset reached California in August of 1850, with the intention of quickly becoming rich. Patrice Dillon, the French Consul in San Francisco, straightened him out on the opportunities in that city, but pushed him to go to Sonora.

Dillon wrote to the French ambassador in Mexico asking him to help Raousset, and through him obtained permission of the

---

[472] The stories of Pindray y Raousset Boulbon are taken from Stout, Allen, op. cit., pp. 58-79, as they are more complete.

Mexican government to take a group of French, supposedly to work in the mines. In the eighteenth century, gold and silver mines had been found on the northern frontier of Sonora in a place called Real de Arizona. The government hoped that the French would find them again, and they would be a cushion against the Apache attacks and North American invaders.

As a result, Raousset signed a contract on April 7, 1852 under the name of Jecker, Torre and Company. From this contract a company called Restored Company of the Mine of Arizona was established. According to the contract, Raousset had to recruit 150 French in San Francisco and travel to Guaymas and meet with government agents who would accompany him to the site. If they found mines or other valuable, half would belong to the company. To protect its investment, the company commissioned an agent who would follow the expeditionaries and who would also get the help of various government authorities of President Mariano Arista. Everyone had high hopes for the expedition.

Raousset returned to San Francisco with the aim of recruiting men, taking advantage of the fact that the central government would discuss with the Sonoran government about donations of land. The Barron and Forbes Company organized a colonization corporation similar to the French, with the only difference being that all its colonists were Mexican. Against the interests of Jecker, Barron and Forbes dedicated themselves to turning the Sonoran government against the French expedition.

When Raousset and his men got to Guaymas, they expected to be received by the authorities, but to their great surprise they only found hostility and obstacles to their projects. They were ordered to do the contrary to what had been planned, and they were prohibited from military operations and finally, governor Cubillas accused them of having violated the laws of the country by bringing two pieces of artillery.

255

Upon the news of what had happened in Sonora, the French ambassador in Mexico withdrew the Restored Company of the Mine of Arizona for fear that the French government would be accused of intervention. Meanwhile, the expedition was held up in Guaymas, and the personality of Raousset made matters worse. He attracted many enemies, as he liked to call himself the Sultan of Sonora, and even governor Cubillas called him a filibusterer.

In July 1852, the French consul in San Francisco announced that he had gotten permission to go to the frontier with Arizona. But there arose a new enemy, General Miguel Blanco, commander of the troops in Sonora. He and Cubillas decided to detain the French, asking that Raousset and the agent of the company, present themselves in Arizpe, with the intent of taking them prisoner. Raousset sent the company agent and one of his men to represent him. As was thought, both were arrested.

At this time, knowing of the intrigues of the Barron and Forbes Company, Raousset understood he could not expect help from the Mexican government and decided to go and look for Manuel Gándara to help him rebel against the government of Sonora. Gándara had participated in various centralist and federalist rebellions and had been governor of Sonora on three or four occasions. Raousset thought he would be a good ally in the rebellion, but Gándara declined to participate, and thus the Frenchman had few possibilities of triumphing.

The pressures against the French continued. When Raousset refused to go before General Blanco, who announced that Raousset could only obtain government protection if he renounced his nationality and obeyed the laws of Mexico, and only in this way could he reach his goal and obtain permission to begin the colonization. Finally, Blanco asked that the French reduce their number to 50 men without arms who would work in the mines. The army would protect them. Raousset refused and Blanco went after him.

The Mexican newspapers were already spreading rumors that France had sent agents to California with the aim of recruiting more men to send to Sonora. Raousset argued that the right was given to him in the contract with Jecker y Torre, but the Sonoran Congress repealed all of the mining petitions and ordered a military expedition against the French. Governor Cubillas tried to calm down the situation by asking the French to accept being civil colonists, lay down their arms, and take Mexican citizenship. At the end of October, 1852, the French decided to fight for what they considered their rights. They took Hermosillo and in this way ended up convincing the Sonorans that they were indeed filibusterers. The Sonoran Congress asked the citizens to expel all of the French. At this critical moment, Raousset fell ill with dysentery while his men obtained free passage to Guaymas, where they surrendered on November 4, 1853. Afterwards, he received a letter from the French consul in San Francisco asking him to organize another expedition. Jecker y Torre had paid the Mexican government for the damage and harm done by the expedition.

The *New York Daily Times* commented that English and French newspapers had paid a lot of attention to the Raousset affair "because they wanted to attract the attention of their citizens and predispose them to asking for a protectorate in Mexico when the time was right."[473]

Count Gastón de Raousset-Boulbon returned to San Francisco at the beginning of 1853, feeling he had been tricked, as he had signed a contract with Jecker y Torre, which the Sonorans did

---

[473] Ibidem, p. 78.

not respect. He wanted vengeance, and thus informed the newspapers and his friends his intentions of returning to Sonora. He planned to organize a true military expedition. Andre Levasseur, ambassador of France in Mexico, wrote him inviting him to come and meet with Santa Anna, who was again in power.

Raousset concluded that the news of his expedition had intimidated the dictator, and he resolved to ask him to form a military government in Sonora, and in July, 1853, he offered to bring to the state several thousand colonists who would defend the frontier. As his offer was not accepted, he proposed soldiers to fight the Indians. Notwithstanding the warnings of Gándara, governor of Sonora, Santa Anna offered Raousset a contract to bring 500 French to work the mines and fight the Indians, but the French refused the contract for not being sufficiently advantageous. In December, 1853, he returned to San Francisco more resentful than ever. There, he tried to organize an expedition against the government of Santa Anna, but did not find much support among the Mexican exiles in California. In addition, the invasion of the North American filibusterer, William Walker, had awakened new nationalist sentiments inciting the Mexican press began to attack Raousset's attempts to organize a second expedition. The government named General José María Yáñez to protect the border of Sonora and prohibited the entry of armed foreigners. Orders were given to closely watch the North Americans living near the coast.

In January, 1854, the Secretary of Exterior Relations, Manuel Díaz de Bonilla, asked the French ambassador that his government send a warship to impede the disembarkment of filibusters, especially Raousset. The French agreed as France considered the acts violations of Mexican territory like piracy.

As a way to stop the effectiveness of Raousset, Santa Anna ordered Luis del Valle, consul in San Francisco, to organize a group of foreigners to colonize the north of Mexico and that among them to include Raousset's men to thus separate them. The Mexican government would promise their enlistment for one year in the Mexican army and a donation of fertile land at the end.

Raousset, hearing of the Mexican government's plan, thought to frustrate it. It was at this time that General John E. Wood, who was commissioned by his government to stop the filibusterer invasions into Mexico, appeared in California. The affair was complicated by Wood who became involved in the tangle of intrigue and ended up accusing Del Valle of treason against the Mexican government for conspiring with Raousset. He ordered him to be arrested based on a law of 1818 that prohibited arming armies on United States territory to attack a friendly country. The North American press criticized their general for resuscitating a totally unknown law. The French consul broke relations with the United States and the affair became a comedy of errors. Wood admitted his error about Del Valle, arrested Dillon (the French consul); and being terrified with the possibility of a French intervention, dedicated himself to fortifying the entrance to the port of San Francisco. The Secretary of War reprimanded him and finally offered his excuses to France.

During this time, Del Valle had sent the first group of one thousand colonists, when in reality Santa Anna had ordered him to send them in small groups. Naturally, loyal Raousset followers, who continued to prepare for the invasion in San Francisco, had infiltrated the group. When they got to Guaymas, the locals were concerned to see such a large group of foreigners. General Yáñez knew he did not have the forces to fight them and the foreigners had come armed with a contract. Therefore, he decided to accept them like soldiers, pay them six reales a day, and arm them with old muskets. Meanwhile, he sped up his preparations to receive Raousset.

In May 1854, Raousset left San Francisco with eight men, 180 rifles, and sufficient ammunition. After many hardships he arrived in Guaymas. There, talks took place ending in threats, and the decisive battle of the 13th of July, 1854, when the French were defeated. Count Gastón Raousset-Boulbon was executed the 12th of August 1854. Thus ended the career of a man determined to invade Sonora in search of riches, adventure and vengeance against the Jecker y Torre company for breach of a signed contract.[474]

William Walker, The Third Expedition

Self-styled lawyer and doctor, William Walker arrived in California at the end of 1850. He was assistant to the publisher of the *San Francisco Daily Herald* and later, due to a duel, for a time lived in Auburn, California. There he met a group interested in establishing a military colony on the Mexican frontier "under the guise of civilian colonists following Mexican colonization laws", for which they commissioned a certain Emory with the end of obtaining donations of land near Arizpe.[475] The petition coincided with the Raousset adventure in Sonora. The local authorities refused to cede the land and the citizens of Auburn abandoned the plan.

After Raousset's fracaso, it was Emory who suggested to Walker the idea of becoming filibusters. Together, they met with General José Castro, who, being exiled, the adventurers believed would be ready to start a revolution in northern Mexico. The general turned them down. It was then that Walker and a certain Watkins decided to go to Guaymas to test the Mexican reaction

---

[474] Ibidem, pp. 101-121.

[475] Ibidem, p. 83.

towards North American colonists. In June, 1853, Walker and Watkins disembarked in Guaymas, where, although they were unable to meet the governor, they became aware that the citizens wanted help against the Apaches. They announced this upon their return to California. The news infuriated the Sonoran authorities. Diez de Bonilla, Secretary of Exterior Relations accused Walker before James Gadsden, ambassador of the United States in Mexico, of selling stock since May 1853 to establish a republic. He asked that he prohibit the granting of documents to travel to the interior.

Many men enlisted in the Walker expedition, as being a filibusterer was very popular in California.[476]
However, President Fillmore had given orders to stop invasions of Mexico, and General Hitchcock was disposed to enforce them and for this reason confiscated Walker's ship. Public opinion rose up against Hitchcock, and while the case was debated in court, Walker and his friends escaped in a smaller vessel in which after passing by Cabo San Lucas, they arrived in La Paz. Surprising the inhabitants they took the defenseless town in less than half an hour and arrested the governor. Walker ordered the raising of the flag of the so-called Republic of Baja California, but as his real aim was to conquer Sonora with its rich gold and silver mines he only stayed a few days in La Paz. On November 8, 1853 they arrived at Cabo San Lucas from where they left almost immediately for Ensenada. Walker wanted to be near the United States to get men and munitions with which to keep his Republic. He sent his Secretary of State, Frederick Emory, to obtain provisions and recruit more men from Alta California. The newspaper, *Daily Alta California* of San Francisco, reported that the people had received the news with great joy, and

---

[476] Ibidem, p. 86.

everyone acclaimed the adventure "as a new step towards accomplishing the Manifest Destiny of the Anglo-Saxon race."[477]

Emory established a recruitment office under the new flag of two red bands, one white, and two stars.

Meanwhile, the diplomatic world discussed the adventure at a time when the governments of Mexico and the United States were concluding discussions on the Gadsden Purchase. Ambassador Gadsden wanted peace for which he asked for all North American warships in the Pacific to intercept the Caroline, Walker's ship. In reality it was not necessary, as the first officer of the ship was aware of the importance of the events and took off with the ship, whose owner was the son of the North American consul in Guaymas.

In Ensenada, Walker was constantly attacked by a group of patriots under the command of Guadalupe Meléndez, who treated him as a bandit. With no more provisions, Walker decided to take the military colony of Santo Tomas, 50 kilometers from Ensenada. The commander, Colonel Francisco del Castillo Negrete, with the people of Meléndez, succeeded in repelling the attack and placed Ensenada under siege for several days. Walker's men were able to break the siege and sent a justification for their conduct to newspapers in California. The *San Diego Herald* and *Daily Alta California* published a declaration by Walker in which he affirmed having taken Baja California and was ready to conquer Sonora to bring the light of civilization and democracy to the region because the Mexican authorities were not in charge and the two provinces would always remain in a half wild state without culture, full of lazy people and only half civilized.

---

[477] Ibidem, p. 91, cited in the *Daily Alta California* of December 9, 1853.

On December 28, 1853, 200 more men arrived in Ensenada, however, for lack of provisions, discipline and money, by January 18, the Republic was on the point of disappearing. On February 13, 1854, Walker decided to abandon Ensenada and to try to take Sonora which he had previously proclaimed to annex. The Republic from this moment on, was called the Republic of Sonora. On February 28, he forced the inhabitants of San Vicente to sign a document in which they renounced their Mexican citizenship and became subjects of the Republic of Sonora; however, problems accumulated. General Wood had arrested Secretary of State Emory, accusing him of filibustering. Until this time, the United States had done little to stop the illegal activities. The local California authorities openly supported the filibusterers, and Fillmore's Secretary of War, Jefferson Davis, took little notice of them. Wood also accused Raousset de Bourbon and took the consuls of France and Mexico prisoner.

Meanwhile, Walker and his men suffered many vicissitudes on the difficult route to Sonora. Without food, dehydrated, and with a large number of deserters, 25 men returned to San Vicente and during the second half of April they saw many confrontations with Meléndez's men. Finally, on May 8, 1854, they returned to the United States and in San Diego were arrested by Mayor McKinstrey. The legal proceedings that took place in San Francisco were epic. They denied having been filibusterers, and accused the Mexicans of having maltreated them! The jury declared them innocent after only eight minutes of deliberation. This experience did not dishearten Walker nor the others who imitated him. Count Gastón de Raousset de Bourbon (the sultan of Sonora), prepared a second expedition. Walker, for his part, then tried to take over Nicaragua, which he later did. Sixteen years after the invasion of Baja California he died by firing squad in Central America.[478]

Mexico complained diplomatically at various times about the actions of Walker. First, it accused the United States government of not stopping Walker's preparations in California; then, of not impeding his sailing when his intentions were notoriously made public; and finally, it asked that the North American authorities be punished "as they were responsible for not suppressing the expeditions against a friendly country." Their negligence had convinced Mexico that the official intentions were to annex more territory.

Bancroft has a long chapter about the activities of the filibusterers, even though his patriotism kept him from condemning them. However, in the last quote of his chapter Bancroft points out the following:

"The United States is accused of complicity in the events for the sole reason of its indifference and negligence to impede or punish them. The principal authorities have to answer for this additional aspect."[479]

---

[478] Ibidem, p. 101.

[479] Bancroft, Hubert Howe, The Works of Hubert Howe Bancroft, History of California, vol. VI, San Francisco, p. 603.

XII. TREATY OF LA MESILLA OR GADSDEN'S PURCHASE

The problem of La Mesilla (Gadsden's Purchase) was the result of the discussions on fixing border limits (Figure 8). According to the Treaty of Guadalupe-Hidalgo, the commissioners charged with settling the line of the frontier had to finish their work within a year of ratification. Work started much later, and the Mexicans did not waste time in accusing North Americans of being more preoccupied with other topics than in tracing the dividing line. But at the end of the decade of the 1840s, the North Americans were very interested in beginning construction of a railroad. Already during the conquest of New Mexico (1846), Lieutenant Emory was put in charge of investigating where the best route would be. According to his studies, an adequate route was the valley of the Gila river, to the southwest of El Paso. This detail was not relayed to Trist, so that the frontier boundary was located to the north of the area indicated by Emory.[480] In the give and take of what followed, this region, called La Mesilla, was occupied by a group of New Mexicans who did not want to live in United States territory, and who decided to found a settlement in the south of New Mexico.

At the same time, the geographers and surveyors ran into many controversies. The map on which they based their discussion during the discussions of the treaty was that of Disturnell, and the Commission determined that it contained measuring errors. Immediately, both sides tried to obtain more territory for their respective countries. They finally reached an agreement, but A.B. Gray, one of the members of the North American commission, who was absent during the discussions, returned and did not accept the accord, and the controversies began again.

---

[480] Luis G. Zorrilla, História de las Relaciones entre México y Estados Unidos, ed. Porrúa, México, 1965, p. 337.

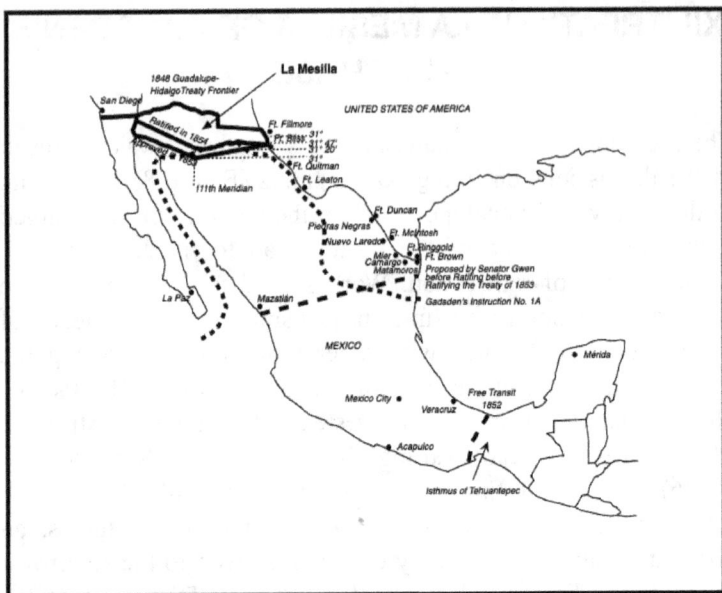

FIGURE 8. PROJECTS FOR THE ACQUISITION OF
TERRITORIES (GADSDENS PURCHASE, ALSO
CALLED THE PURCHASE OF MESILLA) (BASED ON
LUIS G. ZORRILLA, HISTÓRIA DE LAS RELACIONES
ENTRE MÉXICO Y LOS ESTADOS UNIDOS DE
AMÉRICA, 2 VOLS. ED. PORRÚA, 1965

The Mexican commissioners complained that their North
American colleagues were more interested in studying the
possibilities of the region (especially with respect to railroads),
than in the zigzag of the disputed frontier. Emory returned to his
post as a member of the commission and insisted that
Disturnell's map was wrong, and that the frontier was too far
north. Based on his investigations, he knew that the only possible

pass for a railroad between Texas and California was in this region.[481]

Also, following Bemis in *A Diplomatic History of the U.S.*, the proslavery party in the United States Congress wanted to build a railroad along the southern territory so that the land would remain in the hands of pro-slavery farmers. Jefferson Davis, Secretary of War, was determined to obtain this route for a railroad.[482]

Meanwhile, he named William Carr Lane as the new military governor of New Mexico. Lane proceeded to proclaim that all of the area north of El Paso belonged to New Mexico, and had been for many years. The governor of Chihuahua, Trias, then entered the scene. He had received a letter from William Carr Lane in which he asked for him to turn over La Mesilla. The governor notified the Secretary of Exterior Relations that he had travelled through the region of La Mesilla to determine the number of men who could be counted on in case of an invasion. The political chief of the region informed Trias that the governor of New Mexico had asked for a force of volunteers to occupy the area. Trias wanted to know if it would be convenient to move some of his forces to La Mesilla in case the volunteers from New Mexico arrived. [483]

As soon as it received the message from the governor of Chihuahua, the government informed the ambassador of the United States in Mexico. They reminded him that the disputed

---

[481] Tanto Zorrilla como Fred Rippy y César Sepúlveda dan la misma versión.

[482] Bemis, Samuel, A Diplomatic History of the U.S., Henry Holt and Co., New York, 1942, p.324.

[483] ASREM, Expediente 1-2-566, ff. 26-27.

territory was within the limits traced by the commissioners of both countries.

> The general trustee of the Supreme Executive Power has been surprised and disgusted by the conduct of the governor of New Mexico without having orders from his government to assume the grave responsibility of provoking a war between two friendly nations.[484]

In response, the governor of Chihuahua was informed that the Secretary of War had given orders for the delivery of artillery and the money to help him. "If, unfortunately, you are harassed, repel force with force." The ambassador of Mexico in Washington had already been advised to lodge the proper complaints.[485]

Meanwhile, the United States government had begun the usual excuse that the inhabitants of the region preferred to live under the jurisdiction of the United States, as well as those of Isleta, Socorro and San Eleazario. The group of North Americans, the minority among the inhabitants of La Mesilla, declared themselves for union with New Mexico while the Mexicans chose Chihuahua.[486] The division of the population was always one of the most used tactics of the Anglos. On this point, historians diverge: the Mexicans say that the area was always part of Chihuahua, except during the years 1821-1848 when it was part of New Mexico. National biographers insist the territory was in Chihuahua, populated by people who did not want to live in the United States, and that William Carr Lane tried to force a

---

[484] Ibidem, ff. 32-34.

[485] Ibidem, f.26.

[486] Rippy, J. Fred, The U.S. and Mexico, F.S. Crofts and Co., New York, 1931, p.116.

confrontation to take control of Mexican land. The actions of the filibusterers, bitter discussions about Tehuantepec, the protests over violations of the treaty, and the La Mesilla affair, contributed to the resurgence of a warlike atmosphere on the frontier.

North American historians, of course, give a different version. Rippy, who tried to show all the documents, is one of the few who mentions that Conkling, the United States ambassador, wrote to Carr Lane to make him see the grave situation and to ask him to change his mind. The latter did not agree with Conkling.[487] Additionally, Colonel Summer, commander of the territory of New Mexico, had refused to follow the orders to invade La Mesilla. Summer, as well as Conkling, were relieved of their duties in the middle of the discussions. The government of the United States asked Conkling to make it clear that his point of view was strictly personal. The interesting part is that his explanation said that what he had done was to "avoid the perpetration of a great crime and free his country from dishonor."[488] In the archives of the Secretary of Exterior Relations a letter exists from the British ambassador in which he narrates the occurrences in La Mesilla including the threat of occupation on the part of New Mexico, and the delivery of Mexican troops to the region. In response to the Mexican protests, Washington had called in Governor Lane and reproached him for his conduct. Later news, however, reported that the government of the United States ordered General Garland to enter the territory of La Mesilla with his troops. At the same time, Conkling received a note from the Department of State, reproving him for having written to Lane, and also calling him to Washington. They ordered him to inform the Mexican government that his government had doubts about the fairness of

---

[487] Ibidem, p. 119, Zorrilla, p. 339.

[488] Zorrilla, op. cit., p. 340.

the boundaries established by the Treaty of Guadalupe-Hidalgo, of the legality of the naming of Mr. Whipple as surveyor, and of the reasons to suppose that the valley of La Mesilla was part of New Mexico. In addition, the English ambassador to Mexico informed Lord Claredon, that the *New York Inquirer* had published an article together with a map of the disputed region proving that La Mesilla belonged to New Mexico.[489] As we can see the journalistic battle in favor of the purchase of La Mesilla had begun. Soon, all the publications of the neighboring country were publishing articles and maps trying to justify the invasion of the desired territory.

Meanwhile, the government of Mexico supported the position of Trias, governor of Chihuahua, who began to recruit troops. Arrangements were made to prepare militias and for the movement of soldiers towards the frontier. The Mexican press, according to Zorrilla, spread the news and pointed out the necessity of having to defend the integrity of the national territory again.[490] The governor of Chihuahua sent an article translated from the *Heraldo del Norte* to the capital, in which it was mentioned that English bankers counseled the Mexican government to cede Sonora, Chihuahua, and Baja California to avoid bankrupting the country. The article, asking Washington to reason with the Mexican government, supported the suppositions that Mexico was using up the funds coming from the sale of its territory, and that it would become impossible to obtain more for not having credit as an independent country. With the sale of Sonora, Chihuahua, and Baja California a sanitary belt (sic) would be formed populated by Anglos.[491] As we can see, the short but hard-fought battle for La Mesilla had begun. As was

---

[489] ASREM, Expediente 1-2-566, ff. 38-39.

[490] Zorrilla, op. cit., p. 341.

[491] ASREM, 2-1-1823, f. 3.

customary, the United States invoked all kinds of justifications to achieve it.

This was the last time Mexico lost territory, and one has to admire the way it was defended. It repeated time and again the validity of its position. As much through the press as through its representatives in Washington, it repeated with insistence that:

> The territory in which La Mesilla is found has belonged by fact and by right to Mexico from time immemorial, and has constituted part of the ancient province, today the state of Chihuahua [...] since Mexico belonged to Spain to the present day [...] and consequently there is no possible doubt of any kind.

It was pointed out that the Treaty of Guadalupe-Hidalgo had clearly established the territorial limits.[492]

In the United States the age of the railroad had begun and was the most important development at the moment. According to the United States' basic character, all political and economic efforts were directed to the same end, and in this case the United States vitally needed, according to them, a path to transport gold from California, and skins, grains, and cattle to the east of the country. Similarly, they had to bring all types of merchandise to the newly rich in the other direction. The passage through the Rocky Mountains was impossible for the technology of the day, as a result, they contemplated the need to obtain a new cession of Mexican territory. As we have said, the pro-slavery party in Congress considering that California had entered as an anti-slavery state wanted a route by the south to protect the new territory from the anti-slavery party. Also, as noted by historians, the economic progress of the decade of the 1850s made for a

---

[492] ASREM, H/110, 73-0, 858, ff. 247-253.

period of solid expansion. Technical advances, especially the railroad, stimulated economic investment. The rise in the birthrate and the continued European immigration provided the necessary manpower. The North American industrial revolution was ready for a second round of development. To do so, it needed to expand its population to the new territories and acquire more, if that were possible.

All of the foregoing explains why in the middle of internal conflicts around slavery, the government of the United States found itself destined to invade Cuba, infiltrate Hawaii, and to try to buy Baja California and Tehuantepec. President Franklin Pierce, in his inaugural speech declared: "Of course, we should not disguise the fact, that our position as a country and our position in the world makes the acquisition immensely important for our protection."[493]

The ambassadors sent by Pierce to the zones of tension were expansionists. To Mexico he sent James Gadsden, an important official from South Carolina, who had personal interests in the train across La Mesilla.

On the 15th of July, 1853, the Secretary of State of the neighboring country, also an expansionist, sent diplomatic instructions to Gadsden. The principal objective of his mission was related to La Mesilla, even though he was also to seek the repeal of Article XI of the Treaty of Guadalupe-Hidalgo, concerning the Indian invasions. Additionally, he was asked to examine a concession on the Isthmus of Tehuantepec. Thus it was that the diplomatic project of La Mesilla was, from the beginning, embroiled in the Indian invasions, the disputes over Tehuantepec, and the incursions by the North American

---

[493] Bemis, op. cit., p. 320.

filibusterers in the north of the country. Add to this the political situation of Mexico in July, 1853.

In January of that year, a conservative revolt resulted in the defeat of the government of President Mariano Arista. By April, Congress, due to the rising confusion, asked for the return of General Santa Anna to the presidency. This would be his last administration and the most hated, as a result of the sale of La Mesilla. It is curious that in the popular mind Santa Anna was guilty of the sale of Texas, which, as we have seen, did not succeed, while he did sell La Mesilla, which, perhaps for ignorance, was confused with Texas. Santa Anna began his last administration on April 20, 1853. He was not worried about working with Congress, and from the beginning of his administration which pretended to be conservative wanted to have absolute power, and in December, announced by decree that he would assume total power. Various liberal leaders were expelled from the country, among them Ocampo and Juárez; meanwhile, rumors of internal uprisings echoed throughout the Santa Anna period. The sale of La Mesilla took place within this historic, political and social framework. For this we have decided to use as basic material the documents in the archives of the Secretary of Exterior Relations.

Before James Gadsden arrived in the capital, with instructions on the negotiating points with the Mexican government, Santa Anna asked his Secretary of External Relations, Diez de Bonilla, to write to the Mexican ambassadors in London, Madrid, and Paris, asking for help containing North American ambitions. Santa Anna's cabinet was made up of conservatives, so that he used the argument that the North American propaganda against monarchy threatened to defeat them (the conservatives).

> . . . but if this result is considered unlikely, not so that which would produce the progressive extension of the

273

United States against the interests of European commerce, whose products, arts and manufactures could not compete in the markets of all the American countries in the region . . .

Also, he asked them to use the argument that the United States wished for the progressive diminution of the Latin race until it was extinguished.[494] It is a great irony that history has embroiled conservatives in the problem of La Mesilla. They, whose hostility towards the United States is legendary, had to accept the sale of part of the national territory. For this they invoked all possible arguments, including the importation of Swiss mercenaries with the aim of having the Europeans form a dike against the Anglo advance.

The ambassadors of Mexico in Spain, England and France, were unable to obtain the support of these nations to impede the expansion of the United States. Napoleon III jealously guarded the memory of this attempt to justify his intervention in Mexico ten years later. For the moment he would not push it. Spain found itself weakened by the long period of the civil war between Carlistas and Isabelinos, the frequent military uprisings, and the fear of losing Cuba. At the same time, France and England were preparing their intervention in Asia Minor with the so-called Crimean War.

Meanwhile, concern was rising in Chihuahua. The governor wrote to Mexico that, according to recent news, the United States would take La Mesilla no later than September 15, with the seven thousand men at their disposal. Along with this news he sent the documents related to the founding of the La Mesilla colony that indisputably showed their Mexican origin. According to information from the consul in Brownsville, Texas, the whole

---

[494] ASREM, Expediente LE 1096, ff. 92-94.

frontier was being fortified.[495] General Garland's troops arrived in La Mesilla in August.

The Secretary of Exterior Relations tried to change the subject, complaining of the losses caused by the Indians that the United States had the obligation to stop. But Gadsden, as Butler twenty years before, had no other objective than to obtain more territory. He also was not a diplomat, but a large landowner and stockholder in the railroad company that wanted to establish a line to La Mesilla. From this came the answer so disrespectful of the principles of international law: "For some time, the United States had refused all obligations of paying for the destruction of property that was not in its control or was not its obligation to protect." For the North American bureaucrats, Mexico had incorrectly interpreted Article XI that imposed on the United States obligations with which they had no reason to comply. Certainly, Gadsden did not even bother to read the Treaty of Guadalupe-Hidalgo. The only thing that interested him was the possession of what he called an important district, "included, evidently, in the cession made in the treaty".[496]

A month later, Gadsden decided to ask his government authorization not to take up the problem of Tehuantepec and asked that the filibuster invasions in the north of Mexico be restrained, as both things were getting in the way of the problem of La Mesilla. In exchange, he asked for the acquisition of Sonora, Chihuahua and all the territories along the Rio Bravo (Grande), including Baja California. Just like Butler, Gadsden misinterpreted a conversation with Santa Anna by informing his

---

[495] ASREM, 1-2-566, ff. 128-234.

[496] ASREM, Expediente G-R-I-1, ff. 471-479.

Department of State that he recognized La Mesilla as disputed territory.[497]

From the beginning of his term, Gadsden invoked the principle of natural frontiers, that valleys and rivers united settlements while mountains and deserts separated them, thus asking for the territory that extended to the Sierra Madre. In the short six months that the negotiations lasted, the notes of Diez de Bonilla in answer to those of Gadsden are invaluable. Bonilla was a diplomat using diplomacy to defend his country which clashed with Gadsden's insolence. Diez de Bonilla had, according to the documents, a performance, that if not brilliant, at least was professional. Gadsden emerges from the same documents as uncouth, charged to buy that which his masters wanted.

During this time, the country was newly thrown into upheaval by the discord between conservatives and liberals. *The XIX Century* published an article in which the arrangements of the conservatives to obtain a protectorate from Spain and to establish a monarchy came to public attention. Only in this way, they said, would they have protection against the territorial ambitions of the United States that first wanted Texas, then California, now La Mesilla and tomorrow Tehuantepec. The economic situation was disastrous. Desperate for lack of funds, Santa Anna ordered taxes on the numbers of windows and dogs, whose owners would pay a peso a month for each animal. It seems that between June and December of 1853, the government only spent its time creating new taxes, organizing the army, the secret police, and all kinds of festivities to show its authority. Comonfort and Alvarez were already hammering out the Plan de Ayutla to defeat Santa Anna.

497

It was in the middle of such catastrophic confusion, in which things happened one after the other, when the United States sent its representatives instructions for the purchase of La Mesilla. The expansionist government of President Pierce formulated five plans to buy the territory. Without going into geographical details, let's just say that the first plan included 125,000 square miles and included the peninsula of Baja California, half of Tamaulipas, nearly all of Nuevo León and Coahuila, a part of Durango, Chihuahua and Sonora. The price of the purchase would be 50 million pesos. The second proposition, reached 50,000 square miles of territory and included a stretch of land on the south of the dividing line that took land from all of the border states, plus all the land connecting Sonora and Baja California; at the cost of 35 million pesos. The third proposal would include 68,000 square miles, but only 30 million was offered because it only included Baja California. The fourth plan, 18,000 square miles, not including Baja California, for 20 million. In the fifth plan, 15 million was offered for the territory necessary to construct the railroad, leaving in the line connecting Sonora and Baja California. Naturally, all of the plans asked for the repeal of Article XI of the Treaty of Guadalupe-Hidalgo, the annulment of Mexican complaints against the United States government, and permission for free transit across the Isthmus of Tehuantepec.[498]

We have already described the chaotic situation in the country. It only remains to add that Gadsden, knowing of the requests for European aid, threatened a war to annex northern Mexico and Baja California and repeating the threat during the discussions before the treaty. It is understandable that Santa Anna accepted the last proposal. We have already said that his actions during the war with the United States seemed to us treasonous or at least highly suspect. In this treaty he seems to us to have done everything possible to cede the least amount of territory possible.

---

[498] Zorilla, op. cit., p. 346.

On the other hand, the repeal of Article XI was an enormous error in that the United States had assured significant compensation to get rid of it, with the Treaty of La Mesilla (Gadsden Purchase) ending by their offering a tiny amount; it also repealed Article XXIII of the Treaty of Friendship of 1831.

As to the article concerning the Isthmus of Tehuantepec, this was an error that embittered relations between both countries for many years. By it, Mexico authorized the construction of a railroad with a plank road that would cross the isthmus. The government of the United States, confident in its hopes in Tehuantepec, was anxious to obtain a commercial passage between the east and the west of its country. This article of the Treaty of La Mesilla assured that the right of way and the railroad would be built, as well as the assurance that North American citizens would be able to cross it without a passport. In addition, there were assurances that there would be no obstacles to the passage of merchandise and persons; no payments to use the passage. In addition, the United States would have the right to carry mail by bureaucrats and in sealed mailbags; had the promise to open a port where the railroad ended and the promise of a future arrangement for transporting United States troops and munitions. But the most dangerous of those rights and promises for Mexico was the last article, which gave to the United States the right to protect the route.[499]

The treaty found strong opposition in the United States. in that the area obtained was insignificant and desert. Again, we were saved by North American internal politics. The United States found itself in the middle of a great political conflict provoked by the incorporation of Kansas and Nebraska into the union as new states and the country saw itself wrapped up once again in the violent slavery controversy. This problem broke the unity of

---

[499] Ibidem, p. 347.

the Democratic Party and gave rise to the new Republican Party from the ashes of the Whigs. President Pierce took advantage of the moment to threaten the Senate with the responsibility of a war with Mexico if they rejected the treaty and asked for more territory. Congress accepted it, but lowered the sum to 10 million pesos.

As for Mexico, discussions on the treaty had been carried out in secret. In July, 1854, the ratification was announced and it was given out that the land was semidesert and not worth anything. Also, the country was not prepared for a second war with the United States in case they wanted to take La Mesilla by force. There was no public discussion because the dictatorship of Santa Anna had abolished free speech. However, the problem of La Mesilla continued. The United States had paid seven of the ten million pesos with the promise of paying the rest when the border had been demarcated. In January, 1855, Diez de Bonilla, again Secretary of Exterior Relations, complained about the La Mesilla situation. The border had not yet been delimited, and on November 15, General Garland and his troops had taken possession of the region, which constituted an infraction of the treaty given that the remaining three million pesos had not been paid.[500] To such complaints, Gadsden answered defending Garland. If he had occupied La Mesilla it was to save it from the smugglers, murders and thieves who were taking advantage of the situation. According to him, the population had asked for the protection of North American laws. He took advantage of the occasion to blame Mexico since the only cause of disgust in the region were those originated by the Mexican commercial restrictions. It is believed that it was the North American merchants who pushed Garland to invade.

---

[500] ASREM, C-R-1, 2, ff. 581-582.

Of course, the United States government did not pay attention to Mexico's protests. In the face of these facts, the Department of State protested that it knew nothing of what had happened. Later the Mexican ambassador in Washington ended up with the task of recovering the remaining three million pesos. In Mexico, Gadsden tried to add up claims, certainly with the object of diminishing the three million. Diez de Bonilla, exasperated by the continuous interference of the ambassador, asked for his removal.

Whether the United States finally paid the debt or not, we do not know. There is a document in the Archives of Exterior Relations, dated March 1, 1856, and in which Luis de la Rosa gave orders to the chief of negotiations of Mexico in Washington to transfer to the banking house of S.S. Howland R. Aspinall "the three deposits of 500 thousand pesos each owed by the United States of the three million for the Treaty of La Mesilla."[501] The only writer we have found who accuses Santa Anna of taking the money is Alberto María Carreño. The others do not mention the affair.

[501] Ibidem, FF. 1024-1025.

XIII. TEHUANTEPEC, A GREAT DIPLOMATIC ACHIEVEMENT

We have frequently mentioned the Isthmus in relation to the Treaty of Guadalupe-Hidalgo. It is time to explain in depth one of the great triumphs of Mexican diplomacy. Since before the war, the United States had coveted the region, and after the war this greed had become a vital necessity and continued being one until the end of the century, when the Panamanian isthmus supplanted it. However, and despite the pressure applied, Mexico did not allow the isthmus to be taken away. The history of the Mexican defense of the isthmus is long and complicated. We have to go back to the documents in the archives of Exterior Relations, where the papers related to Tehuantepec fill several volumes. Additionally, we have consulted North American archives. The main source in our bibliography is a book of great worth by the Secretary of Exterior Relations, José Fernando Ramirez, in which he relates what happened until 1853. After that year, the story of the conflict is difficult to follow, since even though Zorrilla and Esquivel Obregón discuss it, they do not give a detailed account, chronologically speaking. It is the same with Rippy and Callahan. Other works that speak of the affair exist, but they also are incomplete, such as those of Salado Álvarez and Sodi Álvarez. Although in all of the history books there is mention of the problem, we have tried to synthesize and give a complete picture of what we consider one of the most brilliant pages of our history, the triumph in the defense of the Isthmus of Tehuantepec.

The drama began in 1842 and ended in 1937. Nearly a century of diplomatic battles in which England intervened as it persistently sought, along with the United States a transoceanic passage. Tehuantepec, Nicaragua, and Panama were the most desired routes.

From the establishment of the first Mexican Republic in 1824, the government, conscious of the importance of the isthmus as a transoceanic passage, sent an expedition to study it, along with a recommendation to construct a road. Given the difficulties that accompanied the establishment of a new Republic, no one seriously worked on it until 1842. On February 25, of that year, a certain José de Garay presented a report to the government of Santa Anna asking permission to open a communications network in Tehuantepec. The government agreed to give a concession to construct a route that would connect the two oceans.

Garay had to start the examination of the land within 18 months following February, 1842, and the actual work 10 months later. He had to construct ports, forts, and the necessary storage facilities. The route would be neutral and open to all nations friendly to Mexico. In exchange for these obligations the government of Santa Anna gave Garay the following privileges: the right to charge usage fees for 50 years; the exploitation of the railroad for 60 years; the ownership of vacant lands to 10 leagues on each side of the route; and the power to establish foreigners to develop the industry of the area, on condition that they acquire their property 50 leagues outside the route. Garay's rights were so numerous because of the difficulty of the endeavor.

On January 11, 1843, Garay advised the government that he had finished the reconnaissance of the terrain and asked for the cession of the vacant land that he had been offered to proceed with the opening of the route. The concession would expire on September 30, 1845, if the works did not begin. Ten days before, Ramirez tells us, he asked for two more years and the renewal of the contract, since he had decided that in addition to a railroad he should construct a canal. Paredes' revolution stalled the negotiations. In October, 1846, during the war with the United States, Garay again asked for the concession, begging for the extension of the elimination of taxes from 20 to 50 years. The government, in the hands of General Salas, granted this request and also included the canal without such an important affair being discussed by the Mexican Congress. The Congress also did not know that since August, 1846, Garay had offered to transfer his concession to the English firm of Manning and Mackintosh.[502]

As the United States and England wanted to obtain a transoceanic passage they tried to exclude the other in their negotiations. To this effect, the United States signed a treaty in Colombia in September, 1846, in which they received the right of transit by Panama. However, Colombia insisted that they guarantee their sovereignty over the isthmus of Panama and its neutrality. At the same time England obtained a protectorate on the Mosquito coast on the Caribbean side for a possible Nicaraguan canal.[503]

Meantime, Garay had transferred his concession to the English firm. Immediately afterwards, he asked the government to recognize the concession, and in July, 1847, Manning and Mackintosh became owners of the valuable assignment of which Garay would own 33 percent. When the North American government asked for transit of Tehuantepec during the peace

---

[502] José Fernando Ramirez, *Memorias negociaciones, y documentos para servir a la historia de las dijerencias que se han suscitado entre México y los Estados Unidos, los tenedores de antiguo privilegio para la comunidad de los mares.* Imprenta Ignacio Cumplido,México, 1853, pp. 5-317.

[503] Luis G. Zorrilla, *Historia de las relaciones entre México y los Estados Unidos*, ed.Porrua, México, 1965, pp. 136-317.

conference (of Guadalupe-Hidalgo) they were told that the concession to the English firm had already been granted.[504]

At this moment, the Hargous brothers appeared, rich North American merchants with businesses and properties in Mexico, who had warned of the importance of Tehuantepec. While the proposals of their government were rejected, Louis Hargous, quietly but surely, bought the rights of Manning and Mackintosh. According to Zorrilla, they sold it because they knew that only a month remained of the concession for Garay to begin his works.

In January, 1849, with the concession sold, Manning and Mackintosh asked the Mexican government, which did not know of the sale, to allow them more time to carry out terms of the concession. The answer was negative and the ambassador in Washington was told to tell Garay that his concession had run out.[505] Thus started the problems. Senator Peter Hargous had bought the concession obtained from Manning and Mackintosh from his brother. As a senator he had easy access to Congress and asked for its protection. We do not know if he mentioned the date that Garay's concession would expire. What we do know is that the Mexican government refused to give an extension to Manning and Mackintosh. Whether they had already sold their concession, we do not know either. The important thing was that the North American government took it as an insult and argued that the extension was not extended because the Hargous were United States citizens. This is how their historians have recorded it, with no mention of the denial of extending the length of the concession. They only talk of the cancellation and attribute it to

---

[504] Ramirez, op. cit., p.56.

[505] Zorrilla, op. cit., pp. 318-319.

having been sold to North Americans.[506] Through their ambassador in Mexico, Robert P. Letcher, the government was told that the cancellation of the concession went against the Treaty of Friendship of 1831, to which Mexico responded that its validity should be decided by Mexican laws and not by those of other countries. The date was June, 1849, and it was natural for the Mexican government to look upon the sale of Garay's concession to the North Americans with fear. But we do not believe that they cancelled the concession for that reason, as we repeat, it was not cancelled, it had expired.

Immediately the machine of diplomatic complaints was started up and as on other occasions, the United States complained of the lack of regard for North American citizens by Mexico, of the lack of protection for individual and property rights of North Americans in Mexico, and of the instability of the government. Additionally, they pointed out, as usual, the obligation of the Mexican government to protect its American citizens. Immediately, they asked for an extension for the Hargous company. The Department of State presented the problem as placing Mexico in an embarrassing position. If they did not extend the concession it was because those who had bought it were North Americans attracted by the assurance that Mexico offered them. Finally, the Mexican government declared that a new concession would be made.

In view of the answer and foreseeing that it could have considerable advantages, the North American ambassador, Letcher, proposed a treaty on the passage of Tehuantepec, while the Secretary of State sent him instructions to negotiate a convention that would guarantee the property and rights of United States citizens, and at the same time to refrain from

---

[506] Rippy, Fred J. *The U.S. and Mexico*, F.S. Crofstand Co. New York, 1931, p. 50.

offering any guarantee whatsoever on Mexican sovereignty as they had done on the Colombia treaty.

On June 22, 1850, still during the administration of President Herrera, the first Treaty of Transit of Tehuantepec was signed. Among its most important articles was that the protection of the works, properties and persons could be granted by both nations, and that the United States could only intervene at the express petition of Mexico. Both countries were obligated to maintain neutrality within ten leagues on either side of the route, reserving to Mexico its sovereignty and the right to approve transport fees.[507]

While the treaty was in transit to the United States two things happened. The first was a change in the Secretary of State, John Clayton, whose tenure between 1841-1843 was difficult for Mexico, who was replaced a few months later by Daniel Webster. We have seen that Clayton was an aggressive man and sure of his Anglo superiority as shown by his notes that were generally insulting and full of threats. In 1841, he had sourly discussed the Texas problem and ten years later he was left with Tehuantepec. As a result noting that it was United States citizens who were unlawfully holding the concession of works in Tehuantepec, and having been influenced by the complaints of Hargous, Webster ordered four modifications to the treaty of June 22, 1850. The protection mentioned in the treaty would not only be for the builders, but for all those with an interest in the project. The forces sent to maintain security would have permission to occupy any point within the limits of the cession. Finally, a North American commissioner would live in the zone and would have the right to ask for the protection of his government in case Mexico did not listen to his complaints. Rippy is the only North American historian who called Webster's

---

[507] Zorrilla, op. cit., p. 320.

modifications "amazing", saying that in reality what he was asking for was the establishment of a protectorate over the isthmus. In addition, he threatened the Mexican government if it did not accept his modifications.[508]

Herrera's government did not accept the suggestions, and as to the threats, the Secretary of Exterior Relations, Lacunza, answered, "Your government is strong, ours is weak. You have the power to appropriate whatever part of our territory or all of it if you desire. We do not have the means to resist."[509] The proposed treaty had been made public and was, without the modifications, already under heavy attack. Everyone feared that it was a trick to obtain more territory. Meanwhile, at the beginning of 1850, a company began to be organized in New Orleans. The Tehuantepec Railroad Company of New Orleans bought Hargous' pretended rights and aspired to succeed him. In September, 1850, The Society of Friends of the Country (Mexico) wrote to the Secretary of Exterior Relations to express fear about the projected railroad. They believed that it was only a pretext to obtain territory and that the business of the Isthmus, principally the treaty, would end up resulting in a war. Their fears were based on the excesses already committed by the Company of Tehuantepec in New Granada (Colombia). It was known that they had named authorities as if the territory were theirs. One month later the governor of Veracruz received a letter expressing the same suspicions. In November, it was Oaxaca's turn to disapprove of the treaty:

> We have the honor to send to your excellencies the appeal that this legislature brings to the attention of the august Cámaras de la Union (legislature), asking that

---

[508] Rippy, op. cit., pp. 54-55.

[509] Victoriano Salado Álvarez, Cómo perdimos California y salvamos Tehuantepec., ed. Jus, México, 1968, p. 52.

they do not approve, in its present form, the treaty between the commissioner of Mexico and the ambassador of the United States for the protection of the passage of the Isthmus of Tehuantepec.[510]

In Mexico, the press, the clergy, the opposition party, in a word, everyone, was against the treaty. At the end of 1850, Herrera's government ended and General Mariano Arista was elected President. Shortly after beginning his mandate, he had to execute a group of rebels who had rebelled in Guanajuato against the cession of territory to the United States.[511] It was feared that a problem similar to Texas was developing in Tehuantepec. Arista felt pressured and accepted a second treaty on Tehuantepec that would only assure Garay's concession. The same day he signed it the Mexican Senate began to discuss the affair, deciding in March 1851 that Garay's concession was null since 1846. From this it followed that all the transfers, Manning's as well as Hargous', had been illegal. This decision was like a bomb with Webster violently reacting and accusing the Mexican Congress of acting unconstitutionally. He affirmed that his government would protect North American citizens who had spent great sums to begin the project, sending engineers, material, and provisions to the Isthmus.[512] He threatened Mexico with great disasters if they cancelled the concession. The Company of Tehuantepec did not pay any attention to the fact that the work was suspended. They continued sending ships and provisions without consular permits until they received orders from the Mexican Congress terminating the project. Various schooners trying to unload in Coatzacoalcos and Minatitlan had to be detained.

---

[510] ASREM, Expediente LE-1608, ff. 4-12.

[511] Salado, op. cit., p. 52.

[512] Rippy, op. cit., pp. 57-59.

In August, 1851, José Fernando Ramirez was put in charge of the Secretary of Exterior Relations to whom we owe the copying of documents and information about the Tehuantepec affair. A month after his arrival at the ministry, the Company of Tehuantepec published in the newspapers of the United States that they would not recognize the right of the Mexican government to take away its concession and that they would go ahead with their plans. The declaration was so arrogant and contemptuous that it is obvious that the company was counting on the backing of its government. It was almost equivalent to a declaration of war, something unheard of, especially coming from a private company confronting a foreign government. To the threat of sending a filibuster army to take the Isthmus, the Mexican government answered by decreeing the establishment of military colonies in the region. Also, the general headquarters were moved from Veracruz to Acayucan, the national guard from Veracruz and Oaxaca were called up, and the permits of North American consuls in the region were withdrawn.[513] The Mexico of 1851 prepared to resist a new invasion of its territory. The national press encouraged Mexicans to reject the Anglo attack. *El Universal*, *Siglo XIX*, and *Omnibus* all pointed out the necessity of uniting to stop the theft.[514] In September, 1851, Carvajal's filibuster invasions had begun with the aim of establishing the Republic of the Sierra Madre with the territory of the five states in the north of the country. The situation was difficult, no government could make a concession without the fear of being defeated. Carvajal even declared that his uprising was due to the fact that General Arista "tried to intimidate the Mexican Congress to commit the base and vile deed and treason of ceding the Isthmus of Tehuantepec along with a considerable

---

[513] Zorrilla, op. cit., 324-335v

[514] Rippy, op. cit., p. 60.

part of our sovereignty to a foreign power."[515] The interesting part of the proclamation is that, according to Carvajal, the foreign power was England. Carvajal clearly defended the interests of North American merchants, who at that time feared England would take over the Isthmus.

Meantime, foreseeing a major conflict, the Mexican government tried to find a way to put aside the treaty of concession, making it clear that they would not allow the intervention of a foreign authority to decide controversies subject to international law. President Fillmore, taking part in the affair, wrote to President Arista making him aware of the danger of the controversy. Ramirez, Secretary of Exterior Relations, sent a memorandum to the diplomatic corps explaining the case and making them see the justness of the Mexican position.[516]

In May, 1852, the Mexican Congress sent a decree that opened the competition for the construction of the inter-ocean route. In it, it was left very clear that they would give preference to national companies. It was very careful not to give grounds for claims from foreign governments, specifying that the route would be neutral and its sovereignty would be totally in the hands of Mexican government. It was a valiant act before the repeated threats of the United States.

In national politics, however, it had enormous consequences, as the conservatives already accused the Congress of wanting to provoke a new war with the United States by its intransigence on the Garay concession. What we see as an act of courage to affirm the independence of Mexico, the opposing party saw, or pretended to see, it as an act of arrogance. At that time, they wanted to convince the public that the republican system could

[515] ASREM, Expediente 4-2-5646, f. 4.

[516] Ramirez, op. cit., p. 65.

290

not be applied to Mexico. The conservative press began to talk of the need for a coup d'etat. Added to all this, the economic situation of the country was becoming more difficult. The invasions of the frontier were another weapon in the hands of the conservatives and the news fomented the discontent against the Arista government. Mazatlán, Jalisco, and Veracruz suffered revolts against local governments. Especially important was the taking of Guadalajara in July, 1852.[517]

In April of that same year, Colonel A.G. Sloo of New Orleans had presented to the Mexican government a project to construct a route across Tehuantepec. In May, the competition was announced, and by August they had received five proposals. Congress considered Sloo's to be the best, perhaps because it was a mixed Mexican-American company, and proceeded to examine his proposal to give him a contract. In the United States a new ambassador was named, Alfred Conkling, whose actions we examined when we described the La Mesilla affair. The ambassador brought instructions to obtain a right-of-way across Tehuantepec and salvage the Garay concession. In addition, he had to achieve the repeal of Article XI of the Treaty of Guadalupe-Hidalgo with reference to the Apache invasions. Notwithstanding the change of ambassadors, in the United States a group of senators continued pushing for the protection of the Hargous company, the Tehuantepec Railroad Company, which had been rejected by the Mexican Congress. They insisted to the press that the only reason the Garay concession was attacked was because it was given to a North American company. Much was spoken about the danger of English citizens becoming concessionaires. When they learned of the inclination towards the Mexican-American Sloo company, Senator Brooke presented a resolution to Congress:

---

[517] Enrique Olavarria y Juan de Dios Arias, México a través de los siglos, vol. IV, Editorial Cumbre, México, 1977,p. 750.

Unless Mexico returns their privileges to the American owners of the communications right of way, the United States will proceed to protect them (the owners) in their occupation and enjoyment. (If this attitude provokes an interruption of diplomatic relations) the world will be a witness that it has been caused by the flagrant and indefensible violation by Mexico of individual rights and international law.[518]

Brooke was seconded by other senators, among them Senator Mason, who asked that they take the region by force. The Mexican ambassador in Washington reported that only one senator had defended the rights of Mexico.[519] The newspaper, *Daily Delta*, reported to its readers that the country had suffered so many Mexican attacks that only by taking half of Mexico would the grievances by satisfied.[520] A few days later, Larrainzar, ambassador of Mexico in Washington, worriedly wrote about the articles published in the *New York Herald* concerning Tehuantepec. He thought the most serious thing was that many politicians wanted to take advantage of the Tehuantepec affair to end their obligations under the Treaty of Guadalupe-Hidalgo. He reported that the press, as a faithful voice of its government, was trying to prepare the United States public for the next blow against Mexico.[521]

To avoid more discussions which could have been dangerous, Arista's government, already weakened, invited the United

---

[518] ASREM, Expediente LE-1609, ff. 70-74.

[519] Ibidem, f. 76.

[520] ASREM, LE-1603, ff. 2-4.

[521] ASREM, LE-1605, ff. 116-119.

States to sign a convention on Tehuantepec in January, 1853 to guarantee the neutrality of the route. The political situation had deteriorated to such a point that Arista resigned on January 5, 1853. The government was left in the hands of Juan Bautista Cevallos, president of the Supreme Court. However, the instability of the situation made for the fear of a disastrous ending.

In February, the Mexican government signed a contract with the A.G. Sloo company. In this contract, a railroad was established along the navigable part of the Coatzacoalcos River and the rest by land. It did not contain concessions on lands outside the route necessary to build piers and train stations. In case there was a problem, the company could only take it to the Mexican government. The country would own one-third of the stock, and would build the terminal ports. The contractors could not transfer their rights without the full consent of the government, which had the freedom to approve the tariffs of the company. The contract with A.G. Sloo was well received by Conkling, the North American ambassador in Mexico, so he signed the third treaty of Tehuantepec. As the treaty accepted the concession to Sloo and did not give sufficient importance to North American interests, the United States Senate did not ratify the treaty. Indeed, Conkling was withdrawn from his post, since in addition to his error with respect to Tehuantepec, he had accepted the justice of the Mexican position and for this was replaced by the fanatic expansionist Gadsden. The new ambassador arrived in Mexico insisting that the Garay concession should be recognized.

Meanwhile, the government in Washington, as that in Mexico, had changed. Franklin Pierce assumed the presidency of the United States where his expansionist and pro-Southern tendencies were well known. In Mexico, the government of Cevallos fell and Santa Anna was waiting in the wings from one moment to the next. The Mexican ambassador in Washington sent a message that Pierce, in his inauguration speech, had spoken of the necessity of obtaining the Isthmus of Tehuantepec.[522] One month before, the Secretary of State had explained that the right to ask Mexico for the passage across the Isthmus was not based on the Garay Concession, but rather on the right of nations to have their territories connected. The United States, he said, had bought California and could not reach it. The right of nations was a superior law to that of men, and as such gave them the inviolable right to the passage across Tehuantepec.[523] The secretary was the same one who dared to affirm that the mission of the revolution for the independence of the United States could be compared to the Christian religion. And even more, he said that the beginnings of the revolution constituted a new development in the Christian system "to include the golden rule of benevolence in the science of human government."[524] It was the continuation of Puritan-Calvinist thought, where the ends justified the means.

At the end of March, Santa Anna arrived in Mexico. The North American politicians favorable to Garay hoped that the new president would recognize the concession, given that the president had drawn it up. With his return to power the conservatives returned to the government. Diez de Bonilla, Secretary of Exterior Relations, sent Almonte to Washington with instructions to watch out for North American ambitions.[525] According to the contract with Sloo, in February, the latter was

---

[522] Zorrilla, op. cit., p. 330.

[523] ASREM, LE-1603.

[524] Burns, Edward M. The American Idea of Mission, University of Rutgers Press, New Jersey, 1957, p. 18.

[525] ASREM,LE-1605, f. 48.

supposed to deposit 600,000 pesos as a guarantee fort he contract. He did not do so, and the contract was terminated, but on June 21, 1853 Sloo registered a new mercantile society called Louisiana Tehuantepec Company and renewed the contract. The danger was that he had only been given a year to begin work to fulfill its terms.

The diplomatic discussions on La Mesilla were subordinated to the Tehuantepec problem for the moment. It is enough to say that we were at the point of having a second war with the United States. The government of Santa Anna chose the lesser evil, sold the territory of La Mesilla, repealed Article XI of the Treaty of Guadalupe-Hidalgo and established new terms in reference to Tehuantepec. According to Article VIII of the Treaty of La Mesilla (December, 1853) the United States gained several concessions: Neither government would impose obligations to the transit of persons or goods of either nation; no interest in the passage or in its products could be transferred to a foreign government; no passport, nor letters of security would be asked of Americans in transit; the transit of North American troops and munitions would be permitted; and as a last point they could protect themselves. As we have seen, the United States was favored over other countries. This article was a source of problems between the two countries until it was repealed in 1937.[526] After the concessions in the Treaty of La Mesilla the contract with Sloo's company continued.

Additionally, it was desirable for Mexico to accept the protection of the United States for the communications infrastructure that was projected to be built in the Isthmus.[527] Cué Canovas said

[526] Alvaro Matute, ed. Antología, México en el siglo XIX, UNAM, México, 1973, p. 473-478.

[527] Agustin Cié Canova, El Tratado MacLane-Ocampo, Ed. América Nueva, México, 156, p. 100.

watch out that these stipulations implied a real right of way with respect to the Isthmus of Tehuantepec to the benefit of the neighboring country.

Meanwhile the construction of the passage across Tehuantepec was held up. The history of the transfers, debts, etc. of the concessionaires contributed to a true tangled web. A the end of 1855, the actions of the Sloo company, Louisiana Tehuantepec, had fallen into the hands of an English subject, Francisco Falconnet. The contract expired in February, 1857 without having begun the work. However, Louisiana Tehuantepec alleged that it had constructed a road and asked for a modification of the contract. The North American ambassador intervened in Sloo's petition. He argued that in Article VIII of the Treaty of La Mesilla, the United States had recognized and accepted the contract signed by Sloo, so that now, if it was modified its opinion had to be considered.[528] Sloo's concession ran out and a new consortium came forward, the Company of Tehuantepec, whose partners were the same as before; Garay, Hargous, and Sloo, plus some North American politicians. The North American Secretary of State, Lewis Cass, recommended to John Forsyth, his ambassador in Mexico, that he demand from the Mexican government the approval of any transfer in favor of the North Americans. He also sent a project for a new treaty, in which he would ask Mexico for the transfer in perpetuity of the right of transit across the Isthmus. Additionally, they demanded the right to protect the route in case Mexico could not.[529]

Sebastián Lerdo de Tejada, minister of Exterior Relations, answered the proposals of September 12, 1857, maintaining that

---

[528] Toribio Esquivel Obregón, Apuntes para la historia del derecho en México, vol. V. Antigua Librería de Roberdo, México, 1948, p. 527.

[529] Ibidem, pp. 527-530

Mexico could not grant a concession in perpetuity, the right to pass armed forces, or grant the ability to protect the Isthmus and was ready to develop inter-ocean communications in favor of all nations.[530] One month later, the Mexican government announced two decrees concerning Tehuantepec. The first declared that the privileges given to Sloo had expired on February 5, 1853. The second granted a concession to the company formed in New Orleans on June 30, 1857, called the Company of Tehuantepec.[531] Forsyth complained to his government that the new contract did not stipulate any of his instructions, and that the said contract would not allow the company the passage of troops across the Isthmus without special permission of Mexico.

Forsyth continued insisting in a change of frontiers and in the right of transit in perpetuity. He asked for money from his government because he was sure the temptation would be irresistible for the vacillating government of Comonfort. This was overcome by the fall of the latter in January, 1858, when Forsyth presented himself before the conservative government of Zuloaga with his proposals, which were forcefully rejected, beginning a war to the death between Forsyth and Zuloaga's government.

As for Tehuantepec, the next step was taken by Benito Juárez agreeing to the Treaty of McLane-Ocampo, which stipulated that Mexico cede in perpetuity passage across the Isthmus. He also took on the obligation of establishing ports of deposit which would be paid for by tariffs on the traded goods, and gave permission in perpetuity for the protection of the route to both countries with the stipulation that in case of danger North American forces could enter without previous consent from

---

[530] ASREM, Expediente 3-c-r-l, f. 244.

[531] Ibidem, f. 255.

Mexico.[532] The articles of the McLane-Ocampo Treaty could not have been more humiliating for Mexico. There is only one treaty, it seems to us, worse than Ocampo and that is Corwin-Doblado, which we will see later. Of course we understand the difficult situation confronted by Benito Juárez's government, and we are aware of the justifications that have been used to explain the reasons for signing the treaty, which in our judgement was not only risky but imprudent. We are lucky it was not accepted by the North American Senate for fear it would help the South, which was on the point of declaring war on the North to begin the War of Secession. One of the other articles which was a saving grace, was one that obligated the North American government to provide military aid to Juárez's government in case it needed it. The Senate of the United States led by Buchanan knew that their own Civil War was at the point of breaking out and did not want obligations that might weaken it. Given the fragility of Juárez's government this seemed inevitable. Thus, the North American rejection of a treaty so advantageous to them. We will talk more of this affair in the next chapter.

The North American Civil War was from 1860-1864, during which the North Americans did not officially deal with Tehuantepec. When the war ended they again asked for a concession which was granted to Mr. H.R. de la Reintrie on October 15, 1866. Maximillian accepted the revival of the terms of the Louisiana Tehuantepec Company on October 12, 1866, thus creating again a conflict between two companies. No one could start the construction work and the contracts were revoked. On October 6, 1867, Juárez gave permission for the construction of the route to Emili La Sere. The list of concessionaires was interminable, and the list of failures incomprehensible. En 1870, the Tehuantepec Railroad Company, founded in 1866, obtained a

---

[532] Matute, op. cit., pp. 489-490.

new concession. Its president swore that he could construct a canal even though the climate and health conditions were very bad.[533] However, by 1874, the inauguration ceremonies had not been held, and in December a new extension and a subsidy of 7,000 pesos per kilometer was obtained. Again the United States tried to get a treaty to protect the railroad or canal that would be built, which was refused by the government of Lerdo de Tejada.[534]

In 1878, President Díaz granted the first concession to build the Interoceanic Railroad of Tehuantepec to Edward Learned of New York. It established that the work should be completed within three years with a subsidy of 7,500 pesos per kilometer. In the first three years only 75 kilometers had been built, and the concession was cancelled. The government paid the contractor 127,000 pesos and 1,500 dollars.

In 1880, it was the turn of the North American engineer, James Buchanan Eads, who presented such a fantastic plan that it was unattainable. According to him, his railroad would pick up fully loaded ships and transport them by land to the other ocean. Naturally, it failed. Next was a Mexican, Delfin Sánchez, who also failed, but this time for lack of funds. His work was the first example of a decentralized Mexican company with state participation.

The minister of development, General Carlos Pacheco, shared the desire of President Díaz to construct a route, whether railroad or canal, and decided it should be the Mexican government in charge of it. He obtained a Germano-English loan of 27 million pounds and finally found someone who would continue the

---

[533] Enrique Sodi Álvarez, Istmo de Tehuantepec, s.e. México, 1967, p. 98.

[534] Zorrilla, op. cit., p. 534.

interrupted work. The Anglo-American company of Stanhope, Hampson and Corthell finished the route on July 29, 1894. Its construction took 52 years since it was a technically difficult job and because of the high temperatures that deteriorated the ties. Five years later the concession to use the railroad and the two terminal ports was granted to S. Pearson and Sons.[535] This ended the highly desired route between the two oceans. In 1915, the railroad became secondary when the Panama Canal was inaugurated. Thus ended a period of tremendous hostility between Mexico and the United States caused by the passage across Tehuantepec.

Mexico, its leaders, its newspaper reporters, and the reaction of the general public had been able to save the independence of the region. The battle had been long and difficult, but we had won. Afterwards the United States made themselves owners of Panama by means of tortuous political intrigues which had failed in Mexico. The defense of the Tehuantepec passage and the Isthmus itself, is one of the most glorious pages of our history which for being long and complicated most Mexicans do not know about.

In 1913, a little recognized act repealed Article VIII of the Treaty of La Mesilla that had been on the point of causing a war between the two nations. Mexico was liberated, we hope forever, from an accord that during nearly a century had put the integrity of our national territory in danger.

---

[535] Sodi, op. cit., pp. 120-130.

XIV. THE UNITED STATES AND MEXICO DURING LA REFORMA

The Mexican government, tired of Gadsden's interference in the country's internal politics, asked for his withdrawal. The new ambassador, John Forsyth, arrived on October 11, 1856. One of his first acts was to open again the case of Juan Napoléon Zerman, who had led the first filibuster adventure after the Treaty of La Mesilla, and the third attempt to take Baja California, so the case merits a review.[536]

The expedition of Juan Napoléon Zerman was financed by various North American businessmen, under the pretext of helping the Ayutla revolution, who wanted to take advantage of the situation. There has always been a controversy about the origin of the expedition. Zerman claimed he had received his commission from a so-called provisional government organized by the commercial companies Matherson, Robert, Noah and La Chapelle with offices in San Francisco. Matherson, in turn, said he had an agreement with General Juan Álvarez to obtain a loan of five thousand pesos and supplies and ammunition in exchange for vacant land in Guerrero. Zerman, upon arriving in La Paz, showed a document by which Matherson authorized him to blockade the port supposedly in support of the Ayutla Revolution. General Álvarez later denied having authorized Matherson to do any such thing.

General Blancarte, governor of Southern Baja California, not only refused to accept Zerman's claims, arrested him and later sent him to Mexico City. He also sent along the proclamation of the so-called provisional government, organized by Matherson

---

[536] Jorge Flores, Documentos para la historia de la Baja California, Papeles Históricos Mexicanos, vol. 2, Ed. Intercontinental, México, 1946, p. 41.

and his companions, that declared the port of La Paz free from taxes. This document announced that the foreign merchandise arriving in the port would be met with a new rule that would reduce tariffs. This was the key to the affair, the North American merchants tried to open a lucrative market near their base.

Whether or not he was a filibusterer, it is certain that Zerman tried to blockade La Paz. It was an operetta that made strong waves in the country's diplomacy. James Gadsden took advantage of the situation to claim again what he called illegal procedures. Referring to Zerman and his people as auxiliaries of the Ayutla Revolution, he accused Blancarte of "prejudice and disorderly violence". He asked that everyone arrested be set free "immediately" and sent to the United States.[537]

The Secretary of Exterior Relations at the time, José Antonio de la Fuente, answered Gadsden's claims. He showed him that Zerman and his group were being judged before national courts, and all foreign diplomatic intervention was excluded. He reminded him that an offense against international law would put the defendants beyond the protection of their governments.[538] The Mexican government then asked that Gadsden be withdrawn.

As we have said, the new ambassador, John Forsyth, opened the case against Zerman again. We have a letter from Miguel Lerdo de Tejada in which he answered the ambassador's complaints. The most interesting thing in it is that he accuses the United States of violating the neutrality laws by permitting the organization of this expedition in San Francisco, California. The Mexican government rejected the intervention of the ambassador

---

[537] ASREM, Expediente 3-c-r-l, ff. 440-442

[538] Ibidem, ff. 443-444.

in affairs of internal politics.[539] Lerdo de Tejada tried to show that Zerman had violated international law by changing flags on the high seas, usurping Mexican naval titles and forcing a Mexican ship to join his fleet.[540] In addition, Zerman had started his expedition in supposed support of the Ayutla Revolution two months after it had been won.

Forsyth sent many violent notes in which he defended the Zerman expedition and asked for indemnification. These seem inexplicable, and can only be understood in their historic context. John Forsyth had replaced Gadsden at a difficult time. The ambassador charged with signing the Treaty of La Mesilla had not stopped warning his government for three years of the possibility of a European intervention in Mexico. According to him, the Old World powers were ready to "stop the progress of North American expansion and its ideas in general".[541] In November 1855, the Ayutla Revolution had triumphed. Juan Álvarez was proclaimed president, but the internal peace was broken anew on November 22, when Juárez proclaimed the first law of La Reforma, which abolished parts of the military and the church. Juan Álvarez resigned, perhaps not wanting to confront the problems, and Comonfort was left as the substitute president.

The year 1856 was especially painful for Mexico. It was a year of confrontations between the state and the church, and thus of many pronouncements in favor of the latter. The hate between Conservatives and Liberals became much more intense. In an about face, England presented an ultimatum about pretended injuries to its consul. Spain prepared to send a fleet to Veracruz

---

[539] Ibidem, ff. 452-456.

[540] Ibidem, ff. 326-327.

[541] Rippy, Fred J. The United States and Mexico, F.S. Crofts and Co., New York, 1931, p. 203.

because of the wave of violence against its nationals in the south of the country and for unsatisfied debts. France announced it would cooperate with the other two powers. John Forsyth arrived into this situation in October 1856. It was the last year of Franklin Pierce's presidency, and the desire to obtain more Mexican territory was still alive. When in April, 1856, the law confiscating the property of the clergy was passed, the New York press lamented: the Mexican government, they said, would have money and that would frustrate the attempts to buy more territory. In that year, the United States offered six million for a change in the frontier from the Rio Bravo (Grande) to the 31st parallel and from there to the Gulf of California.[542] This was the second time after the Treaty of La Mesilla that they officially tried to acquire Sonora and Baja California. Gadsden had already presented their proposal at the end of 1854, less than a year after the purchase of La Mesilla. There is a note from Diez de Bonilla to Gadsden dated January 25, 1855, referring to the proposition of the North American government for the cession of a portion of territory, "more or less to the Sierra Madre." In it he remarked about the rumors going around about the North American acquisition of Yucatan and other Mexican territories. At the same time he explained the motives of why Mexico had sold La Mesilla, and tried to make Gadsden see that the arguments in favor of the cession were without grounds. The note ended with another Mexican rejection of selling its territory.[543]

From what we have seen, the North American government did not see the rejection as final, as they presented the petition again the next year through their ambassador, John Forsyth.

---

[542] Luis Zorrilla, Historia de las relaciones entre México y los Estados Unidos, Ed. Porrua, México, 1965, p. 355.

[543] ASREM, Expediente 2-c-r-l, ff. 926-935.

In March, 1857, James Buchanan became president. With his election the desire for expansion at the cost of Mexico returned. He authorized Forsyth to offer twelve to fifteen million dollars for Baja California and a large part of Sonora and Chihuahua.[544] The Constitution of February, 1857, had caused a great revolt as it recognized the anti-clerical measures of two years earlier. In the second half of the year, Comonfort was elected president and Benito Juárez vice president with the Conservative reaction against the constitution growing. In December, 1857, after innumerable riots, the Conservatives made a coup d'etat and announced the Plan of Tacubaya. Various states joined in the abolition of the Constitution of 1857.

The Conservative government of General Zuloaga took power in January, 1858 to February, 1859. Benito Juárez, a Liberal president, installed his government in Veracruz from May 5, 1858, until his entrance into the capital in January, 1861. Ambassador John Forsyth again presented his petitions to buy territory before the government of Zuloaga. Comonfort, before he resigned after the coup d'etat, had not accepted the sale of territory to the United States, but perhaps the Conservatives made him do so in return for recognition by the United States of the Conservative government. On March 22, 1858, the ambassador wrote a long letter to Zuloaga's government in which he spoke of the need to establish "natural frontiers" through a cession or sale of Sonora and Baja California, again asking for the right to cross Tehuantepec in perpetuity. On April 5, the Secretary of Exterior Relations, Luis G. Cuevas, rejected both proposals.[545] Next, Cuevas wrote to the Mexican ambassador in Washington to tell him what had happened. "Mr. Forsyth proposed to the new government a new demarkation of limits that, of course, would involve a great loss of territory."

---

[544] Rippy, op. cit., p. 214.

[545] Zorrilla, op. cit., p. 379.

305

Cuevas told Forsyth that the president was not willing to cede territory. The North American then threatened the government for not paying the claims before, to which he was told that his tone was not new, and in fact, it was normal in negotiations with "whatever administration or agencies of the country (United States)."[546] Forsyth's threats to help the Liberals were not taken seriously, as he treated them in the same manner.

Rippy in his history of the relations between Mexico and the neighbor to the north, published a note from Forsyth urging his government to not remain passive and that if they wanted Sonora, they should raise an international scandal over the execution of the filibusterer Crabb. If they wanted more territory, all they had to do was present Mexico with an ultimatum over the debt for the diplomatic claims.[547] Forsyth's aggressiveness, hardly diplomatic, is only understandable in its historic context. President Buchanan, whose government was the last before the Civil War and also the last to be the openly predatory, had declared, "Expansion is the future policy of our country, and only cowards fear and oppose it."[548]. After the war, North American governments, conscious of their growing industrial power were more preoccupied with economically infiltrating their neighbors. Buchanan's government, however, was a preindustrial regime, for which he dreamed of more and more land.

In April, 1858, the Mexican ambassador in Washington wrote to Luis G. Cuevas with some surprising news. The senator of Texas, Samuel Houston, had submitted a proposal on the creation

---

[546] ASREM, Expediente 3-c-r-l, f. 821.

[547] Rippy, op. cit., p. 216.

[548] Albert Weinberg, Destino Manifiesto, Ed. Paídos, Buenas Aires, 1968, p. 185.

of a protectorate by the United States in Mexico! He explained that this was the only measure that could end the anarchy that reigned in the country and keep it from falling into the hands of a foreign power "against the interests of the United States." A force of five thousand men would be enough, and *would not cost the United States government anything as Mexico would pay the expenses. (italics by the translator)*[549] Not finding any support in the Senate, Houston tried to form a filibuster expedition to invade Mexico.[550] Since February, the Mexican Ambassador in Washington had been worried about invasions, writing to Lewis Cass, Secretary of State, asking that he break up an expedition being prepared in New York.[551] Zerman, the erstwhile filibusterer after the Treaty of Mesilla prepared a new attempt that Zuloaga's government frustrated. In March, Luis G. Cuevas wrote to the ambassador in Washington asking him to redouble his vigilance over the expeditions with "notes relevant to the North American projects to send filibuster expeditions to Mexico have been received under the pretext of helping the constitutional government."[552] Then in April, he was notified that they had received news that in New Orleans, Texas, and several other points of the United States, that filibuster expeditions were being organized to invade the national territory.[553]

Meanwhile, Ambassador Forsyth looked for more excuses to attack Zuloaga's government. Soon, an occasion presented itself in May, 1858, when Zuloaga published a decree that all landowners had to contribute one percent of their capital to

---

[549] ASREM, Expediente 6-12-14, f. 1.

[550] Ibidem, f. 16.

[551] ASREM, Expediente 5-c-r-l, f. 7.

[552] ASREM, Expediente 3-c-r-l, f. 816.

[553] Ibidem, f. 602.

defray the costs of the government. Forsyth and the English ambassador protested against the decree saying that it was really a "forced loan" and according to them, the Treaty of 1826 exempted English subjects and North Americans from such taxes under a favored nation clause.[554]

The decree deadline was postponed, but in July, 1858, the first deportations of those who refused to pay the tax were made. Among them was a Salomón Miguel, whom Forsyth decided to protect. On July 17, he wrote to Luis G. Cuevas saying that Miguel's rejection was due to his decision to formally protest against the legality of the decree. He reminded him that he himself had counseled disobedience of the decree and ended by threatening the government with grave consequences that the expulsion of a North American citizen would have.[555] This note was the beginning of a series of communications between Forsyth and Cuevas who in a letter to the ambassador in Washington said:

> Forsyth is determined to create all types of complications for the present government and in discrediting it in the least excusable way. The government believes that this conduct illustrates the desire of the United States to intervene in our internal affairs.

Such aggressiveness on Cuevas' part was attributed to rejection of ceding anymore territory with the hope that the North American government would not approve Forsyth's conduct.[556]

---

[554] Ibidem, f. 818.

[555] Ibidem, f. 845-847.

[556] Ibidem, ff. 835-837.

Learning of the issue, Secretary of State Lewis Cass did not consider the tax to have been a "forced loan" in the strict sense; however, given the bad relations between the two countries he instructed Forsyth to break off diplomatic relations. In his note, he told him that in no way did he think the tax was just, given that Zuloaga's administration was only recognized in part of the Mexican territory. If it was accepted, every local government could assume the same powers and oppress foreigners. *He asked that the Mexican regime not impose taxes before asking the opinion of the United States. (italics by the translator)*[557]

The tax problem was added to the arrest of several North American citizens in various places in the Republic. Forsyth denounced the imprisonment of a certain Roncari, accused of swindling the public in his role as theatrical impresario, as unjust. He also complained of the arrest of Jesús Ainra, accused of sedition. To this the Mexican government answered that Ainra was a Mexican caught in Mexican territory and as such there was no reason to complain. In his note to the Mexican ambassador in Washington, Luis G. Cuevas answered:

> You know that there is a system of agglomerating successive charges against the Republic, and that for a hostile spirit as well as to prepare public opinion so as to lessen the surprise of the intended aggression when it happens. It is often repeated that the United States government requires much from Mexico in defense of its citizens and their property. This system has been followed for thirty years.

Cuevas then ordered that the Mexican ambassador should request that Forsyth be relieved of his post.[558] In August, 1858,

---

[557] Ibidem, ff. 699-670.

[558] ibidem, ff. 871-879.

Forsyth communicated with Castillo Lanzas, the new Secretary of Exterior Relations, to inform him that his government had approved the suspension of relations while Luis G. Cuevas was in charge. The North American president ordered the legation in Mexico to close and to go to Veracruz where a warship would pick him up.[559]

Meanwhile, Forsyth had converted the legation in Veracruz into a center of conspirators. Miguel Lerdo de Tejada had lived there for several months, and Forsyth saw him as the leader of a revolution on the point of breaking out. He then informed his government that he had arms and thirty North Americans ready to defend the legation in case Zuloaga's government tried to take Lerdo de Tejada.[560] After unnecessarily bothering Zuloaga's government, Forsyth left the country on October 20, 1858. Two months later in December, Castillo Lanzas reported that 46 bars of gold stolen by the Constitutionalists (Juarez) from the cathedral in Morelia had been found in Forsyth's house.[561]

The pressure from Washington however did not end with the exit of Forsyth. Congressman Cox proposed the establishment of a protectorate over Mexico, as Samuel Houston had done in the Senate, and formed what he called an inexorable law in which "weaker, disorganized nations must be absorbed by the stronger and more organized."[562] In December, President Buchanan spoke of Mexico in his state of the union message and recommended the organization of a North American protectorate over the north

---

[559] Ibidem, ff. 701-706.

[560] Callahan, James Morton, American Foreign Policy in Mexican Relations, The Macmillan Co., New York, 1932, p. 258.

[561] ASREM, Expediente 3-c-r-l, f. 815.

[562] Weimberg, op. cit., p. 205.

of Chihuahua and Sonora to control the violence in Arizona and New Mexico. On January 11, 1859 he sent the presidential recommendation to the Foreign Relations Committee of the House of Representatives which gave him permission to use force to protect North American citizens in Mexico. Finally, and after lively debate, Congress defeated the motion by a vote of 31 to 25.[563] Again it was the growing division of Congress on the eve of the Civil War, that saved us from being invaded. The politicians from the north regarded with apprehension the desire to expand to the south because what was most important to them at the moment was to prevent the expansion of the slave states.

The withdrawal of Forsyth did not mean the breaking of relations with Mexico, only with the government of Zuloaga. On December 27 1858, Buchanan sent William M. Churchwell as special agent to investigate the Mexican situation. As with all presidential agents, before and since, Churchwell already brought prior instructions as to the results of his investigations. The Secretary of State, Lewis Cass told him:

> The message from the president to Congress will be understood to be the opinion of the administration in Mexican affairs. The Liberal Party has our cordial sympathies, and we are ready to give them moral help resulting in the recognition of its supremacy, as soon as this recognition can be done in conformity with our policies.[564]

Zuloaga's last Secretary of Exterior Relations, Miguel Arroyo, wrote to the ambassador in Washington asking him, by means of the press, to reject the ideas in the President's state of the union message to Congress. He called the message a direct attack on the integrity of the national territory and future sovereignty of

---

[563] Rippy, op. cit., p. 219.

[564] Ibidem, p. 219.

the nation,[565] and was replaced by Diez de Bonilla when General Miramón assumed the presidency on February 2, 1859. Zuloaga had probably lost power because of the weak stances he had taken in the situation. The Conservatives thought that with the audacity and youth of Miramón they would defeat the Liberals, with him assuring them that the taking of Veracruz (where the Liberals Juárez was) would end with a battle.

Meanwhile, as Churchwell and the government of Juárez were in talks, North American pressure continued. The Secretary of Exterior Relations of Miramón, Diez de Bonilla, directed himself to Washington to protest the events happening in Guaymas when the Sinaloan government informed him that two North American warships were headed to the Sonoran port with instructions to take it. The pretext was to punish the Liberals of Guaymas for having taken, without compensation, 500 rifles, property of a North American, found in the house of the United States consul. Diez de Bonilla protested to the Secretary of State:

> If this story is true, the United States' government should address a claim in the normal way to that of the Republic, and it would have been properly attended to, but in no case try to take a port of the nation for an act committed by rebels for which the supreme government cannot be held responsible.

Additionally, he energetically protested about the news that three to four thousand North Americans were posted on the Sonoran frontier.[566] These protests were not answered. When the Mexican ambassador in Washington went to the Secretary of State to ask why, he was told that they were waiting for the results of the conflict in Mexico to know which was the real government and

[565] ASREM, Expediente 3-c-r-l, ff. 575-576.

[566] ASREM, Expediente 6-2-21, ff. 7-8.

312

to direct itself to it.[567] In reality, what they were waiting for was to know the results of the mission of their envoy to President Juárez.

In December, 1858, we saw that President Buchanan had sent Churchwell to the government in Veracruz, which resulted in sending an ambassador, Robert McLane, to undertake talks with Melchor Ocampo, Juárez' Secretary of Exterior Relations. McLane was authorized to offer ten million dollars for Baja California and privileges of transit across the north of Mexico and Tehuantepec.[568] On April 14, 1859, Diez de Bonilla sent a circular to the diplomatic corps accredited in Mexico protesting because the United States government had recognized Benito Juárez' government as legitimate with the circular summarizing how the North American policy had led to this ending. In great detail he accused the North Americans of having broken relations with the Conservative government because this latter had rejected selling them national territory. Upon recognizing the Juárez government, "the conduct of the United States could not have had another reason than to acquire territory that the Conservatives had rejected. The circular ended with the declaration that they considered null all the treaties on cession of territory that had been established between the two countries.[569]

Much has been written about the McLane-Ocampo Treaty (Figure 9) with hundreds of pages filled to defend or attack Juárez in that regard. It seems to us that, as with all treaties, it must be examined as part of what was happening at the time. Juárez' government was bankrupt, there was a threat of European intervention, the Conservatives were actively fighting, and the United States wanted part of the country. There were rumors that

---

[567] Ibidem, ff. 3-5.

[568] Rippy, op. cit., p. 220.

[569] ASREM, Expediente LE-81, ff. 8-10.

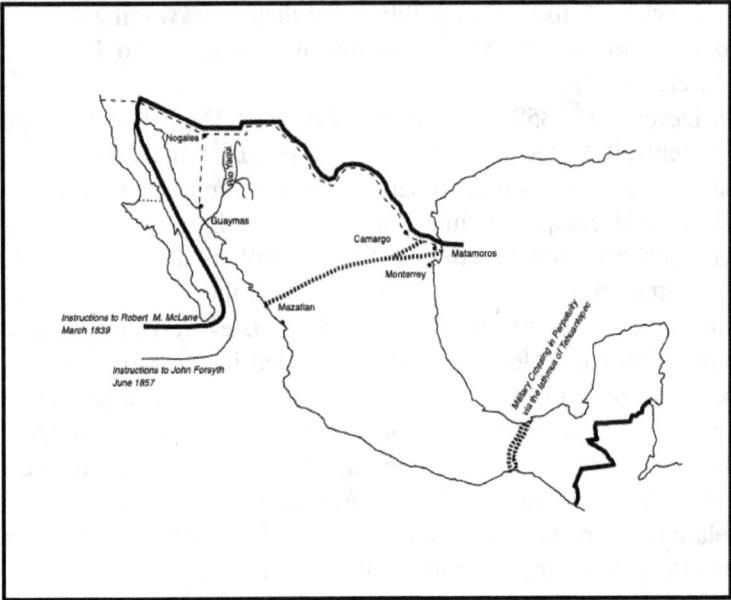

FIGURE 9. RIGHT OF TRANSIT GRANTED BY THE
TREATY OF MCLANE-OCAMPO, 1857-1859. (BASED
ON LUIS G. ZORRILLA, HISTÓRIA DE LAS
RELACIONES ENTRE MÉXICO Y LOS ESTADOS
UNIDOS DE AMÉRICA, ED. PORRÚA, VOL. 1965.)

Miramón had bought ships to attack Juárez from the sea. Many
are the historians recounting the Juárezist resignation to turn
over Baja California. The Juárezist resignation is what caused
the tardiness, during which the discussions on the treaty began in
April and ended in December. It is understood that what Juárez
wished for was to obtain a means by which he could get a loan
making a treaty unnecessary. This is what explains why, in the
middle of the discussions, the property of the clergy was
expropriated. In addition the church economically helped the
Conservative Party and this would be a good way to weaken it.

314

There was also the hope of getting a loan using the clerical property as a guarantee.meanwhile, the Conservatives asked for the intervention of Europe, while the North Americans insisted on their claims: right of transit in perpetuity across Tehuantepec; right of transit along the northern frontier to the Gulf of Mexico; authority to militarily protect the right of way across Tehuantepec, with or without the consent of the Mexican government; and the sale of Baja California.[570] For its part, the government of Juárez wanted a treaty of alliance that would be added to the convention under discussion, by which both countries would be obligated to help each other mutually in case of an attack by a third party. In addition, Juárez asked that the two Republics help each other to sustain order and security in the territory of the other. This was equivalent to permission to openly intervene, which of course, would be bilateral in theory.[571]

On September 26, 1859, the Treaty of Mon-Almonte was signed in Paris, and with it the European answer to the United States. On October 29, Miramón settled a large loan with the Swiss banker Jecker. As we know, this loan resulted in being more disastrous in practice than the McLane-Ocampo Treaty. At the same time, the Conservative victories including the great victory of Miramón in the Estancia de las Vacas continued: Oaxaca on November 7, Zacatecas the same day, then Tepic, and on November 13. Until this moment, it was clear that the Constitutionalist government could not win by itself and it was then that Juárez had to accede to the demands of the North Americans to save the Liberal cause. It took him eight months to

[570] Jose Fuentes Mares, Juárez y los Estados Unidos, Ed. Jus, México, 1972, p. 221, Cita el documento de "Proyecto de Tratado Robert McLane."

[571] Álvaro Matute, ed., Antologia. México en el sigo XIX, UNAM, México, 1973, p. 491.

decide, obviously with the hope of not having to sign the treaty which he signed when he saw no other way out, as was the case with Miramón and the Treaty of Mon-Almonte. Both chose what they saw as the lesser evil with the end justifying the means. The McLane-Ocampo Treaty was signed on December 14, 1859, with Juárez not ceding Baja California, nor parts of Sonora and Chihuahua that the North Americans had asked for. However, he had to accede to the transit in perpetuity in Tehuantepec and the right to protect it militarily, with or without consent from the Mexican government. In addition, and this was much more dangerous, he approved the right of passage from Guaymas to Nogales. In the seventh article he ceded in perpetuity transit between Camargo and Matamoros to a point in Tamaulipas, and from Monterrey to Mazatlán.[572]

Even Justo Serra, a good friend of Juárez, came out against the treaty in writing. I, however, do not intend to revive the old Liberals-Conservative quarrels. I only want to point out that Juárez like Miramón were imprudent their respective actions. The first was very lucky that Congress rejected the treaty. Many argue that the mutual aid clause was subscribed to, knowing that the United States could not intervene in Mexico as it was close to a civil war and that the clause was a trick to get military aid against the Conservatives. If those were his intentions, Juárez kept them to himself. The documents of his ambassadors do not refer to the clause in the same way. José María Mata, ambassador in Washington wrote to Ocampo on January 6, 1860 that he was worried about the possible rejection of the treaty and presented a summary of what its enemies, the Republican party, the Catholic party, and the bureaucrats who wanted the conflict to continue so they could keep selling arms, were saying. He even asked for money to find supporters for the treaty.[573]

---

[572] Ibidem, p. 490.

[573] ASREM, Expediente c-r-l 40 bis, ff. 162-164.

In a later letter, Mata reported that he had had published the letter of Gutiérrez Estrada in which he wanted a European monarch. This was the key to the problem: for the Liberals, a North American protectorate was preferable to a European monarch. For the Conservatives, it was just the opposite. Neither can be accused of treason. What both groups suffered was the profound pain of seeing the Mexican incapacity to govern themselves. Both wanted what was right for the country from different ideologies. As José María Mata wrote, he would do anything to get approval of the treaty, "because from my point of view, the pacification and the future growth of my country depend on it."[574]

At the end of January, Mata reported that opposition to the treaty had been developing, because those interested in a transoceanic passage via Nicaragua or Panama saw the opening of the Isthmus as a dangerous obstacle. They worked actively to impede confirmation of the treaty as the most efficient way to prevent the opening of Tehuantepec.[575]

While the ratification of the treaty was being debated in the North American Senate the incident of Antón Lizardo took place. Miramón, at the time president of the Conservatives, sent Admiral Tomás Marín to buy ships in La Habana to attack Veracruz once and for all, to impede the ratification of the treaty, and to end the war. Juárez' government heard about the departure of Marín through the ex-consul of the United States, who had remained in the capital even though it was in Conservative hands. They informed José María Mata in Washington so that he could with all the resources at his command keep Marín from buying armaments and war supplies in the United States. Tomás

---

[574] Ibidem, ff. 14-14.

[575] ASREM, Expediente c-r-l 40 bis, f. 165.

Marín did not go to the United States but to Cuba and from there to Spain. Mata reported that "a North American navy officer told me that if he were given an armed steamship of enough strength he would promise to capture Marín and all of his ships."[576]

On March 10, 1860, the Department of State answered the Mexican government with respect to Mata's information about the (Conservative) blockade of Veracruz established by Marín:

> Previously Mr. McLane, ambassador of the United States in Mexico, had called our attention to this business, and he was told to not respect the authority of the blockade, and he was given the necessary instructions to protect North American commerce in the Gulf of Mexico. [577]

A few days later, the North Americans informed Ocampo that the English ambassador in Washington had assured them that their ships would not accept a blockade.[578]

Meanwhile, Juárez proclaimed a decree in which he declared Marín's ships to be pirates. The representative of McLane in Veracruz was informed that he should make known the decree to the captains of the North American ships located near Veracruz so that they could "actively and effectively" chase Marin's ships, "because those ships are carrying projectiles and munitions of war for the rebels that they will use against this place and against the interests and persons of North American citizens and their respectable legation."[579]

---

576 Ibidem, f. 37.

577 Ibidem, f. 51.

578 Ibidem, f. 52

579 Fuentes Mares, op. cit., p. 175.

On March 6, 1860, two Conservative ships, the General Miramón and the Marques de la Habana, anchored in Antón Lizardo (near Veracruz). At the same time, Miramón and his forces appeared before Veracruz in hopes of a coordinated attack. The Secretary of Exterior Relations wrote to the North American Secretary of State:

> The Mexican ship, General Miramón, was anchored in Mexican waters when the North American Saratoga approached to examine its nationality by which it deduced without any doubt that it was his (the Saratoga's captain's) judgement that (the ship) was purposely placed to provoke a battle between the North American naval forces and the Mexican steamships.[580]

We know that the North Americans ended up capturing the Mexican ships, and the cargo of pirates, who were sent to New Orleans. They had decided to help the Liberal government, and this meant their salvation even though it was an act of interference in the internal politics of the country. However, it should be pointed out that the intervention was at the behest of the Benito Juárez' government. Both sides, Liberals and Conservatives, asked for help from foreign governments. The two parties sought the intervention of a third party to break the stalemate in which they found themselves. The intervention of the United States did not have disastrous consequences, however, as its own Congress rejected the ratification of the McLane-Ocampo Treaty. Hence, the Juárez group has been exonerated by history. In the final analysis, the end is judged, not the means in a historical event. Juárez had the enormous luck that his treaty, for reasons internal to the United States, was rejected. This luck has been called political vision; perhaps it was. Until now, we do not

---

[580] ASREM, Expediente LE-81, ff. 74-76.

know for certain. What is unjust is to attack the Conservatives for being unlucky. I firmly believe that both parties were profoundly patriotic and looked for the well being of the country according to their ideology.

One month later, in January, 1861, Juárez rejoined his government in Mexico City. In South Carolina, northerners and southerners found themselves on the point of breaking from the American Union. In March, Abraham Lincoln came to power and on April 12, 1861, the Civil War began. This is where we stop our narrative. For a while the Secretaries of State stopped communicating. The Civil War made them look inward and leave their neighbors in peace, . . . for the moment.

BIBLIOGRAPHY

Books

Baylin, Bernard, et al., *The Great Republic*, Little Brown and Co., Boston, 1977

Bancroft, Hubert Howe, *History of Arizona and New Mexico*, The History Co., San Francisco, 1889.

____, *History of California*, vol. VI, The History Co.San Francisco, 1886.

Basave, Agustin, *Visión de Estados Unidos*, De Diana, México, 1974

Bautista Pino, Pedro, *Noticias históricas y estadísticas de la antigua provincia de Nuevo México, presentadas por su diputado de las Cortes de Cádiz en el año de 1812*, Imprenta de Lara, México, 1849.

Beck, Warren, *New Mexico, a History of Four Centuries*, University of Oklahoma Press, Oklahoma, 1962.

Bemis, Samuel, *A Diplomatic History of the U.S.*, Henry Holt and Co., New York, 1942.

Benton, Thomas Hart, *Thirty Years View, vol. 1*, I.D. Appleton, New York, 1958.

Boorstin, Daniel J., *Historia de los norteamericanos: La experiencia colonial*, Tipográfia Editorial Argentina, Buenos Aires, 1973.

Bosch Garcia, Carlos, *Material para la historia diplomática de México*, UNAM, México 1957.

____, *Historia de las relaciones entre México y los Estados Unidos*, UNAM, México, 1961.

____, *La base de la política exterior estadounidense*, UNAM, México, 1969.

Bravo Ugarte, José, *Compendio de historia de México*, Editorial Jus, México, 1972.

Burns, Edward M., *The American Idea of Mission*, Rutgers University Press, New Jersey, 1957.

Bustamente, Carlos M., *Gabinete Mexicano, vol. 3*, Ed. José M. Lara, México, 1842.

Callahan, James, *American Foreign Policy in Mexican Relations*, Cooper Square, New York, 1967.

Canales, Isidro, *Invasión de los indios bárbaros*, Universidad de Nuevo Leon, Monterrey, 1964.

Caughey, John Walton, *Early Federal Relations with Mexico*, Doctoral Thesis, University of California, Los Angeles, 1923.

Cleland Robert G., *From Wilderness to Empire*, Alfred Knopf, New York, 1944.

____, *History of California, The American Period*, The MacMilland Co., New York, 1922.

Connors, Seymour, et al., *La intervención norteamericana*, Ed. América Nueva, México, 1956.

Cutts, James M., *The Conquest of California and New Mexico*, Horn and Wallace, Albuquerque, 1966.

Duffins, R.L., *The Santa Fe Trail*, Longmans Green and Co., New York, 1930.

Esquivel Obregón, Toribio, *Apuntes para la historia de derecho en México, vol. IV (Relaciones Internacionales)*, Antigua Librería Robredo, México, 1948.

Emory, William H., *Notes of a Military Reconnaissance*, Wendell and Van Behthuysen, Washington D.C., 1848.

Fuentes Mares, José, *Poinsett, historia de un gran intriga*, Editorial Jus, México, 1951.

Flores, Jorge, *Documentos para la historia de la Baja California, vol. 2*, Ed. Intercontinental, México, 1946.

Garrad, Lewis H., *Wha-to-Yah and the Taos Trail*, Ed. Ralph Bieber, The Arthur H. Clark Co., Glendale, California, 1938.

Gregg, Josiah, *Commerce of the Prairies*, J.W. Moore, Philadelphia, 1849, y Norman Press, Oklahoma, 1954.

Heyman, Max L., *Prudent Soldier, a Biography of Major General Camby 1817-1873*, The Arthur H. Clark Co., Glendale, California, 1959.

Lavender, David, *Bent's Fort*, University of Nebraska Press, Lincoln, Nebraska, 1972.

López y Rivas, Gilberto, *La guerra del 47*, Ed. ERA, México, 1976.

Long, Robert, *Life and Times of José Matias Moreno*, Doctoral Thesis, Western University, San Diego, California, 1972.

Magoffin, Susan Shelby, *Down the Santa Fe Trail and into Mexico*, Yale University Press, New Haven, 1926.

Martinez Pablo, *Historia de Baja California*, Libros Mexicanos, México, 1956.

Matute, Álvaro, ed. Antología, *México en el siglo XIX*, UNAM, México, 1973.

McDonald, Decker, *The Last Best Hope*, Addison, Wesley and Goon, Reading, Massachusetts, 1972.

McNickle, D'Arcy, *Las tribus indios de los Estados Unidos*, Eudeba, Buenos Aires, 1976.

McWilliams, Carey, *Al norte de México, Siglo XXI*, México, 1972.

Merck, Frederick, *Manifest Destiny and Mission in American History*, Alfred A. Knopf, New York, 1963.

Moorhead, Max, *New Mexico's Royal Road*, Norman Press, Oklahoma, 1958.

Morton, A.L., *A People's History of England*, Lawrence and Wishart, London, 1956.

Moyano, Angela, *El comercio de Santa Fe y la guerra del 47*, Sepsetenta, México, 1975.

Nance, Joseph Milton, *After San Jacinto the Texas-Mexican Frontier, 1836-1841*, University of Texas Press, Austin, 1964.

Nunis, Doyce, Jr., ed. *The Mexican War in California: Memorandum of Captain Henry Halleck*, Dawson's Bookshop, Los Angeles, 1977.

O'Donovan, Patrick, *Los Estados Unidos*, Biblioteca Universal de Life en español, Offset Multicolor, S.A., México, 1966.

O'Gorman, Edmundo, *México, el trauma de su historia*, UNAM, México, 1977.

Olavarria, Enrique, *México a través de los siglos, vol. IV*, Ed. Cumbre, México, 1977.

Orozco Farias, Rogelio, *Fuentes históricas de México, 1821-1867*, Edición del autor, México, 1952.

Ortega y Medina, Juan, *Destino Manifiesto*, Sepsetentas, México, 1973.

Paredes, Mariano, *Proyectos de leyes sobre colonización en el estado de Sonora, presentados a la Cámara de Diputados por el representante de aquel estado en la sesión extraordinaria del día . . . 1850*, Ignacio Cumplido, México, 1850.

Perkins, Dexter, *Historia de la doctrina Monroe*, Ed. Universitaria de Buenos Aires, Buenos Aires, 1964.

Pitt, Leonard, *The Decline of the Californias*, University of California Press, Los Angeles, 1966.

Polk, James, ed. Luis Cabrera, *Diario del Presidente Polk*, Antigua Libreria Robredo, México, 2 vols., 1948.

Pourade, Richard, *The Silver Dons, the History of San Diego*, Union-Tribune Publishing Co., San Diego, 1963.

Powell, Philip, *El arból del odio*, Ed. José Porrua Turanzas, Madrid, 1972.

Price, Glenn, *Orígenes de la guerra con México*, Fondo de Cultura Económica, México, 1967.

Ramirez, José Fernando, *Memorias, negociaciones y documentos para servir a la historia de las diferencias que se hand suscitado entre México y los Estados Unidos, los tenedores del antiguo privilegio para la comunicación de los mares*, Imprenta Ignacio Cumplido, México, 1853.

Rippy, Fred. J. *The U.S. and Mexico*, F.S. Crofts and Co. New York, 1931.

Ruxton, George, *Adventures in Mexico and the Rocky Mountains*, ed. Perey R. Hafen, Norman Press, Oklahoma, 1950.

Salado Álvarez, Victoriano, *Cómo perdimos California y salvamos Tehuantepec*, Ed. Jus., México, 1965.

Sánchez, José M., *Viaje a Texas*, s.c.e., México, 1829.

St. Cooke, George, *The Conquest of New Mexico and California*, Horn and Wallace, Albuquerque, 1964.

Schmitt, Karl, *México y Estados Unidos*, Ed. LIMUSA, México, 1978.

Sepúlveda, César, *Tres ensayos sobre la frontera septentrional de la Nueva España*, Ed. Porrúa, México, 1977.

__, *La frontera norte*, Ed. Porrúa, México, 1976.

Sodi Álvarez, Enrique, *Istmo de Tehuantepec*, s.e. México, 1967.

Stout, Allen Joseph, *The Last Years of Manifest Destiny, Filibustering in Northern Mexico*, Barton Books, New York, 1962.

Twitchell, Ralph E., *Leading Fact of New Mexico History*, Rio Grand Press, Chicago, 1963.

Urbina, Manuel, *Effects of the Independence of Texas on the Government, Politics and Society in Mexico*, 1836-1846, Doctoral Thesis, University of Texas, Austin, 1976.

Webb, Prescott, *The Great Plains*, Wedel W.R., New York, 1931.

Weber, David, *The Taos Trappers, The Fur Trade in the Far South West 1540-1846*, Norman Press, Oklahoma, 1954.

Weber, Max, *The Protestant Ethic and the Spirit of Capitalism*, George Allen Ltd. London, 1976.

Weimberg, Albert, *Destino Manifiesto*, Ed. Paidós, Buenas Aires, 1968.

Wright, Louis, *Breve historia de los Estados Unidos*, Ed. LIMUSA, 1972.

Woodward, William, *The Way Our People Lived*, Washington Square Press.

Valdés, José C., *Alamán, estadista e historiador*, Antigua Libreria Robredo, México, 1938.

Vaughan, Alden T., *The Puritan Tradition in America*, Harper and Row, New York, 1972.

Velasco Márquez, Jesus, *La guerra del 47 y la opinión pública*, Sepsetentas, México, 1975.

Zorrilla, Luis G., *Historia de las relaciones entre México y los Estados Unidos de América*, Ed. Porrúa, 2 vols., México, 1965.

Journals

Cazadero, Manuel, "¿Pudo México ganar la guerra contra los Estados Unidos?", *Anglia, num.* 5, Armario de Estudios Angloamericanos, Facultad de Filosofía y Letras, UNAM, México, 1978.

Knapp, Frank A., "Preludios de la pérdida de California", *Historia Mexicana, IV, (14)*, El Colegio de México, México, 1956.

Marshall, Thomas Maitland, "Commercial Aspects of the Texan-Santa Fe Expedition", *The South-Western Historical Quarterly*, University of Texas Press, Austin, vol II, 1917.

McNitt, Frank, "Navajo Campaigns and the Occupation of New Mexico 1847-1848", *New Mexico Historical Review*, University of New Mexico, vol. LIII, 1952.

Rippy, Fred, "The Indians of the Southwest in the Diplomacy of the United States and Mexico", *Hispanic American Historical Review, II*, August, 1919.

Vázquez de Knauth, "El congreso de los Estados Unidos y la guerra de 47", *Anglia, num.* 5, Facultad de Filosofia y Letras, UNAM, México, 1973.

Newspapers

Gaceta Diaria de México, México, D.F., 4 de junio de 1825.

El Republicano, México, D.F., 5 de febrero de 1847.

Daily Missouri Republican, Liberty Mississippi, 5 de diciembre de 1846.

Weekly Tribune, Missouri, 5 de diciembre de 1846.

Archives

Archivo de la Secretaria de Relaciones Exteriores de México, (ASREM).

Archive of the University of New Mexico, *Benjamin Read Collection* and *Ritche Papers Collection*.

Record of the War Department, *The National Archives*, Wendall and Van Benthysen, 1872.

Message from the President of the United States to the 2 houses of Congress at the Commencement of the 1st Session of the 30th Congress, December 7, 1847. Wendall and Van Benthysen, Washington, 1847.

State Records Center and Archives, Santa Fe, File numbers 170, 35, 295, Benjamin Read Collection.

Archivo Historico de La Paz "Pablo L. Martinez", Northamerican file.

Document Collection of the House of Representatives Executive num. 1, Series 537, Congress 30, Second Session, Washington, 1848.

Bancroft Library Archives, Cowen Collection, University of California, Berkeley, Microfilms, num 12 y 13, 1847

APPENDICES

APPENDIX I-TRANSCRIPT OF THE TREATY OF GUADALUPE-HIDALGO (1848)

TREATY OF PEACE, FRIENDSHIP, LIMITS, AND SETTLEMENT BETWEEN THE UNITED STATES OF AMERICA AND THE UNITED MEXICAN STATES CONCLUDED AT GUADALUPE HIDALGO, FEBRUARY 2, 1848; RATIFICATION ADVISED BY SENATE, WITH AMENDMENTS, MARCH 10, 1848; RATIFIED BY PRESIDENT, MARCH 16, 1848; RATIFICATIONS EXCHANGED AT QUERETARO, MAY 30, 1848; PROCLAIMED, JULY 4, 1848.

IN THE NAME OF ALMIGHTY GOD
The United States of America and the United Mexican States animated by a sincere desire to put an end to the calamities of the war which unhappily exists between the two Republics and to establish Upon a solid basis relations of peace and friendship, which shall confer reciprocal benefits upon the citizens of both, and assure the concord, harmony, and mutual confidence wherein the two people should live, as good neighbors have for that purpose appointed their respective plenipotentiaries, that is to say: The President of the United States has appointed Nicholas P. Trist, a citizen of the United States, and the President of the Mexican Republic has appointed Don Luis Gonzaga Cuevas, Don Bernardo Couto, and Don Miguel Atristain, citizens of the said Republic; Who, after a

328

reciprocal communication of their respective full powers, have, under the protection of Almighty God, the author of peace, arranged, agreed upon, and signed the following: Treaty of Peace, Friendship, Limits, and Settlement between the United States of America and the Mexican Republic.

ARTICLE I

There shall be firm and universal peace between the United States of America and the Mexican Republic, and between their respective countries, territories, cities, towns, and people, without exception of places or persons.

ARTICLE II

Immediately upon the signature of this treaty, a convention shall be entered into between a commissioner or commissioners appointed by the General-in-chief of the forces of the United States, and such as may be appointed by the Mexican Government, to the end that a provisional suspension of hostilities shall take place, and that, in the places occupied by the said forces, constitutional order may be reestablished, as regards the political, administrative, and judicial branches, so far as this shall be permitted by the circumstances of military occupation.

ARTICLE III

Immediately upon the ratification of the present treaty by the Government of the United States, orders shall be transmitted to the commanders of their land and naval forces, requiring the latter (provided this treaty shall then have been ratified by the Government of the Mexican Republic, and the ratifications exchanged) immediately to desist from blockading any Mexican ports and requiring the former (under the same condition) to commence, at the earliest moment practicable, withdrawing all troops of the United States then in the interior of the Mexican Republic, to points that shall be selected by common agreement, at a distance from the seaports not exceeding thirty leagues; and such evacuation of the interior of the Republic shall be completed with the least possible delay; the Mexican Government hereby binding itself to afford every facility in its power for rendering the same convenient to the troops, on their march and in their new positions, and for promoting a good understanding between them and the inhabitants. In like manner orders shall be despatched to the persons in charge of the custom houses at all ports occupied by the forces of the United States, requiring them (under the same condition) immediately to deliver possession of the same to the persons authorized by the Mexican Government to receive it, together with all bonds and evidences of debt for duties on importations and on exportations, not yet fallen due. Moreover, a faithful and exact account shall be made out, showing the entire amount of all duties on imports and on exports, collected at such custom-houses, or elsewhere in Mexico, by authority of the United States, from and after the day of ratification of this treaty by the Government of the Mexican Republic; and also an account of the cost of collection; and such entire amount, deducting only the cost of collection, shall be delivered to the Mexican Government, at the city of Mexico, within three months after the exchange of ratifications.

The evacuation of the capital of the Mexican Republic by the troops of the United States, in virtue of the above stipulation, shall be completed in one month after the orders there stipulated for shall have been received by the commander of said troops, or sooner if possible.

ARTICLE IV

Immediately after the exchange of ratifications of the present treaty all castles, forts, territories, places, and possessions, which have been taken or occupied by the forces of the United States during the present war, within the limits of the Mexican Republic, as about to be established by the following article, shall be definitely restored to the said Republic, together with all the artillery, arms, apparatus of war, munitions, and other public property, which were in the said castles and forts when captured, and which shall remain there at the time when this treaty shall be duly ratified by the Government of the Mexican Republic. To this end, immediately upon the signature of this treaty, orders shall be despatched to the American officers commanding such castles and forts, securing against the removal or destruction of any such artillery, arms, apparatus of war, munitions, or other public property. The city of Mexico, within the inner line of entrenchments surrounding the said city, is comprehended in the above stipulation, as regards the restoration of artillery, apparatus of war, & c.

The final evacuation of the territory of the Mexican Republic, by the forces of the United States, shall be completed in three months from the said exchange of ratifications, or sooner if possible; the Mexican Government hereby engaging, as in the foregoing article to use all means in its power for facilitating such evacuation, and rendering it convenient to the troops, and for promoting a good understanding between them and the inhabitants.

If, however, the ratification of this treaty by both parties should not take place in time to allow the embarkation of the troops of the United States to be completed before the commencement of the sickly season, at the Mexican ports on the Gulf of Mexico, in such case a friendly arrangement shall be entered into between the General-in-Chief of the said troops and the Mexican Government, whereby healthy and otherwise suitable places, at a distance from the ports not exceeding thirty leagues, shall be designated for the residence of such troops as may not yet have embarked, until the return of the healthy season. And the space of time here referred to as, comprehending the sickly season shall be understood to extend from the first day of May to the first day of November.

All prisoners of war taken on either side, on land or on sea, shall be restored as soon as practicable after the exchange of ratifications of this treaty. It is also agreed that if any Mexicans should now be held as captives by any savage tribe within the limits of the United States, as about to be established by the following article, the Government of the said United States will exact the release of such captives and cause them to be restored to their country.

ARTICLE V

The boundary line between the two Republics shall commence in the Gulf of Mexico, three leagues from land, opposite the mouth of the Rio Grande, otherwise called

Rio Bravo del Norte, or Opposite the mouth of its deepest branch, if it should have more than one branch emptying directly into the sea; from thence up the middle of that river, following the deepest channel, where it has more than one, to the point where it strikes the southern boundary of New Mexico; thence, westwardly, along the whole southern boundary of New Mexico (which runs north of the town called Paso) to its western termination; thence, northward, along the western line of New Mexico, until it intersects the first branch of the river Gila; (or if it should not intersect any branch of that river, then to the point on the said line nearest to such branch, and thence in a direct line to the same); thence down the middle of the said branch and of the said river, until it empties into the Rio Colorado; thence across the Rio Colorado, following the division line between Upper and Lower California, to the Pacific Ocean.

The southern and western limits of New Mexico, mentioned in the article, are those laid down in the map entitled "Map of the United Mexican States, as organized and defined by various acts of the Congress of said republic, and constructed according to the best authorities. Revised edition. Published at New York, in 1847, by J. Disturnell," of which map a copy is added to this treaty, bearing the signatures and seals of the undersigned Plenipotentiaries. And, in order to preclude all difficulty in tracing upon the ground the limit separating Upper from Lower California, it is agreed that the said limit shall consist of a straight line drawn from the middle of the Rio Gila, where it unites with the Colorado, to a point on the coast of the Pacific Ocean, distant one marine league due south of the southernmost point of the port of San Diego, according to the plan of said port made in the year 1782 by Don Juan Pantoja, second sailing-master of the

Spanish fleet, and published at Madrid in the year 1802, in the atlas to the voyage of the schooners Sutil and Mexicana; of which plan a copy is hereunto added, signed and sealed by the respective Plenipotentiaries.

In order to designate the boundary line with due precision, upon authoritative maps, and to establish upon the ground land-marks which shall show the limits of both republics, as described in the present article, the two Governments shall each appoint a commissioner and a surveyor, who, before the expiration of one year from the date of the exchange of ratifications of this treaty, shall meet at the port of San Diego, and proceed to run and mark the said boundary in its whole course to the mouth of the Rio Bravo del Norte. They shall keep journals and make out plans of their operations; and the result agreed upon by them shall be deemed a part of this treaty, and shall have the same force as if it were inserted therein. The two Governments will amicably agree regarding what may be necessary to these persons, and also as to their respective escorts, should such be necessary.

The boundary line established by this article shall be religiously respected by each of the two republics, and no change shall ever be made therein, except by the express and free consent of both nations, lawfully given by the General Government of each, in conformity with its own constitution.

ARTICLE VI

The vessels and citizens of the United States shall, in all time, have a free and uninterrupted passage by the Gulf of California, and by the river Colorado below its confluence with the Gila, to and from their possessions situated north of the boundary line defined in the preceding article; it being understood that this passage is to be by navigating the Gulf of California and the river Colorado, and not by land, without the express consent of the Mexican Government.

If, by the examinations which may be made, it should be ascertained to be practicable and advantageous to construct a road, canal, or railway, which should in whole or in part run upon the river Gila, or upon its right or its left bank, within the space of one marine league from either margin of the river, the Governments of both republics will form an agreement regarding its construction, in order that it may serve equally for the use and advantage of both countries.

ARTICLE VII

The river Gila, and the part of the Rio Bravo del Norte lying below the southern boundary of New Mexico, being, agreeably to the fifth article, divided in the middle between the two republics, the navigation of the Gila and of the Bravo below said boundary shall be free and common to the vessels and citizens of both countries; and neither shall, without the consent of the other, construct any work that may impede or interrupt, in whole or in part, the exercise of this right; not even for the purpose of favoring new methods of navigation. Nor shall any tax or contribution, under any denomination or title, be levied upon vessels or persons navigating the same or upon merchandise or effects transported thereon, except in the case of landing upon one of their shores. If, for the purpose of making the said rivers navigable, or for maintaining them in such state, it should be necessary or advantageous to establish any tax or contribution, this shall not be done without the consent of both Governments.

The stipulations contained in the present article shall not impair the territorial rights of either republic within its established limits.

ARTICLE VIII

Mexicans now established in territories previously belonging to Mexico, and which remain for the future within the limits of the United States, as defined by the present treaty, shall be free to continue where they now reside, or to remove at any time to the Mexican Republic, retaining the property which they possess in the said territories, or disposing thereof, and removing the proceeds wherever they please, without their being subjected, on this account, to any contribution, tax, or charge whatever.

Those who shall prefer to remain in the said territories may either retain the title and rights of Mexican citizens, or acquire those of citizens of the United States. But they shall be under the obligation to make their election within one year from the date of the exchange of ratifications of this treaty; and those who shall remain in the said territories after the expiration of that year, without having declared their intention to retain the character of Mexicans, shall be considered to have elected to become citizens of the United States.

In the said territories, property of every kind, now belonging to Mexicans not established there, shall be inviolably respected. The present owners, the heirs of these, and all Mexicans who may hereafter acquire said property by contract, shall enjoy with respect to it guarantees equally ample as if the same belonged to citizens of the United States.

ARTICLE IX

The Mexicans who, in the territories aforesaid, shall not preserve the character of citizens of the Mexican Republic, conformably with what is stipulated in the preceding article, shall be incorporated into the Union of the United States. and be admitted at the proper time (to be judged of by the Congress of the United States) to the enjoyment of all the rights of citizens of the United States, according to the principles of the Constitution; and in the mean time, shall be maintained and protected in the free enjoyment of their liberty and property, and secured in the free exercise of their religion without restriction.

ARTICLE X
[Stricken out]

ARTICLE XI

Considering that a great part of the territories, which, by the present treaty, are to be comprehended for the future within the limits of the United States, is now occupied by savage tribes, who will hereafter be under the exclusive control of the Government of the United States, and whose incursions within the territory of Mexico would be prejudicial in the extreme, it is solemnly agreed that all such incursions shall be forcibly restrained by the Government of the United States whensoever this may be necessary; and that when they cannot be prevented, they shall be punished by the said Government, and satisfaction for the same shall be exacted all in the same way, and with equal diligence and energy, as if the same incursions were meditated or committed within its own territory, against its own citizens.

It shall not be lawful, under any pretext whatever, for any inhabitant of the United States to purchase or acquire any Mexican, or any foreigner residing in Mexico, who may have been captured by Indians inhabiting the territory of either of the two republics; nor to purchase or acquire horses, mules, cattle, or property of any kind, stolen within Mexican territory by such Indians.

And in the event of any person or persons, captured within Mexican territory by Indians, being carried into the territory of the United States, the Government of the latter engages and binds itself, in the most solemn manner, so soon as it shall know of such captives being within its territory, and shall be able so to do, through the faithful exercise of its influence and power, to rescue them and return them to their country. or deliver them to the agent or representative of the Mexican Government. The Mexican authorities will, as far as practicable, give to the Government of the United States notice of such captures; and its agents shall pay the expenses incurred in the maintenance and transmission of the rescued captives; who, in the mean time, shall be treated with the utmost hospitality by the American authorities at the place where they may be. But if the Government of the United States, before receiving such notice from Mexico, should obtain intelligence, through any other channel, of the existence of Mexican captives within its territory, it will proceed forthwith to effect their release and delivery to the Mexican agent, as above stipulated.

For the purpose of giving to these stipulations the fullest possible efficacy, thereby affording the security and redress demanded by their true spirit and intent, the Government of the United States will now and hereafter pass, without unnecessary delay, and always vigilantly enforce, such laws as the nature of the subject may require. And, finally, the sacredness of this obligation shall never be lost sight of by the said Government, when providing for the removal of the Indians from any portion of the said territories, or for its being settled by citizens of the United States; but, on the contrary, special care shall then be taken not to place its Indian occupants under the necessity of seeking new homes, by committing those invasions which the United States have solemnly obliged themselves to restrain.

ARTICLE XII

In consideration of the extension acquired by the boundaries of the United States, as defined in the fifth article of the present treaty, the Government of the United States engages to pay to that of the Mexican Republic the sum of fifteen millions of dollars.

Immediately after the treaty shall have been duly ratified by the Government of the Mexican Republic, the sum of three millions of dollars shall be paid to the said Government by that of the United States, at the city of

Mexico, in the gold or silver coin of Mexico. The remaining twelve millions of dollars shall be paid at the same place, and in the same coin, in annual installments of three millions of dollars each, together with interest on the same at the rate of six per cent per annum. This interest shall begin to run upon the whole sum of twelve millions from the day of the ratification of the present treaty by--the Mexican Government, and the first of the installments shall be paid-at the expiration of one year from the same day. Together with each annual installment, as it falls due, the whole interest accruing on such installment from the beginning shall also be paid.

ARTICLE XIII

The United States engage, moreover, to assume and pay to the claimants all the amounts now due them, and those hereafter to become due, by reason of the claims already liquidated and decided against the Mexican Republic, under the conventions between the two republics severally concluded on the eleventh day of April, eighteen hundred and thirty-nine, and on the thirtieth day of January, eighteen hundred and forty-three; so that the Mexican Republic shall be absolutely exempt, for the future, from all expense whatever on account of the said claims.

ARTICLE XIV

The United States do furthermore discharge the Mexican Republic from all claims of citizens of the United States, not heretofore decided against the Mexican Government, which may have arisen previously to the date of the signature of this treaty; which discharge shall be final and perpetual, whether the said claims be rejected or be allowed by the board of commissioners provided for in the following article, and whatever shall be the total amount of those allowed.

ARTICLE XV

The United States, exonerating Mexico from all demands on account of the claims of their citizens mentioned in the preceding article, and considering them entirely and forever canceled, whatever their amount may be, undertake to make satisfaction for the same, to an amount not exceeding three and one-quarter millions of dollars. To ascertain the validity and amount of those claims, a board of commissioners shall be established by the Government of the United States, whose awards shall be final and conclusive; provided that, in deciding upon the validity of each claim, the boa shall be guided and governed by the principles and rules of decision prescribed by the first and fifth articles of the unratified convention, concluded at the city of Mexico on the twentieth day of November, one thousand eight hundred and forty-three; and in no case shall an award be made in favour of any claim not embraced by these principles and rules.

If, in the opinion of the said board of commissioners or of the claimants, any books, records, or documents, in the possession or power of the Government of the Mexican Republic, shall be deemed necessary to the just decision of any claim, the commissioners, or the claimants through them, shall, within such period as Congress may designate, make an application in writing for the same, addressed to the Mexican Minister of Foreign Affairs, to be transmitted by the Secretary of State of the United States;

and the Mexican Government engages, at the earliest possible moment after the receipt of such demand, to cause any of the books, records, or documents so specified, which shall be in their possession or power (or authenticated copies or extracts of the same), to be transmitted to the said Secretary of State, who shall immediately deliver them over to the said board of commissioners; provided that no such application shall be made by or at the instance of any claimant, until the facts which it is expected to prove by such books, records, or documents, shall have been stated under oath or affirmation.

ARTICLE XVI

Each of the contracting parties reserves to itself the entire right to fortify whatever point within its territory it may judge proper so to fortify for its security.

ARTICLE XVII

The treaty of amity, commerce, and navigation, concluded at the city of Mexico, on the fifth day of April, A. D. 1831, between the United States of America and the United Mexican States, except the additional article, and except so far as the stipulations of the said treaty may be incompatible with any stipulation contained in the present treaty, is hereby revived for the period of eight years from the day of the exchange of ratifications of this treaty, with the same force and virtue as if incorporated therein; it being understood that each of the contracting parties reserves to itself the right, at any time after the said period of eight years shall have expired, to terminate the same by giving one year's notice of such intention to the other party.

ARTICLE XVIII

All supplies whatever for troops of the United States in Mexico, arriving at ports in the occupation of such troops previous to the final evacuation thereof, although subsequently to the restoration of the custom-houses at such ports, shall be entirely exempt from duties and charges of any kind; the Government of the United States hereby engaging and pledging its faith to establish and vigilantly to enforce, all possible guards for securing the revenue of Mexico, by preventing the importation, under cover of this stipulation, of any articles other than such, both in kind and in quantity, as shall really be wanted for the use and consumption of the forces of the United States during the time they may remain in Mexico. To this end it shall be the duty of all officers and agents of the United States to denounce to the Mexican authorities at the respective ports any attempts at a fraudulent abuse of this stipulation, which they may know of, or may have reason to suspect, and to give to such authorities all the aid in their power with regard thereto; and every such attempt, when duly proved and established by sentence of a competent tribunal, They shall be punished by the confiscation of the property so attempted to be fraudulently introduced.

ARTICLE XIX

With respect to all merchandise, effects, and property whatsoever, imported into ports of Mexico, whilst in the occupation of the forces of the United States, whether by citizens of either republic, or by citizens or subjects of any neutral nation, the following rules shall be observed:

(1) All such merchandise, effects, and property, if imported previously to the restoration of the custom-houses to the Mexican authorities, as stipulated for in the third article of this treaty, shall be exempt from confiscation, although the importation of the same be prohibited by the Mexican tariff.

(2) The same perfect exemption shall be enjoyed by all such merchandise, effects, and property, imported subsequently to the restoration of the custom-houses, and previously to the sixty days fixed in the following article for the coming into force of the Mexican tariff at such ports respectively; the said merchandise, effects, and property being, however, at the time of their importation, subject to the payment of duties, as provided for in the said following article.

(3) All merchandise, effects, and property described in the two rules foregoing shall, during their continuance at the place of importation, and upon their leaving such place for the interior, be exempt from all duty, tax, or imposts of every kind, under whatsoever title or denomination. Nor shall they be there subject to any charge whatsoever upon the sale thereof.

(4) All merchandise, effects, and property, described in the first and second rules, which shall have been removed to any place in the interior, whilst such place was in the occupation of the forces of the United States, shall, during their continuance therein, be exempt from all tax upon the sale or consumption thereof, and from every kind of impost or contribution, under whatsoever title or denomination.

(5) But if any merchandise, effects, or property, described in the first and second rules, shall be removed to any place not occupied at the time by the forces of the United States, they shall, upon their introduction into such place, or upon their sale or consumption there, be subject to the same duties which, under the Mexican laws, they would be required to pay in such cases if they had been imported in time of peace, through the maritime custom-houses, and had there paid the duties conformably with the Mexican tariff.

(6) The owners of all merchandise, effects, or property, described in the first and second rules, and existing in any port of Mexico, shall have the right to reship the same, exempt from all tax, impost, or contribution whatever.

With respect to the metals, or other property, exported from any Mexican port whilst in the occupation of the forces of the United States, and previously to the restoration of the custom-house at such port, no person shall be required by the Mexican authorities, whether general or state, to pay any tax, duty, or contribution upon any such exportation, or in any manner to account for the same to the said authorities.

ARTICLE XX

Through consideration for the interests of commerce generally, it is agreed, that if less than sixty days should elapse between the date of the signature of this treaty and the restoration of the custom houses, conformably with the stipulation in the third article, in such case all merchandise, effects and property whatsoever, arriving at the Mexican ports after the restoration of the said custom-houses, and previously to the expiration of sixty days after the day of signature of this treaty, shall be admitted to entry; and no other duties shall be levied thereon than the duties established by the tariff found in force at such custom-houses at the time of the restoration of the same. And to all such merchandise, effects, and property, the rules established by the preceding article shall apply.

ARTICLE XXI

If unhappily any disagreement should hereafter arise between the Governments of the two republics, whether with respect to the interpretation of any stipulation in this treaty, or with respect to any other particular concerning the political or commercial relations of the two nations, the said Governments, in the name of those nations, do promise to each other that they will endeavour, in the most sincere and earnest manner, to settle the differences so arising, and to preserve the state of peace and friendship in which the two countries are now placing themselves, using, for this end, mutual representations and pacific negotiations. And if, by these means, they should not be enabled to come to an agreement, a resort shall not, on this account, be had to reprisals, aggression, or hostility of any kind, by the one republic against the other, until the Government of that which deems itself aggrieved shall have maturely considered, in the spirit of peace and good neighbourship, whether it would not be better that such difference should be settled by the arbitration of commissioners appointed on each side, or by that of a friendly nation. And should such course be proposed by either party, it shall be acceded to by the other, unless deemed by it altogether incompatible with the nature of the difference, or the circumstances of the case.

ARTICLE XXII

If (which is not to be expected, and which God forbid) war should unhappily break out between the two republics, they do now, with a view to such calamity, solemnly pledge themselves to each other and to the world to observe the following rules; absolutely where the nature of the subject permits, and as closely as possible in all cases where such absolute observance shall be impossible:

(1) The merchants of either republic then residing in the other shall be allowed to remain twelve months (for those dwelling in the interior), and six months (for those dwelling at the seaports) to collect their debts and settle their affairs; during which periods they shall enjoy the same protection, and be on the same footing, in all respects, as the citizens or subjects of the most friendly nations; and, at the expiration thereof, or at any time before, they shall have full liberty to depart, carrying off all their effects without molestation or hindrance, conforming therein to the same laws which the citizens or subjects of the most friendly nations are required to conform to. Upon the entrance of the armies of either nation into the territories of the other, women and children, ecclesiastics, scholars of every faculty, cultivators of the earth, merchants, artisans, manufacturers, and fishermen, unarmed and inhabiting unfortified towns, villages, or places, and in general all persons whose occupations are for the common subsistence and benefit of mankind, shall be allowed to continue their respective employments, unmolested in their persons. Nor shall their houses or goods be burnt or otherwise destroyed, nor their cattle taken, nor their fields wasted, by the armed force into

whose power, by the events of war, they may happen to fall; but if the necessity arise to take anything from them for the use of such armed force, the same shall be paid for at an equitable price. All churches, hospitals, schools, colleges, libraries, and other establishments for charitable and beneficent purposes, shall be respected, and all persons connected with the same protected in the discharge of their duties, and the pursuit of their vocations.

(2). In order that the fate of prisoners of war may be alleviated all such practices as those of sending them into distant, inclement or unwholesome districts, or crowding them into close and noxious places, shall be studiously avoided. They shall not be confined in dungeons, prison ships, or prisons; nor be put in irons, or bound or otherwise restrained in the use of their limbs. The officers shall enjoy liberty on their paroles, within convenient districts, and have comfortable quarters; and the common soldiers shall be dispose(in cantonments, open and extensive enough for air and exercise and lodged in barracks as roomy and good as are provided by the party in whose power they are for its own troops. But if any office shall break his parole by leaving the district so assigned him, or any other prisoner shall escape from the limits of his cantonment after they shall have been designated to him, such individual, officer, or other prisoner, shall forfeit so much of the benefit of this article as provides for his liberty on parole or in cantonment. And if any officer so breaking his parole or any common soldier so escaping from the limits assigned him, shall afterwards be found in arms previously to his being regularly exchanged, the person so offending shall be dealt with according to the established laws of war. The officers shall be daily furnished, by the party in whose power they are, with as many rations, and of the same articles, as are allowed either in kind or by commutation, to officers of equal rank in its own army; and all others shall be daily furnished with such ration as is allowed to a common soldier in its own service; the value of all which supplies shall, at the close of the war, or at periods to be agreed upon between the respective commanders, be paid by the other party, on a mutual adjustment of accounts for the subsistence of prisoners; and such accounts shall not be mingled with or set off against any others, nor the balance due on them withheld, as a compensation or reprisal for any cause whatever, real or pretended Each party shall be allowed to keep a commissary of prisoners, appointed by itself, with every cantonment of prisoners, in possession of the other; which commissary shall see the prisoners as often as he pleases; shall be allowed to receive, exempt from all duties a taxes, and to distribute, whatever comforts may be sent to them by their friends; and shall be free to transmit his reports in open letters to the party by whom he is employed. And it is declared that neither the pretense that war dissolves all treaties, nor any other whatever, shall be considered as annulling or suspending the solemn covenant contained in this article. On the contrary, the state of war is precisely that for which it is provided; and, during which, its stipulations are to be as sacredly observed as the most acknowledged obligations under the law of nature or nations.

ARTICLE XXIII

This treaty shall be ratified by the President of the United States of America, by and with the advice and consent of the Senate thereof; and by the President of the Mexican Republic, with the previous approbation of its general

Congress; and the ratifications shall be exchanged in the City of Washington, or at the seat of Government of Mexico, in four months from the date of the signature hereof, or sooner if practicable. In faith whereof we, the respective Plenipotentiaries, have signed this treaty of peace, friendship, limits, and settlement, and have hereunto affixed our seals respectively. Done in quintuplicate, at the city of Guadalupe Hidalgo, on the second day of February, in the year of our Lord one thousand eight hundred and forty-eight.

N. P. TRIST
LUIS P. CUEVAS
BERNARDO COUTO
MIGL. ATRISTAIN
National Archives

APPENDIX II-GADSDEN PURCHASE (1853)

BY THE PRESIDENT OF THE UNITED STATES OF AMERICA

A PROCLAMATION.

WHEREAS a treaty between the United States of America and the Mexican Republic was concluded and signed at the City of Mexico on the thirtieth day of December, one thousand eight hundred and fifty-three; which treaty, as amended by the Senate of the United States, and being in the English and Spanish languages, is word for word as follows:

IN THE NAME OF ALMIGHTY GOD:

The Republic of Mexico and the United States of America desiring to remove every cause of disagreement which might interfere in any manner with the better friendship and intercourse between the two countries, and especially in respect to the true limits which should be established, when, notwithstanding what was covenanted in the treaty of Guadalupe Hidalgo in the year 1848, opposite interpretations have been urged, which might give occasion to questions of serious moment: to avoid these, and to strengthen and more firmly maintain the peace which happily prevails between the two republics, the President of the United States has, for this purpose, appointed James Gadsden, Envoy Extraordinary and Minister Plenipotentiary of the same, near the Mexican government, and the President of Mexico has appointed as Plenipotentiary "ad hoc" his excellency Don Manuel Diez de Bonilla, cavalier grand cross of the national and distinguished order of Guadalupe, and Secretary of State, and of the office of Foreign Relations, and Don Jose Salazar Ylarregui and General Mariano Monterde as scientific commissioners, invested with full powers for this negotiation, who, having communicated their respective full powers, and finding them in due and proper form, have agreed upon the articles following:

ARTICLE I

The Mexican Republic agrees to designate the following as her true limits with the United States for the future: retaining the same dividing line between the two Californias as already defined and established, according to the 5th article of the treaty of Guadalupe Hidalgo, the limits between the two republics shall be as follows: Beginning in the Gulf of Mexico, three leagues from land, opposite the mouth of the Rio Grande, as provided in the 5th article of the treaty of Guadalupe Hidalgo; thence, as defined in the said article, up the middle of that river to the point where the parallel of 31° 47' north latitude crosses the same; thence due west one hundred miles; thence south to the parallel of 31° 20' north latitude; thence along the said parallel of 31° 20' to the 111th meridian of longitude west of Greenwich; thence in a straight line to a point on the Colorado River twenty English miles below the junction of the Gila and Colorado rivers; thence up the middle of the said river Colorado until it intersects the present line between the United States and Mexico.

For the performance of this portion of the treaty, each of the two governments shall nominate one commissioner, to the end that, by common consent the two thus nominated, having met in the city of Paso del Norte, three months after the exchange of the ratifications of this treaty, may proceed to survey and mark out upon the land the dividing line stipulated by this article, where it shall not have already been surveyed and established by the mixed commission, according to the treaty of Guadalupe, keeping a journal and making proper plans of their operations. For this purpose, if they should judge it necessary, the contracting parties shall be at liberty each to unite to its respective commissioner, scientific or other assistants, such as astronomers and surveyors, whose concurrence shall not be considered necessary for the settlement and of a true line of division between the two Republics; that line shall be alone established upon which the commissioners may fix, their consent in this particular being considered decisive and an integral part of this treaty, without necessity of ulterior ratification or approval, and without room for interpretation of any kind by either of the parties contracting.

The dividing line thus established shall, in all time, be faithfully respected by the two governments, without any variation therein, unless of the express and free consent of the two, given in conformity to the principles of the law of nations, and in accordance with the constitution of each country respectively.

In consequence, the stipulation in the 5th article of the treaty of Guadalupe upon the boundary line therein described is no longer of any force, wherein it may conflict with that here established, the said line being considered annulled and abolished wherever it may not coincide with the present, and in the same manner remaining in full force where in accordance with the same.

ARTICLE II

The government of Mexico hereby releases the United States from all liability on account of the obligations contained in the eleventh article of the treaty of Guadalupe Hidalgo; and the said article and the thirty-third article of the treaty of amity, commerce, and navigation between the United States of America and the United Mexican States concluded at Mexico, on the fifth day of April, 1831, are hereby abrogated.

ARTICLE III

In consideration of the foregoing stipulations, the Government of the United States agrees to pay to the government of Mexico, in the city of New York, the sum of ten millions of dollars, of which seven millions shall be paid immediately upon the exchange of the ratifications of this treaty, and the remaining three millions as soon as the boundary line shall be surveyed, marked, and established.

ARTICLE IV

The provisions of the 6th and 7th articles of the treaty of Guadalupe Hidalgo having been rendered nugatory, for the most part, by the cession of territory granted in the first article of this treaty, the said articles are hereby abrogated and annulled, and the provisions as herein expressed substituted therefor. The vessels, and citizens of the United States shall, in all time, have free and uninterrupted passage through the Gulf of California, to and from their possessions situated north of the boundary line of the two countries. It being understood that this passage is to be by navigating the Gulf of California and the river Colorado, and not by land, without the express consent of the Mexican government; and precisely the same provisions, stipulations, and restrictions, in all respects, are hereby agreed upon and adopted, and shall be scrupulously observed and enforced by the two contracting governments in reference to the Rio Colorado, so far and for such distance as the middle of that river is made their common boundary line by the first article of this treaty.

The several provisions, stipulations, and restrictions contained in the 7th article of the treaty of Guadalupe Hidalgo shall remain in force only so far as regards the Rio Bravo del Forte, below the initial of the said boundary provided in the first article of this treaty; that is to say, below the intersection of the 31° 47'30'/ parallel of latitude, with the boundary line established by the late treaty dividing said river from its mouth upwards, according to the fifth article of the treaty of Guadalupe.

ARTICLE V

All the provisions of the eighth and ninth, sixteenth and seventeenth articles of the treaty of Guadalupe Hidalgo, shall apply to the territory ceded by the Mexican Republic in the first article of the present treaty, and to all the rights of persons and property, both civil and ecclesiastical, within the same, as fully and as effectually as if the said articles were herein again recited and set forth.

ARTICLE VI

No grants of land within the territory ceded by the first article of this treaty bearing date subsequent to the day-twenty-fifth of September-when the minister and subscriber to this treaty on the part of the United States, proposed to the Government of Mexico to terminate the question of boundary, will be considered valid or be recognized by the United States, or will any grants made previously be respected or be considered as obligatory which have not been located and duly recorded in the archives of Mexico.

ARTICLE VII

Should there at any future period (which God forbid) occur any disagreement between the two nations which might lead to a rupture of their relations and reciprocal peace, they bind themselves in like manner to procure by every possible method the adjustment of every difference; and should they still in this manner not succeed, never will they proceed to a declaration of war, without having previously paid attention to what has been set forth in article twenty-one of the treaty of Guadalupe for similar cases; which article, as well as the twenty-second is here reaffirmed.

ARTICLE VIII

The Mexican Government having on the 5th of February, 1853, authorized the early construction of a plank and railroad across the Isthmus of Tehuantepec, and, to secure the stable benefits of said transit way to the persons and merchandise of the citizens of Mexico and the United States, it is stipulated that neither government will interpose any obstacle to the transit of persons and merchandise of both nations; and at no time shall higher charges be made on the transit of persons and property of citizens of the United States, than may be made on the persons and property of other foreign nations, nor shall any interest in said transit way, nor in the proceeds thereof, be transferred to any foreign government.

The United States, by its agents, shall have the right to transport across the isthmus, in closed bags, the mails of the United States not intended for distribution along the line of communication; also the effects of the United States government and its citizens, which may be intended for transit, and not for distribution on the isthmus, free of custom-house or other charges by the Mexican government. Neither passports nor letters of security will be required of persons crossing the isthmus and not remaining in the country.
When the construction of the railroad shall be completed, the Mexican government agrees to open a port of entry in addition to the port of Vera Cruz, at or near the terminus of said road on the Gulf of Mexico.

The two governments will enter into arrangements for the prompt transit of troops and munitions of the United States, which that government may have occasion to send from one part of its territory to another, lying on opposite sides of the continent.

The Mexican government having e agreed to protect with its whole power the prosecution, preservation, and security of the work, the United States may extend its protection as it shall judge wise to it when it may feel sanctioned and warranted by the public or international law.

ARTICLE IX

This treaty shall be ratified, and the respective ratifications shall be exchanged at the city of Washington within the exact period of six months from the date of its signature, or sooner, if possible.

In testimony whereof, we, the plenipotentiaries of the contracting parties, have hereunto affixed our hands and seals at Mexico, the thirtieth (30th) day of December, in the year of our Lord one thousand eight hundred and fifty-three, in the thirty-third year of the independence of the Mexican republic, and the seventy-eighth of that of the United States.

JAMES GADSDEN,
MANUEL DIEZ DE BONILLA
JOSE SALAZAR YLARBEGUI
J. MARIANO MONTERDE,

And whereas the said treaty, as amended, has been duly ratified on both parts, and the respective ratifications of the same have this day been exchanged at Washington, by WILLIAM L. MARCY, Secretary of State of the United States, and SENOR GENERAL DON JUAN N. ALMONTE, Envoy Extraordinary and Minister Plenipotentiary of the Mexican Republic, on the part of their respective Governments:

Now, therefore, be it known that I, FRANKLIN PIERCE, President of the United States of America, have caused the said treaty to be made public, to the end that the same, and every clause and article thereof, may be observed and fulfilled with good faith by the United States and the citizens thereof

In witness whereof I have hereunto set my hand and caused the seal of the United States to be affixed.

Done at the city of Washington, this thirtieth day of June, in the year of our Lord one thousand eight hundred and fifty-four, and of the Independence of the United States the seventy-eighth.

BY THE PRESIDENT:
FRANKLIN PIERCE,
W. L. MARCY, Secretary of State.

Avalon Project
Yale University

APPENDIX III-MCLANE-OCAMPO TREATY (1859)

(NEVER RATIFIED)

The treaty concluded with the Liberal Government of Mexico by Hon. ROBEAR McLANE, as Plenipotentiary of the United States, Dec. 14, 1859, is now awaiting ratification in the Senate. Conceiving it to be equally important that the public should be prepared to pass not only upon the stipulations of this Convention, but upon the action of the Senate in regard to it, we this morning lay the authentic text before the readers of the TIMES. Having been the first to present to the world a synopsis of these negotiations, it is quite proper that we should also be the first to make public the entire instrument.

ARTICLE I.

As an amplification of the eighth article of the treaty of the 30th of December, 1853, the Mexican Republic cedes to the United States and its citizens and property, in perpetuity, the right of way, by the Isthmus of Tehuantepec, from one ocean to the other, by any kind of road now existing, or that may hereafter exist, both Republics and their citizens enjoying it.

ARTICLE II.

Both Republics agree to protect all routes now existing, or that shall hereafter exist, over the said Isthmus, and to guarantee the neutrality of the same.

ARTICLE III.

Simultaneous with the first bona fide use of any route across the said Isthmus for purposes of actual transit, the Republic of Mexico shall establish two ports of deposit -- the one on the east, the other on the west of the Isthmus. No duty shall be levied by the Government of Mexico upon foreign effects and merchandise which may pass bona fide by the said Isthmus, and which may not be intended for the consumption of the Mexican Republic. No incumbrance or tolls shall be imposed upon foreign persons and property which may pass by this road beyond those that may be imposed upon the persons and property of Mexicans. The Republic of Mexico will continue to allow the free and untrammeled transit of the mails of the United States, provided they pass in closed mail bags, and they be not for distribution on the road. Upon such mails none of the charges imposed, nor of those which may hereafter be imposed, shall be applied in any case.

ARTICLE IV.

The Mexican Republic agrees that it will establish for each of the two ports of deposit -- the one on the east, the other on the west of the Isthmus -- regulations that will permit the effects and merchandise belonging to citizens or subjects of the United Slates or of any foreign country to be entered and stored in warehouses, which shall be erected for that purpose, free of all tonnage or other duties whatever, except the necessary charges for cartage and storage, which said effects and merchandise may be subsequently withdrawn for transit across the said Isthmus, and for shipment from either of the said ports of deposit to any foreign port, free of all tonnage or other duties whatever; and they may likewise be withdrawn from the said warehouses for sale and consumption, within the territory of the Mexican Republic, on the payment of such duties or imposts as the said Mexican Government may be pleased to enact.

ARTICLE V.

The Republic of Mexico agrees that Should it become necessary at any time to employ military forces for the security and protection of persons and property passing over any of the routes aforesaid, it will employ the requisite force for that purpose; but upon failure to do this, from any cause whatever, the Government of the United States may, with the consent, or at the request of the Government of Mexico, or of the Minister thereof at Washington, or of the competent legally-appointed local authorities, civil or military, employ such force for this and for no other purpose; and when, in the opinion of the Government of Mexico, the necessity ceases, such force shall be immediately withdrawn.

In the exceptional case, however, of unforeseen or imminent danger to the lives or property of citizens of the United States, the forces of said Republic are authorized to act for their protection without such consent having been previously obtained; and such forces shall be withdrawn when the necessity for this employment ceases.

ARTICLE VI.

The Mexican Republic grants to the United States the simple transit of its troops, military stores and munitions of war by the Isthmus of Tehuantepec, and by the transit or route of communication referred to in this Convention from the city of Guaymas, on the Gulf of California, to the Rancho de Nogales, or some suitable point on the boundary line between the Republic of Mexico and the United States near the one hundred and eleventh degree west longitude from Greenwich, immediate notice thereof being given to the local authorities of the Republic of Mexico. And the two Republics agree, likewise, that it shall be an express stipulation, with the companies or enterprises to whom hereafter the carriage or transportation is granted, by any railroads or other means of communication, on the aforesaid transits, that the price for conveying the troops, military stores and munitions of war of the two republics shall be, at most, one-half the ordinary fare paid by the passengers or merchandise which may pass over the said transits; it being understood that if the grantees of privileges already granted, or which hereafter may be granted, upon railroads or other means of conveyance over said transits, refuse to receive for one-half the price of conveyance the troops, arms, military stores, and munitions of the United States, the latter government will not impart to them the protection spoken of in articles second and fifth, nor any other protection.

ARTICLE VII.

The Mexican Republic hereby cedes to the United States in perpetuity, and to their citizens and property, the right of way or transit across the territory of the Republic of Mexico, from the Cities of Camargo and Matamoras, or any suitable point on the Rio Grande, in the State of Tamaulipas, via Monterey, to the port of Mazatlán, at the entrance of the Gulf of California, in the State of Slnaloa, and from the Rancho de Nogales, or any suitable point on the boundary line between the Republic of Mexico and the United States, near the one hundred and eleventh degree west longitude from Greenwich, via Magdalena and Hermosillo, to the City of Guaymas, on the Gulf of California, in the State of Sonora, over any railroad or route of communication, natural or artificial, which may now or hereafter exist or be constructed, to be used and enjoyed in the same manner and upon equal terms by both Republics, and their respective citizens, the Mexican Republic reserving always for itself the right of sovereignty which it now has upon all the transits spoken of in the present Treaty. All the stipulations and regulations of every kind applicable to the right of way or transit across the Isthmus of Tehuantepec, that are or have been agreed upon between the two Republics, are hereby extended and applied to the foregoing transits or rights of way, excepting the right of passing troops, military stores, and munitions of war, from the Rio Grande to the Gulf of California.

ARTICLE VIII.

The two Republics likewise agree that, from the list of merchandise here annexed, the Congress of the United States shall select those which, being the natural, industrial, or manufactured product of either of the two Republics; may be admitted for sale and consumption in either of the two countries, under conditions of a perfect reciprocity, whether they be considered free of duty, or at a rate of duty to be fixed by the Congress of the United States; it being the intention of the Mexican Republic to admit the articles in question at the lowest rate of duty, and even free, if the Congress of the United States consents thereto. Their introduction from one to the other

Republic shall be made at the points which the Governments of both Republics may fix upon, at the limits or boundaries thereof ceded and granted for the transits, and in perpetuity, by this Convention, either across the Isthmus of Tehuantepec or from the Gulf of California, to the interior frontier between Mexico and the United States. If any similar privileges should be granted by Mexico to other nations at the termini of the aforesaid transits upon the Gulfs of Mexico and California, and upon the Pacific Ocean, it shall be in consideration of the same conditions and stipulations of reciprocity which are imposed upon the United States by the terms of this Convention.

List of Merchandise annexed to Article VIII.

Animals of all kinds.
Plows and loose iron bars.
Rice.
Poultry and fresh eggs.
Quicksilver.
Stone coal.
Fresh, salted, and smoked meats.
Wood and iron houses.
Raw hides.
Horns.
Chile or red peppers
Drawings and models of large machinery, buildings, monuments, and boats.
Boats of all sizes and classes, for the navigation of the rivers on the frontier.
Brooms and material for their manufacture.
Bridle bits.
Fresh, dried, and sugared fruits.
Type, spaces, plates for printing or engraving, rules, vignettes, and printing ink.

Printed books of all classes bound in paper, (pamphlet bound.)
Hops.
Timber, unwrought, and firewood.
Butter and cheese.
Geographical and nautical maps and topographical plans.
Marble, wrought and unwrought.
Machines and implements for agriculture, farming, mining, for the development of the arts and sciences, and their fixtures, either loose or for their repair.
Dyewood.
Fish, tar, turpentine and ashes.
Plants, trees and shrubbery.
Slates for roofing purposes.
Common salt.
Riding-saddles.
Palm-leaf heats.
Plaster of Paris, (gypsum.)
Vegetables.
Undressed sheepskins.
Grain of all kinds, and from which bread is made,
Flour.
Wool.
Lard.
Tallow.
Leather, and manufactures of leather.
Every species of textile or woven fabric of cotton, excepting that called brown sheeting, (mantatriguena.)

ARTICLE IX.

As an amplification of the fourteenth and fifteenth Articles of the Treaty of the fifth of April, one thousand eight hundred and thirty-one, in which that which relates to the exercise of their religion by the citizens of Mexico was stipulated, the citizens of the United States will be permitted to exercise freely in Mexico their religion, either in public or in private, within their houses or in the churches and places which may be assigned to worship, as a consequence of the perfect equality and reciprocity which the second Article of the same treaty states was taken for its basis. The chapels or places for public worship may be purchased, and shall be field as the property of those who may purchase them, as any other common property is purchased or held, excepting there from, however, the religious communities and corporations to whom the present laws of Mexico have prohibited entirely and forever and a day the obtaining and holding anything whatever in propriety. In no case shall citizens of the United States residing in Mexico be subject to have forced loans levied upon them.

ARTICLE X.

In consideration of the foregoing stipulations, and in compensation for the revenue surrendered by Mexico on the goods and merchandise transported free of duty through the territory of that Republic, the Government of the United States agrees to pay to the Government of Mexico the sum of $4,000,000, of which two millions shall be paid immediately upon the exchange of the ratifications of this treaty, and me remaining two millions shall be retained by the Government of the United States for the payment of the claims of citizens of the United States against the Government of the Republic of Mexico, for injuries already inflicted, and which may be proven to be just, according to the law and usage of nations and the principles of equity; and the same shall be paid pro rata, as far as the said sum of two millions will permit, in pursuance of a law to be enacted by the Congress of the United States for the adjudication thereof, and the remainder of this sum shall be returned to Mexico by the United States, in case there be any such remainder after the payment of the claims thus found to be just.

ARTICLE XI.

This Treaty shall be ratified by the President of the United States, by and with the advice and consent of the Senate of the United States, and by the President of Mexico, in virtue of his extraordinary and actual executive functions, and the respective ratifications shall be exchanged at the City of Washington, within the exact period of six months from the date of its signature, or sooner if possible, or at the seat of the Constitutional Government, if any alterations or amendments be proposed by the President and Senate of the United States, and accepted by the President of the Republic of Mexico.

New York Times
A version of this archive appears in print on February 15, 1860, on Page 1 of the New York edition with the headline: OUR RELATIONS WITH MEXICO.; Text of the McLane-Ocampo Treaty. Supplementary Articles Authorizing American Intervention. TREATY OF PEACE AND COMMERCE BETWEEN THE UNITED STATES AND THE MEXICAN REPUBLIC.

APPENDIX IV-LIST OF TREATIES
by Translator

Name	Date Signed or Ratified	Purpose and Parties
Treaty of San Lorenzo	1795	Spain and the United States defined West Florida boundary.
Treaty of Paris	1783	Peace Treaty between Britain and the United States ending Revolutionary War
Treaty of San Ildefonso	1800	Spain agreed to return Louisiana to France
Treaty of Louisiana Purchase	1803	Between France and the United States
Adams-Onis Treaty	1819	Between Spain and the United States ceding Florida to the United States and establishing other boundaries with Mexican territory. (also, Transcontinental Treaty), never ratified.
Treaty of Limits	1828	Between Mexico and the United States, using limits established in the Adams-Onis Treaty

Name	Date Signed or Ratified	Purpose and Parties
Treaty of Friendship and Commerce and Navigation	1831	Between Mexico and the United States
Peace Treaty of the Pastry War	1839	Peace Treaty between France and Mexico
Treaty of Texas Annexation	1845	Treaty between Mexico and the Republic of Texas
Treaty of Guadalupe-Hidalgo	1848	Treaty between Mexico and the United States, giving away half of Mexico
1st Treaty of Transit of Tehuantepec	1850	Between Mexico and the United States, never ratified
Treaty of la Mesilla (Gadsden's Purchase)	1854	Between Mexico and the United States
McLane-Ocampo Treaty	1859	Between Mexico and the United States, transit of Tehuantepec, Sonora, Sinaloa, etc. never ratified

Name	Date Signed or Ratified	Purpose and Parties
Treaty of Mon-Almonte	1859	Re-established relations between Mexico and Spain

APPENDIX V-ANGLO-SAXON AND SPANISH HERITAGE

by Translator

Anglo-Saxon Colonies	New Spain
Heritage:	**Heritage:**
England	Spain
Colonies founded in 17th c	Colonies founded in 16th c
England in peace since the 15th c	Spain at war until Moors conquered in 1492
England had a modern economic system	Spain had a feudal economic system
Mercantile businesses and hostility towards Spain, "black legend"	Business was conquest and evangelization and hostility towards England, pirates
Thousands of religious colonists (250,000) in first half century	Colonists numbered only 300,000 after 300 years
Rejection of the indigenous peoples from politics and religion	Assimilation of the indigenous population politically and religiously
Calvinist philosophy, many denominations (salvation through faith and work)	Catholic philosophy, only one religion (salvation by liturgy)
13 autonomous colonies	One centralized colony

Education required for all, but at a lower level.	Education only for a prosperous elite, universities in the 16 c
Free commerce in private ships	Commerce controlled from Seville in Spanish ships
Free internal and external immigration	Internal and external immigration controlled from Spain
White and black laborers, virtually no Indians	Indigenous labor, encomienda system in 16th c
Economy based on agriculture and commerce	Economy based on mining
Local authorities (except governors) by elected assemblies of landowners	Authority from Spain (Spanish born governed the church and the state in New Spain
All equal before the law (English and later nationalized Europeans)	No civilian participation
African slavery	Castes, little slavery beyond the encomienda system in 16th c
Culture:	**Culture:**
Pioneering spirit and money was all important	"From poverty comes the heavenly kingdom"
Becoming rich was the goal, but wealth was to be used for good	Wealth as a means, not an end
Time is sacred and to be used for work	Little sense of time and change (better the bad you know the good you do not)

Religious tolerance	Insistence on a single religion
Concept of private property	Roman concept that the state owns everything
Object is owning the truth	Object is belonging to a great church
Optimistic "architects of their lives"	Fatalist "as God demands"
Mission:	**Mission:**
To regenerate the world (American way of life)	To evangelize (monks)
Priorities: first religion and then republicanism	Did not exist
Right to unused land (including Mexican)	Took land, but not because they believed they had the right
Belief in being God's chosen as an example to the world	Chosen as being different from Spain
Vocation to be free and develop liberty for others	Vocation to obey the law of the church
American interests are the interests of the world	Did not exist
The American cause is the cause of humanity	Did not exist
Type of Government:	**Type of Government:**
Government b the free voting citizens who increased over time	Absolute centralism

The governor was sent by the owner of the colony, whether by the king or a company	Governor and government named by Spain, and the highest posts filled only by Spaniards born in Spain
Law by the governor and his counsel, but purse strings rested in the general assembly, upper and lower houses. Each colony became self governing over time	All authority came from Spain

www.ingramcontent.com/pod-product-compliance
Lightning Source LLC
Chambersburg PA
CBHW062153270326
41930CB00009B/1521